AF449154

Reason, Culture, Religion

Culture and Religion in International Relations

Series Editors
Yosef Lapid and Friedrich Kratochwil

Published by Palgrave Macmillan

Dialogue Among Civilizations: Some Exemplary Voices
By Fred Dallmayr

Religion in International Relations: The Return from Exile
Edited by Fabio Petito and Pavlos Hatzopoulos

Identity and Global Politics: Empirical and Theoretical Elaborations
Edited by Patricia M. Goff and Kevin C. Dunn

Reason, Culture, Religion: The Metaphysics of World Politics
By Ralph Pettman

Reason, Culture, Religion

THE METAPHYSICS OF WORLD POLITICS

Ralph Pettman

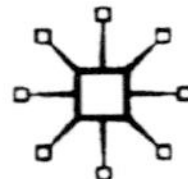REASON, CULTURE, RELIGION

First published 2004 by
PALGRAVE MACMILLAN™
175 Fifth Avenue, New York, N.Y. 10010 and
Houndmills, Basingstoke, Hampshire, England RG21 6XS
Companies and representatives throughout the world

PALGRAVE MACMILLAN is the global academic imprint of the Palgrave
Macmillan division of St. Martin's Press, LLC and of Palgrave Macmillan Ltd.
Macmillan® is a registered trademark in the United States, United Kingdom
and other countries. Palgrave is a registered trademark in the European
Union and other countries.

ISBN 978-1-4039-6505-9

Library of Congress Cataloging-in-Publication Data
Pettman, Ralph.
    Reason, culture, religion : the metaphysics of world politics / Ralph Pettman.
       p. cm.
    Includes bibliographical references and index.
    ISBN 1-4039-6505-6
       1. International relations and culture. 2. International relation–Philosophy.
       3. World politics–Philosophy. I. Title.

JZ1249.P48 2004
327.1′01—dc22   2003060176

A catalogue record for this book is available from the British Library.

Design by Newgen Imaging Systems (P) Ltd., Chennai, India.

First edition: April 2004
10 9 8 7 6 5 4 3 2 1

Transferred to Digital Printing in 2008

*This book is dedicated to Dominic Astronomer
and Tasha Sudan*

CONTENTS

Preface   ix

Introduction   The Metaphysics of World Affairs   1

PART I
MODERNITY   13

  1. World Affairs—The Modernist Project   15
  2. World Affairs—The Movie   35

PART II
COMMUNITY   49

  3. The World Politics of World Heritage   51
  4. The World Politics of World Heritage—Japan   69

PART III
SPIRITUALITY   79

  5. Taoist Strategics   83
  6. Buddhist Economics   93
  7. Islamic Civics   103
  8. Confucian Marxism   115
  9. Hindu Constructivism   125
 10. Pagan Feminism   135
 11. Animist Environmentalism   145

Conclusion   A World Affairs for All the World   157

References   163
Index   183

Preface

What *is* world politics? Most Euro-Americans would tend to answer this question by highlighting the politics of the globalization process whereby a particular cultural project, the Euro-American project, is being transformed into a global one. They would do so, what is more, in a characteristically Euro-American way, promoting in the process the sort of person Euro-Americans tend to represent.

What, then, is *world* politics? Read with the word "world" italicized, other agendas begin to emerge, that locate these politics in larger contexts. Such a reading not only suggests the possibility of seeing world affairs as world ones. It also anticipates a world affairs discipline more worthy of the name.

This study attempts to answer the questions posed above, though to answer the second reading (what is *world* politics?) it must first of all answer the first. It begins, then, by briefly outlining the modernist study of world affairs. It goes on to compare these world affairs—and the culture of which they are a part—with world affairs as described and explained from other politico-cultural perspectives. It ends by comparing these world affairs, and the religion of which modernist culture is part, with world affairs as described and explained from other politico-spiritual perspectives.

The key purpose of this work is to show how the modernist prioritization of reason as an end in itself not only clarifies and extends our capacity to explain world affairs, but also constrains and skews every relevant explanation. These limits and distortions are most clearly demonstrated by subjecting modernist world affairs to analyses from communalist and sacralist perspectives, analyses that not only transgress the limits modernity sets, but also compensate for the distortions they create.

In attempting to extend the reach of the discipline, this is a study that moves outside the discipline's mainstream concerns. The discipline itself continues to grow, however, as the singular character of the cultural milieu in which these particular world affairs arose becomes more apparent, and as the singular character of the sacral milieu in which this particular cultural milieu arose becomes more apparent too.

When particular current events challenge the discipline's construction of its own mainstream, the need for a more comprehensive account of world affairs is seen to be acute. The need is a chronic one, however, since the modernist project never ceases to skew and constrain how world affairs are described, explained, and prescribed for in policy terms.

In seeking to augment what the discipline represents, the following study is obliged to interrogate the theoretical integrity of the foundations of modernist world affairs. It should be said at the outset, however, that it does not seek to abandon these foundations. Rather, it seeks to understand the consequences these foundations have for the study of the subject, to bring to bear upon them some relatively unfamiliar cultural and spiritual outlooks and insights, to extend the perimeters that modernist analyses impose, and to counter the misrepresentations that modernist analyses make.

While it would not be possible to do justice to the generosity of all those who helped, this is a work that confirms that, whatever else they might be, very many people are extremely kind. I would like to thank specifically those who award Japan Foundation Fellowships and those who administer the Japanese Peace, Freedom and Exchange Program. For assistance far beyond the call of duty, I would also like to thank an academic colleague from whom I never cease to learn, Paul Morris, as well as Christiane Havel, then of the French Ministry of Culture and Communication, and Yoshinobu Yamamoto, then of the University of Tokyo.

Introduction

The Metaphysics of World Affairs

One pushes upward into an empty city

— I Ching

In his *Course in Positive Philosophy*, Auguste Comte, the nineteenth-century French philosopher, surveyed human thought from its first "trial flights" up to the present day (Andreski, 1974 [1842], 19). In doing so he believed he was able to discern a law that applied to every branch of human knowledge, a law he found confirmed not only by reflections on the nature of human nature, but also by historical research. In short, he saw every discipline progressing from a Theological or fictitious stage, through a Metaphysical or abstract stage, to a Positivist or scientific stage (Kolakowski, 1972, 67–73).

In discussing this sequence of ways of knowing, Comte not only said that each way was different from the others, but that the last one was superior to those preceding it. He not only thought human intelligence had three "essentially different and even . . . mutually exclusive" ways of thinking about the truth. He saw these ways as forming a progressive series, and he saw Positivism as the last and highest stage in this series (Andreski, 1974 [1842], 20).

The last stage was the highest, Comte said, since it allowed us to arrive at conclusions that are open to public scrutiny, and that obtain whether we believe in them or not. (Somewhat paradoxically, an admiration for Catholic universalism prompted him to refer to this conclusion in theological terms. Though he deemed theological knowing to be fictitious, that is, Comte professed a belief in a Religion of Humanity. He proclaimed absolute faith in the systematic study of "facts" and the laws to which "facts" pertain, and he anointed himself the first "positivist pope" (Andreski, 1974 [1842], 13, 138–40; Kolakowski, 1972, 80–3).)

Comte subsequently compared the theological/metaphysical infancy of the study of politics (which now includes the study of world politics) with the mature discipline he believed we get when our analyses are reliable enough to provide social stability on a regular basis. He saw the discipline's infancy as analogous to astrology, alchemy, or the use of cure-alls. Its potential maturity, on the other hand, he saw as analogous to contemporary astronomy, chemistry, or medicine. He looked forward to a study of the subject capable of subordinating the imagination to observation, and of turning "superstition" into "science." In so doing, he sought to highlight what he considered to be a fundamental difference between a belief in final causes (supernatural agents, abstract forces, inherent qualities, and the like), and a belief in the efficacy of using the mind to observe and reflect upon the real world in an externalized way (Andreski, 1974 [1842], 20).

Comte carries forward a tradition of thought that extends back, in the Western canon, through Descartes and Galileo to the Greeks, though the nineteenth-century Comtean preference for Positivism was carried forward in turn to become the twentieth-century neo-Comtean preference for Rationalism. As a meta-language for scientific analysis Rationalism continues to dominate the study of world affairs, particularly in the United States where the desire, after World War II, to defeat the Soviet Union in the Cold War so-called, led the Americans to prioritize the most reliable knowledge they knew of relevant to such a task, namely, scientific knowledge. They subsequently set about scientizing the discipline. The "behavioralist revolution" was the result. Most contemporary analysts of the subject, both American and non-American, continue to promote the Positivist approach, even those who turn reason back on itself to mount postmodernist critiques of it (George, 1994).

It should be noted at this point that every analytic language is a site of contending analytic dialects, and Rationalism is no exception. Once Rationalism was established in the seventeenth century as a specific analytic language, a difference soon emerged within it between rationalists with a small "r" (those who see Rationalism as being furthered best by abstract/deductive reflection) and positivists with a small "p" (those who see Rationalism as being furthered best by empirical/inductive experimentation). As a mentalist mind-gaze Rationalism has an obvious affinity with the Rationalist dialect that highlights deduction (rationalism with a small "r"). Nineteenth-century Positivism, on the other hand, is not only the antecedent of twentieth-century Rationalism, but because of its high regard for "facts," resurfaces there in the form of the Rationalist dialect that highlights induction (positivism with a small "p"). There is Positivism, therefore, and there is positivism. With a capital "P," the word refers to the nineteenth-century version of Rationalism. With a small "p," the word refers to the empiricist dialect within Rationalism that is most directly at odds with rationalism with a small "r." It is possible, as a consequence, to talk about a positivist attack on rationalism. This refers to an argument, within the modernist project, between two of its most prominent analytic dialects. It refers, that is, to an attack by those who prefer an empirical appreciation of the "facts," upon those who attempt to arrive at scientific conclusions by mental means alone. This argument highlights a long-standing philosophic difference that the present study is not about to try and resolve. It is worth noting, however, that a philosophic synthesis was attempted by Kant (Cottingham, 1984, 82–9), and that it was this synthesis that was ultimately made the basis for the hypothetico-deductive scientism currently much favored by mainstream American analysts of world affairs.

Can the eschewal of the metaphysical and the theological go too far, however? Can Comte be accused of wanting to throw out some perfectly good epistemological babies, along with what he saw as being some particularly grubby epistemological bathwater?

What, in other words, if Comte's progressive sequence does not obtain? What if the study of world affairs should exhibit scientific, metaphysical, and theological *dimensions*, rather than scientific, metaphysical, and theological *stages*?

Then it ought to be possible to talk of Theological ("fictitious") and Metaphysical ("abstract") components to the discipline, without jeopardizing the Positivist ("scientific") project. It should be possible to exploit different ideas about how best to understand the subject, without being seen as reverting to some kind of disciplinary infantilism. This, in turn, should permit explorations of parts of the discipline, in ways that Positivism/Rationalism has long sought to occlude or reject. There is more than one way to know about the world. As well as the scientific way, for example, there are emotional, experiential, intuitive, traditional, and spiritual ways. All of these, by their own particular lights, describe, explain, and prescribe for, what goes on in the world (Shweder and Levine, 1984; Smith, 1999). They are not Rationalist but they are ways to know nonetheless. Should they be eschewed just because Comte and the neo-Comteans say so?

First we must ascertain if Comte is doing justice to metaphysics. And this means asking what metaphysics might be.

The Oxford English Dictionary defines metaphysics as the "ultimate science of Being and Knowing." More particularly, it defines it as "that branch of speculative inquiry" that deals with the "first principles" of concepts like "being, substance, essence, time, space, cause, [and] identity . . . " (OED, Def. 1[a]).

To do metaphysics in this regard is to ask what reality might ultimately be, and how it might ultimately work. Thus we find Heidegger explaining metaphysical reflection as the "essence of what is . . . ," even though, as he says, this requires having the courage to make "the truth of our own presuppositions . . . into the things that most deserve to be called in[to] question" (which is what the postmodernists do) (Heidegger, 1977, 115, 116). Mohanty defines metaphysics as simply the "science of beings *qua* beings" (Mohanty, 1993, 18, 21). Neither sees metaphysics as being incompatible with a Positivist approach.

The second of the OED's definitions of metaphysics refers to the "theoretical principles or higher philosophical rationale of some particular branch of knowledge" (OED, Def. 1[b]). For example, the study of world politics can be seen as a "particular branch of knowledge," where analysts articulate "theoretical principles" (like realism or liberalism), with reference to a "higher philosophic rationale" (like Rationalism). This is also compatible with a Positivist approach.

The third of the OED's definitions is different, however. According to this definition, metaphysics represents whatever cannot be verified (OED, Def. 1[c]).

This is to counterpose science and nonscience. It is to use metaphysics, much as Comte did, to refer to nonscience alone.

The OED's editors say that this is incorrect. They say it is based upon an etymological error since Aristotle, who first used the word, did not use it like this. Metaphysics was first used to describe what Aristotle wrote after the *Physica*, writings that were subsequently called the *Metaphysica* (though saying so does not make metaphysics peculiar to "the West"). Aristotle did make a distinction between the initial part of his treatise, which was about natural things (and is known as the second philosophy), and the latter part of his treatise, which was about the basis and cause all that is intelligible (and is known as the first philosophy.) However, he did not see any radical difference between these two parts. Not so neo-Comteans. Unlike Aristotle, they see this distinction as representing a significant difference. They also extend the realm of the natural to include all of reality, construing, as it were, everything as *Physica*. This allows them to make *Metaphysica* into their preferred term for the realm of the unnatural, that is, for whatever they deem to be magical, mystical, super-sensible, superstitious, or occult.

What the OED says is technically correct, but the scientific success of the Positivist approach has given metaphysics a negative meaning now, and this in turn has had radical consequences. Every observation about world affairs, for example, is not scientific, since it can be falsified once cast in falsifiable terms. There is no hypothesis about world affairs, that is, that has yet survived every attempt to disprove it. For example, the hypothesis that democracies do not go to war with each other is said to have survived falsification attempts long enough to qualify as a scientific conclusion, and is as close as the discipline gets to a scientific law. Uncertainties remain, however, about the quality of this claim. This suggests that the entire discipline should be lumped in with religion, and subsequently shunned.

Comte dealt with this problem by saying that a discipline like world politics was in its Positivist infancy, while neo-Comteans say that scientific methods can deliver superior outcomes, even when they fail to result in a Rationalist science of world affairs. They remain convinced of the importance of reaching in this direction, despite their manifest lack of success in generating reliable knowledge on par with that of physics or chemistry or biology. Thus they say that the more precise the description and explanation of world affairs, the more exact the ability to predict and control it will be, and that only the hypothetico-deductive method can deliver in this regard.

Positivist/Rationalists also highlight the appalling policy consequences that non-Positivist/Rationalist knowing can have, particularly in the hands of the credulous or the malign. To wit, the Nazi notion of "thinking with the blood," and the utterly fallacious "science" that the Nazis used to discriminate against, and ultimately to try and exterminate, Jews, gypsies, communists, gays, the disabled, and any others they deemed non-Aryan, "impure," and therefore biologically "unfit." Even when widely endorsed (as Rationalists never tire of pointing out), the results of non-Rationalist research can be "trashy, false, or deceptively sophisticated . . . ." If there are "prophets, messiahs and apocalyptic dawns," they say, then "there are also false prophets, false messiahs and false dawns . . . [R]eciprocal acknowledgement, however passionate, is no guarantee against delusion" (Ree, 2000, 167). Hence their own preference for Rationalism, and for the skeptical and critical appraisal it allows of non-Rationalist illusions.

While good beginners are said to be skeptics, skepticism is only a beginning, however. Positivism/Rationalism is not as unassailable as its proponents may think. For example, the neo-Comtean notion that the more scientific the method, the more certain the result, is seen by non-Rationalists as being self-serving. More specifically, they see this notion as radically compromised by the kind of limiting and distorting factors fundamental to the Rationalist project as a whole. Because of these factors (which will be outlined below), non-Rationalists see Rationalism as being "too crude" an approach to reliably assess world affairs with alone (Stevenson and Haberman, 1998, 20). Such factors can only ensure, they say, a kind of "elegant messiness" (Bryson, 2003, 147). In addition, non-Rationalists argue that there are non-Rationalist epistemologies that provide accounts of world affairs of direct relevance to our knowledge of world affairs, accounts that reaching in the direction of Rationalism actively precludes. The knowledge that these other epistemologies provide is not *necessarily* false, either. It may not be open to public scrutiny, in the way that Rationalist knowledge ostensibly is, but this does not make it *inevitably* untrue. Indeed, it may be just this kind of knowledge that takes us beyond the limits and distortions Rationalism creates, beyond the "horizon of science," as it were, to make possible the very "survival of humanity as we know it" (Kolakowski, 1990b, 135). To repeat: scientific Rationalism is not "science itself." It is a philosophic doctrine, an analytic language, an ideology. And though its practitioners shun all ways of knowing other than their own because they do not " 'deliver the goods' as science does" (Kolakowski, 1990b, 105), this does not make Rationalism any less of an analytic language, and any less susceptible, as a consequence, to the limits and distortions that the presuppositions underpinning all analytic languages can cause.

There are at least six factors, seemingly intrinsic to the Positivist/Rationalist approach, that non-Rationalists say limit and distort it. These factors pertain to the more moderate British and Continental forms of Rationalism, as well as to the more extreme American ones. Positivist/Rationalists themselves see the doctrine's advantages outweighing any such disadvantages (assuming they acknowledge that the latter even exist). Non-Rationalists disagree.

The first compromising factor is the assumption Positivist/Rationalists make about the efficacy of the objectifying mind-gaze (see chapter 1). Objectifying is an extremely powerful mind-tool, particularly when applied to the natural world (though even here, principles like that of quantum indeterminacy suggest the presence of important limits and distortions). The Rationalist mind-gaze means detachment. Detachment in turn means an improved capacity to see patterns of cause and effect. However, detachment also removes us from our social context, and therefore what we learn by being part of that context (Devetak, 1995).

Diagram 0.1 depicts the construction of the modernist/Rationalist self. Those born into a modernist society—represented here by the little circles inside the ellipse labeled *non-modernity/pre-modernity*—start off culturally unspecified. In a modernist context they are taught to pull away mentally from the communal one, as if from a rubber sheet, the better to prioritize reason as an end in itself. They remain part of that context, being gendered, for example, and/or ethnocentric, in the way their society might be. They learn to push away regardless, though.

Having been taught to objectify, they then converse with other individuals, similarly mentally constructed. In so doing they become part of a

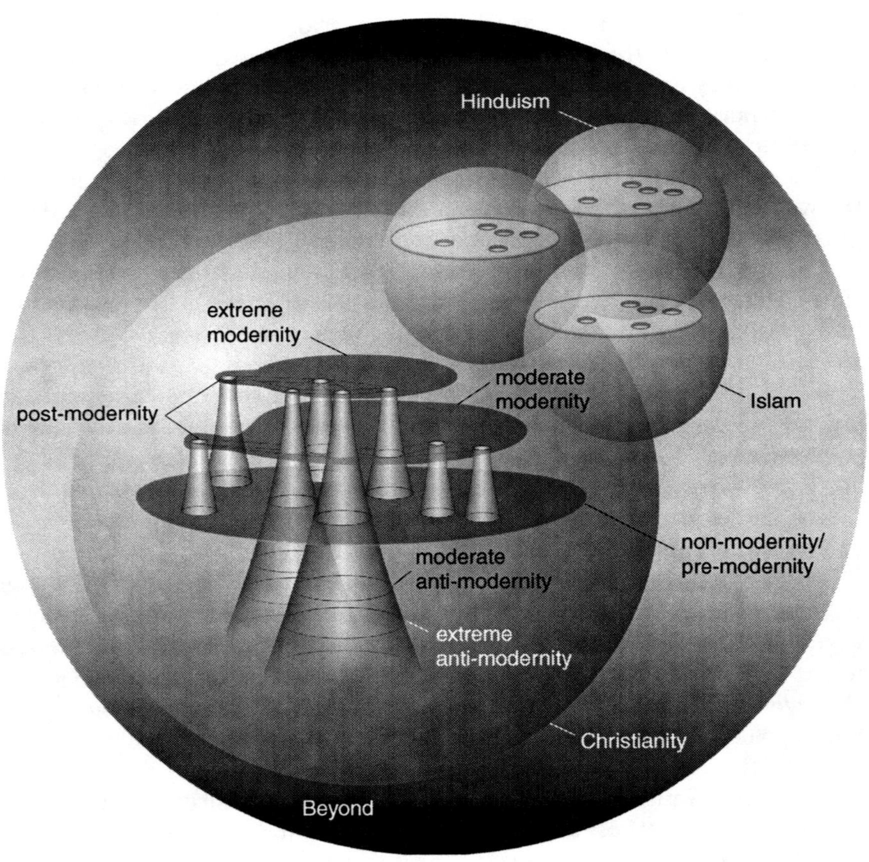

Diagram 0.1

notional meta-society, depicted here by the superordinate ellipse: *moderate modernity*. The lines that represent their mental conversations are marked, and it is here that we find modernist world affairs being made. The conclusions they come to get read back upon the world as policy prescriptions (see diagrams 1.1 and 1.2).

The individuation process can be valorized so highly that a second-order meta-society results, represented above by the superordinate ellipse: *extreme modernity*. We find modernist world affairs being made here too, though in more abstract versions, and mostly in the United States.

Some modernists choose to move off to one side, to turn reason back on itself. This is the ultimate rationalist critique of Rationalism, and is shown as a distortion of both the moderate and extreme ellipse, that is, as *postmodernity*. Others reject Rationalism in favor of emotivism, however, seeking, in their romantic fashion, a return to the experience of the lived world and of the primacy of sentiment. Others again reject Rationalism in favor of an embedded and embodied use of reason, seeking, in their phenomenological fashion, a return to the experience of the lived world, while continuing to espouse the primacy of the intellect.

The making of the modernist form of the self occludes the extent to which the construction process is embedded in the non-modernist context of Christianity. As modernists learn to objectify, they learn to eschew their sacralist instincts. For most of them, the Christian mind-move is an antimodernist one, opposed to their own. For Christians, however, modernity is simply part of being Christian. The Christian mind-move is to meditate, worship, pray, or adore. It is represented here by the first of the sacralist ellipses and is called, in deference to the modernist project, *moderate anti-modernity*. Those who go further become saints. This is shown here as the second of the sacralist ellipses, and is called, again in deference to the modernist project, *extreme anti-modernity*. Beyond this is the *Beyond*, where the self becomes the *Self*. This is where the prophets and divines come from and go.

The Christian context is not the only one in which modernist projects are currently constructed. There are other politico-spiritual contexts (Islamic, Hindu, Buddhist, Taoist, Confucian, Pagan, Animist, and so on). Modernity impinges upon all of them, and they impinge upon modernity. Hence the overlap between them all, and the "multiple" forms contemporary modernity now takes. These contexts are represented here as other spheres. Each sphere hosts its own form of modernity where it overlaps modernity, a form expressive of its own ontology. This is shown by the ellipse drawn within each overlap domain.

This diagram could well have been constructed the other way around. In this case, each particular modernist would be seen as sinking into a discrete pit of individuation, as he or she comes to prioritize reason as an end in itself. He or she would then tunnel toward others to make mental contact. The sacralist/antimodernists would then be seen as rising toward the *Beyond*, as they succeed in their faith.

The gendered nature of this self, and the cognate significance of patriarchy, is well hidden. So, too, is its neo-imperial, racial, ecological, and anarchistic significance. Being well hidden does not mean that these aspects are not there, however, or not important.

Objectifying is closely related to the second compromising factor, which results from the individuation required to make objectifying possible (see also chapter 1). Absolute individuation would require complete asociality. It would require us to renounce our humanity completely. Therefore, individuation is usually relative. Even so, becoming the kind of person capable of being an objectifying one means learning to detach ourselves, not only from our social context but also from each other. The valorization of this sense of self results in politico-strategic, -economic, and -social liberalism. It is personally emancipatory. It is also alienates, however. It only succeeds at the expense of a diminution in our sense of communalism. Nor, non-Rationalists argue, is the individuated self that Positivism/Rationalism fosters as fixed an entity as its proponents seem to think (Gupta and Ferguson, 1997, 20). For example, there is evidence to suggest that it remains more "decentred" and "multiple" than Rationalists suggest (Edkins, 1999, 22; Jameson, 2000, 68, fn. 16). To the extent that this is so, we might expect the "I" who speaks these words to fail to communicate successfully with the "not-I" who reads them (Levinas, 1961), and the Rationalist project to be radically compromised to the extent that this is the case. There is also evidence to suggest that the "I" only exists in relationship, which would limit and distort our ability to objectify in another way, and with it, the Rationalist mind-gaze again.

This leads to the third compromising factor, which is to do with how we remain imbued with the values and prejudices of our social environment, even as we learn to detach ourselves from it and become more personally autonomous there. We do not, by becoming individuated, become a kind of mental blank slate. We do not become people without qualities. The individuated self remains a product of its social context. We remain engendered and embodied, for example, and ethnocentric and class conscious, and open to intuition. This, in turn, limits and distorts the objectivity of our outlook, whether we realize it or not.

The fourth compromising factor has to do with the point of all this objectifying and individuating, which is to give reason as free a rein as possible. Big "R" Rationalism requires the prioritization of reason as an end in itself. This requires the eschewal of emotion, which once again may not matter much where study of the natural world is concerned (though there are scientists who argue otherwise—see chapter 11). Appropriate emotion does provide a check on the illusions that untrammeled reason is prone to, however. Conclusions arrived at without reference to the feelings that let us know what particular facts mean (and this is particularly so with regard to world affairs) can result in descriptions and explanations that are simply not true. Reason used without the relevant emotional associations can result in virtual versions of reality that may be intellectually plausible, but are actually false. This can happen to the individual, for example, when specific brain lesions prevent reason and emotion relating in the normal way (Capgras syndrome). It can also happen to whole cultures, however, particularly where hypertrophy of the intellect, of the kind that Rationalism entails, prevents reason and emotion relating in the usual way. This, in turn, prevents the appropriate feelings being used to check for deluded thoughts (which is not to eschew the use of reason to dispel the illusions created by untrammeled emotion, but rather to highlight how emotion can dispel the illusions created by untrammeled reason).

The fifth compromising factor has to do with the ability of language to correspond to reality closely enough for it to be a correlate thereof. We converse with each other about world affairs, for example, as objectively as we can, but language itself is not a neutral tool. There is no language that does not involve presumptions, and does not, therefore, limit or distort our capacity to know world affairs with scientific certainty. What English-speaking Rationalists are taught from birth with regard to the priority to be given objectifying thinking, for example, is exacerbated in their particular case by a language that consistently depicts the world as "things." (It is instructive to compare English with classical Chinese in this regard, the latter being a language that depicts the world as a "persistently episodic one," and the experience of that world as being "processional, transformative, and always provisional . . . " (Ames and Rosemont, 1998, 20–1, 23, 30).)

Like the postmodernist mind-gaze, which carried through to its logical endpoint means death of the intellect, the poststructuralist concern for language, carried through to its logical endpoint, renders us mute. By stopping short of self-extinction, postmodernists are able to unsettle modernist stories about the telling of ultimate truths, and to open thinking and speaking spaces for those whom modernity marginalizes. By stopping short of self-negation, poststructuralists are able to do likewise. They are able to deploy their profoundly reflexive interest in the talking and writing of world affairs *per se* to expose the pretensions of those who would posit an external reality that can be definitively described and explained, thereby unsettling modernist certainty in another way, and opening similar spaces for analysis and dissent (Campbell, 1992; Edkins, 1999).

The sixth, and final compromising factor is intrinsic to the Positivist/Rationalist approach only because it is not possible to be completely Rationalist without having the eye and ear of a god. Divine status is given to few. Most fall short, and never acquire the scientific perspective such status makes possible. Falling short, however, we invariably make assumptions about human nature and nurturing practices that trammel our use of reason in the same way that our socially acquired prejudices do.

Limiting and distorting factors like these would suggest the need to escape Rationalism's "invisible shadow," if we are to know as much as possible about the way the world works (Heidegger, 1977, 136). The particular assumptions required to make Rationalism operative not only preclude it from grasping the Grail of universal, eternal, and absolute Truth. They also render problematic even the attempt to reach in this Grail's direction.

Mabbott once likened Rationalism to climbing a cathedral tower. As we ascend, he said, we glimpse from the little windows that open along the way ever more comprehensive views of the surrounding countryside. We are lured on, he argued, by the belief that there is a little room at the top, with windows all around, where the whole world is wide open to our ever curious gaze. Mabbott did not believe that we ever make it to this place of ultimate clarity. He did consider the climb worthwhile, though (Mabbott, 1958, 9–10).

The problematic nature of the assumptions that underpin Mabbott's metaphor make his tower much less solid than it seems, however. All such towers only appear to be built upon firm ground. They are built in swamps, or seas, or even mid-air, and the compromised character of their foundations arguably affects the standing of the whole subsequent structure.

Which is why Carse suggests that we use a different image entirely. Why not look at knowing not as tower climbing, he says, but as a kind of mind gardening? Why not see analysts as nurturing thoughts in the way gardeners grow plants? Why not highlight how mental horticulture can be used to weed out undesired ideas, to water and fertilize the ones that are wanted, and to watch as the preferred crop fruits or flowers, and then falls back to earth to be dug in to further the next one, and to further the efforts of mind-gardeners yet to come? (Carse, 1986, 118–35). It is we who decide what fields to leave fallow, and whether to nurture a host of analytic daffodils, or one huge scientific zucchini. There is no single, eternal, universal crop of knowledge, to be harvested forever and by all (Kolakowski, 1990a, 240–1).

If, as Carse seems to urge, we decide not only to compensate for the shortcomings of the Positivist/Rationalist approach, but also to allow for ways of knowing that its proponents eschew, what does this mean with regard to knowing world affairs? How do we proceed from here?

The first step away from Positivist/Rationalist orthodoxy is to remain within the purview of the modernist (Positivist/Rationalist) mind-gaze. As such, it is a relatively modest step. It invites us to construct cycles of knowing, rather than pursue science in the linear, unidirectional, seemingly elevated way that objectifying recommends. It is, in effect, to climb up and down Mabbott's tower. It is to seek, as well as the views afforded by the "superior" windows higher up, the news afforded by listening to what is said at the "inferior" cafes at the tower's foot. It is to pursue the kind of understanding that comes from living among the tower's own builders and users.

There are two cycles of knowing in this regard. Together, they make a double epistemological helix. One cycle seeks to combine Positivist knowing with "negativist" knowing of the *romantic* kind (see chapter 2). This involves standing back to look at world affairs from a scientific distance (Positivism/Rationalism), then trying to experience these affairs emotionally (the irRational form of "negativism"), before standing back to look from a scientific distance again. The other cycle combines Positivist knowing with "negativist" knowing of the *phenomenological* kind. It involves standing back to look at world affairs from a scientific distance (Positivism/Rationalism), then choosing to experience these affairs mentally (the rational, as opposed to the irRational form of "negativism"), then standing back to look from a scientific distance again.

The second step away from Positivist/Rationalist orthodoxy is to step outside this particular cultural milieu to entertain non-Rationalist ways to know (see chapters 3 and 4). This puts the Rationalist project in its own politico-cultural context, and in the light of other such contexts, then asks what communalists, for example, might have to say.

The third and most radical step away from Positivist/Rationalist orthodoxy is to move even further outside the Rationalist milieu to entertain not only "negativist," not only non-Rationalist, but also *anti*-Rationalist ways to know (see chapters 5 through 11). This puts the Rationalist project in its own politico-spiritual context, and into the light of non-Christian sacralist discourses as well.

Comte eschewed all three of these steps, though he eschewed the third step in particular. Neo-Comteans do likewise. What follows tries to show what we gain by eschewing the likes of Comte and the neo-Comteans.

What follows, then, outlines the neo-Comtean approach to world affairs (what in mainstream parlance is called the modernist project, or "modernity"). It then briefly explores the epistemological possibilities of subjectifying as well as objectifying the subject.

After that it explores some communalist alternatives to modernist world affairs. More specifically, it explores the range of epistemological possibilities presented by a study of the world politics of world heritage.

It then explores some non-Christian accounts of particular aspects of modernist world affairs. More specifically, it explores the range of epistemological possibilities presented by a study of Taoist strategics, Buddhist economics, Islamic civics, Confucian marxism, Hindu constructivism, Pagan feminism, and Animist environmentalism.

Part I

Modernity

Most contemporary world affairs are part of the modernist project. They are mostly, that is, part of a historically unique and analytically radical attempt to prioritize reason as an end in itself, not as the province of a privileged few, but in principle, at least, as a whole cultural undertaking. Comte was part of this project. He was one of those who promoted its epistemological preferences and its ontological assumptions. He was one of those determined to establish the primacy of the analytical claims it makes. Neo-Comteans do likewise, though they are better known as Rationalists now (or as they like to depict themselves, as "modernists").

The proponents of this project consider it uniquely characteristic of contemporary times, hence their appropriation of the term "modern," and of the concept of "modernity." This renders any other project non-modern, and seemingly less innovative and up-to-date, though this can also be seen as a self-serving bid to capture the positive connotations of this word for the exclusive use of the proponents of the Rationalist mind-gaze.

The modernist project is first of all European and Christian. As it impinges globally, however, its proponents encounter other cultural practices and other sacral discourses. There are many modernities now as peoples around the world choose, or are obliged to choose, to adapt to, and to adopt modernist principles, and then do so in their own inimitable fashion (Eisenstadt, 2000).

This section focuses on the modernist project as it pertains to the contemporary (Euro-American) discipline of world affairs. It outlines the ways in which these affairs are described and explained, sketching briefly the analytical languages articulated by modernist analysts, and the key features of the politico-cultural milieu in which they articulate them. Later the work will explore the ongoing significance of the Christian milieu in which this project arose, as well as the sacral insights that seem to have been the inspiration for a number of the world's great faiths, and what these insights reveal when brought to bear upon the modernist project in general, and modernist world affairs in particular. At the moment, however, it simply seeks to analyze the modernist construction of these world affairs, and the culture of reason they promote and protect.

Chapter 1

World Affairs—The Modernist Project

What does it mean to say that world affairs are part of a modernist politico-cultural project centered on the twentieth-century version of Positivism, namely, Rationalism? What does it mean to prioritize reason as an end in itself, as a whole cultural value, which is what Rationalism entails? What is modernity, and what kind of world affairs are modernist ones?

Rationalism is more than mere awareness of the human capacity for reason, since reason was manifest by *homo sapiens* long before axial times (Jaspers, 1953). More is also involved than the placing of a priority upon the human capacity for reason as an end in itself, since individuals in all societies and cultures, and in all historic epochs, have eschewed authoritative traditions to explore what might be known with an intellect as untrammeled as possible. Rather, it means the placing of a priority upon the use of the rational abilities of the mind as an end in itself, by whole societies, that is, by the whole culture that informs such societies (if not in practice, then at least in principle).

The philosophic rationale for this kind of thinking and speaking has been called Objectivism, since Rationalism is predicated upon intellectual detachment and an objectifying mind-gaze (Husserl, 1970, 68–9). This requires (somewhat paradoxically) the social construction of a de-sociated sense of the self, however. The more autonomous and individuated the sense of the self, Rationalists argue, the more possible it is to give reason free rein (Mehta, 1985, 2). And though such a self could not be manifest completely without the person concerned going mad, or becoming a god, or both, it is the ongoing attempt to construct such selves *en masse* that makes for Rationalism *en masse*. It is the cultural Grail modernists reach toward, even though it could not be grasped without the individual becoming completely detached, completely objective, and therefore divine or insane (see diagram 0.1).

The individuation of the individual that Rationalist objectifying requires has to be taught for. The ability to stand back mentally from the society in which the individual is born has to be inculcated from birth. It is not easy knowledge to acquire, but a persistent social emphasis placed upon the priority of seeing the world from a mental distance does ensure that the individual is able, in due course, to participate more fully in the modernist project, and in modernist world affairs (Bull, 1999).

It is a moot point which one came first, Rationalism/Objectivism or individuation/subjectivism. They are now two sides of one emergent politico-cultural coin, however, with the modernist individual being the one who subsequently "sees," while everything else (including the self that still resides in the world) is "seen."

Across whole societies, and even between them, objectifying minds learn at the same time to converse with each other, creating in the process a mental meta-society. It is here, using reason that is as untrammeled as we can make it, that the contemporary natural sciences are constructed. It is here, too, that the contemporary social sciences are devised, including modernist world affairs. It is here, that is, that we talk across to each other, in a relatively disembedded and disembodied way, in analytical languages that articulate our ideas about good rule, sound commerce, and appropriate global behavior (this talk is represented by the lines drawn between the modernist selves, at both moderate and extreme levels, in diagram 0.1). The relative character of such talk (as poststructuralists point out) is an important issue in itself.

The result of giving reason relatively free rein has been a series of scientific, technological, industrial, and social revolutions. It was these revolutions that so markedly augmented the European capacity to project its military power, making it possible for Europeans to build vast and invasive empires, as they did in the nineteenth century. When these empires fell apart, after two major wars, they left many monuments behind, which continue to dominate world affairs. These monuments include the contemporary state and state-system, the global market and world capitalism, nationalized civic identities, internationalized class identities, a stressed planetary ecology, various "first peoples" rendered radically marginal, and universal forms of male hegemony.

Those heartened rather than alienated by the emancipatory feel of Rationalism valorize even more highly the use of reason as an end in itself. They place an even greater value upon the en-selving process, becoming doubly detached. They aspire to a mental distance twice removed from the society in which they were born, where they create among themselves an even more abstract mental meta-society, and articulate even more abstract forms of the modernist project and modernist world affairs (Taylor, 1989).

It is analysts of the latter sort who tend to entertain the more abstract and scientifically rigorous notions of social studies. Doubly convinced of the sovereign status of the objectifying mind-gaze, they tend to cast all policy preferences in hypothetico-deductive terms, talking across to each other about "rational actor" theories, human rights, market freedoms, international regimes, and other such profoundly individuated thought-forms.

Historically, this involved a move away from the "old" world (British and Continental) to the "new" (the United States). Rationalism in America is notably more reflexive than in Europe and Britain, and the "observing subject" in the former is given notably greater politico-cultural prominence than in the latter (Foucault, 1994, xiii, xiv). As a consequence, there are two relatively discrete sets of modernist conversation about contemporary world affairs, as well as two relatively discrete sets of policy preferences, one (the American) being notably more rarified and abstracted than the other (the Anglo-European).

This can clearly be seen, for example, in the debate that took place in the 1960s between British "traditionalists" and American "behavioralists." While the British traditionalists were content to stand mentally apart from the world at one remove, and to construe scientific thinking in terms of systematic thinking, the American behavioralists preferred to apply much more strict scientific criteria, and much more explicit and quantifiable formulations of cause and effect (Bull, 1966; Kaplan, 1966a; Smith, 2002). The same sort of difference became apparent in the attempt made in the 1970s to prise neorealism (Waltz, 1979) apart from classical realism (Morgenthau, 1972 [1948]; Bull, 1977; Aron, 1966), and again in the 1980s in the attempt to distinguish internationalism in its "English school" format (Bull and Watson, 1984; Little, 2000) from parallel efforts by the American mainstream (Keohane and Nye, 1977).

It should be noted at the beginning, as well, that to make modernity, and hence modernist world affairs, is to make some notable margins to this project at the same time. Most obviously, it is to make margins of those deemed (by modernists, not themselves) pre- and postmodernist. Less obviously, it is to make margins of women, environmentalists, "first peoples," postcolonialists, anarchists, and the poor.

There are, for example, those who continue to resist or reject the modernist penchant for reason as an end in itself, and who prefer wherever possible not to adopt or adapt to the kind of world affairs that modernity entails. These premodernists, so-called, remain more or less resolutely determined not to convert to modernity as a politico-cultural doctrine. Though they may be obliged to manifest alternate or hybrid identities in global arenas, they attempt to retain as much as they can of their own ways of living (Smith, 1999).

Then there are those who take reason and turn it back on itself. These are those modernists who would use untrammeled reason to question the assumptions Rationalism itself is predicated upon, and the conclusions that Rationalists tend to come to.

The danger here is of a degree of reflexivity so extreme that it ends up refuting itself (Esteva and Prakash, 1998; Tallis, 2002, 4). By stopping short of the self-refutation point, however, these postmodernists, so-called, are able to contest modernist claims to have made our knowing singularly reliable, universal, eternal, absolute, and true (George, 1994). They are able to contest what is seen to be the modernist preclusion of a "wider and more effective" sense of life (Tallis, 2002, 4). And they are able to provide thinking and speaking spaces for those marginalized by modernity in general, and by aspects of modernist world affairs in particular (Darby, 1997).

If we look closer at modernity's margins, conspicuous at once are women. The modernist project is gendered, and so are modernist world affairs, since the (mostly male, white, well-off and "Western") proponents of this project tend to assume that women are less rational than men. This makes it possible for them to discriminate against women, to make that discrimination seem natural and normal, and to make the central contribution of women to world affairs seem like a peripheral one. As a consequence women do not, overall, enjoy anywhere near the same advantages as men. Gender-specific disparities in terms of relative command of power, status, or wealth are manifest, for example, in terms of who the contemporary state-makers are, who controls the contemporary state-system, and the ratio of women to men in this regard. They are also obvious in terms of who possesses capital power, who gets the bulk of the market's rewards, and who gets most respect accorded their human rights claims (Pettman, 1996). The entire modernist project is patently sexist, and militates against women's life chances and choices. Which is why most (but not all) feminists would want to couch the whole discussion of world affairs in terms of gender distortion, and why feminists, whether on the margins made within the modernist project (like liberal or marxist ones), or on the margins constructed outside of this project (like the pre- or post-modernist ones), highlight the male-made nature of the modernist project, and see men as the main problem with the kind of world affairs modernists make (Zalewski and Parpart, 1998).

The modernist project is also ethnocentric, and so, as a consequence, are modernist world affairs. Which is why it is argued that world affairs "cannot be adequately represented through the existing categories of Western thought. . . ." A "different order of political possibilities" is prefigured by non-Western ways of thinking, particularly given the way they push the discipline "up to and beyond" the limits Rationalism sets (Seth, 2000, 226). Postcolonialists understand this ethnocentricity well. So, too, do indigenous peoples, as they struggle to conserve what remains of their language, their preferred ways of living, their resources, and their land. For postcolonials and indigenes on the margins within this project, the fight-back strategies might be modernist ones. They might, for example, involve contesting Euro-American hegemony in liberalist or marxist ways. For those on the margins outside of this project, however, pre- and postmodernist fight-back strategies might be used to contradict what Rationalists say about their capacity to access superior knowledge, and to highlight the partial nature of what is considered to be a costly epistemological conceit (Smith, 1999; Bugotu, 1976).

The modernist project is one that is also relatively indifferent to its environmental consequences. Environmentalists who look at the impact of modernist world affairs on the health of the planet as a whole, for example, and who fear for our capacity to sustain life on earth, tend to be characterized as uncommitted to the modernist cause, and marginalized accordingly. A concern for global pollution, resource depletion, and population growth, though, or the ecological threats represented by nuclear, chemical, and biological weapons, can be sufficient to see those expressing such concerns consigned to the periphery of the modernist project. From outside of this project, premodernist environmentalists seek to reinstate what they consider to be sustainable ecological practices, and postmodernist environmentalists question the Rationalistic certainty that underpins scientific attempts to say the planet's ecology is surviving modernist onslaughts. Within the modernist project, meanwhile, collectivist environmentalists confront liberalist ones, internationalist environmentalists confront realist ones, and so on.

Nor is the modernist project particularly amenable to anarchists. Humankind abhors chaos, since it precludes what human life ordinarily entails, so we continually organize our environment at every level to provide for order. The character of that order can vary widely, however, from the most centrist and authoritarian to the most diffused and anarchistic. Anarchists are those who see sovereign states, managed markets, and collective attempts to define our civic identity as preventing us from living free, ungoverned, self-determined lives. This puts them at odds with those who would institute a state-made, marketeering, nation-based form of world affairs, and ensures their peripheral status.

As for the poor, the injustice and inequity that modernist world affairs involve is evidenced by a growing disparity in global wealth, and by an ongoing failure to alleviate the worst examples of global poverty. This is not to deny the material prosperity and well-being that the various modernist revolutions have made possible. It is rather to note how poverty continues to spread as modernist world affairs do, and how the attempts made so far to bring the productive largesse of this extraordinary project to the majority of humankind, via the contemporary construction of world affairs, continues to fail. The modernist project can be a singularly uncharitable one in this regard, the poor often being blamed for their poverty, and for not embracing wholeheartedly enough the solutions offered by the dominant modernist analytical languages.

If we look not at their margins, but at modernist world affairs themselves, it is striking how the attempt to use reason as an end in itself has resulted, over the last 300 years, in a wide range of ways in which to account for these affairs. These diverse ways generally present as a complex minestrone of doctrines and concepts, which is why the discipline as a whole can seem analytically as chaotic as the world system itself.

What sense can be made of this profusion (and confusion) of ideas and ideologies? The first clue is provided by the division of modernist mental labor that has been emerging for 300 years between those who study "politics," "economics," and "sociology" (Milbank, 1990, 4). By now, for example, it is possible to differentiate between world affairs analysts who highlight state-making and politico-strategic accounts of the subject, and who tend to talk about military and diplomatic affairs, world affairs analysts who highlight market making and the politico-economy of the subject, and who tend to talk about demand and supply issues, and world affairs analysts who highlight the making of the self-in-society and politico-social accounts of the subject, and who tend to talk about issues of identity and socialization. ("Politico-" appears as a prefix throughout because politics is taken here to mean the art of getting one's own way, whether individually or collectively. As such it is seen to refer to a form of human behavior that is truly ubiquitous.)

Human Nature

A second clue as to the kind of systematic overview that might apply to modernist world affairs is one that was given by Martin Wight. He was the first to suggest a differential reading of the politico-strategic dimension to world affairs, and to identify three main doctrines as component parts of this particular dimension. He labeled these doctrines realism, rationalism, and revolutionism (Wight, 1967).

These three doctrines seem to correspond to three different assumptions about human nature. There is a basic difference, that is, between those modernists who assume that we are basically bad (base/fearful/aggressive), and who talk as a consequence about competitive power politicking; those modernists who assume that we are basically calculating (neutral/canny), and who talk as a consequence about more reciprocal and cooperative forms of conducting world affairs; and those modernists who assume that we are basically good (benign/caring/altruistic), and who talk as a consequence about more collaborative forms of conducting world affairs.

While Wight's term for the first clump of analysts was realism, and this remains common analytic parlance to this day, his term for the second clump, rationalism, confuses the modernist's underlying commitment to reason as an end in itself, with one of the ways in which reason gets brought to bear upon world affairs, namely, internationalism. It is no surprise that Wight's use of rationalism has not endured.

If Wight had been more concerned to understand the way world politics are constructed within the modernist project, and the Rationalist character of that project, he would probably not have used rationalism the way he did. He would likely have reserved the word to denote the ideology of modernity itself, as is done here, and used another term (like internationalism) to denote the analytical language used to articulate world affairs by those who see human nature as essentially calculating (see diagram 1.1).

Wight also used revolutionism to refer to what is more accurately called globalism. Revolutionism has marxist connotations. It tends, therefore, to confuse a doctrine derived from the assumption that we are essentially good (globalism), with a doctrine whose proponents tend to argue that we are not by nature essentially anything (marxism). Globalism can certainly seem revolutionary, especially when compared to realism. This is no doubt why Wight chose to use it. However, globalism is less revolutionary than the outcome of the class struggle described by classical marxists would be, and it is therefore a better term for what Wight meant.

		Politico-strategic	Politico-economic	Politico-social
	Bad	Realism	Mercantilism	Nationalism
Human nature	Calculating	Internationalism ("idealism")	Liberalism	Individualism
	Good	Globalism ("idealism")	Socialism	Collectivism

Diagram 1.1

	Materialist	Marxism
Human nurture	Less materialist/ more idealist	Neo-marxism
	Idealist	Neo-Hegelianism (Constructivism)

Diagram 1.2

Our second clue as to how to order modernist thinking about world affairs was provided by Robert Gilpin, who was the first to popularize a Wight-style reading of the second dimension to world affairs, the politico-economic one. Political economists converge on three specific doctrines, he said, which he called mercantilism, liberalism, and marxism (Gilpin, 1987).

Only two of these doctrines articulate assumptions about our essential human nature, however. One is mercantilism, which is the politico-economic version of a commitment to state interest (the concomitant of realism). Mercantilists tend to assume that human beings are basically bad, in the same way realists do. The other doctrine is liberalism, which is the politico-economic version of a commitment to the market (the concomitant of internationalism). Liberalists tend to assume that human beings are basically calculating, in the same way internationalists do (see diagram 1.1).

The problem category here is marxism, since marxists make assumptions about the essential nature of human nurturing practices, not about our essential human nature. The politico-economic concomitant of politico-strategic globalism is socialism not marxism (i.e., socialism of the non-marxist sort). It is the socialists, like the globalists, who tend to assume that human beings are basically good. It is socialism, not marxism, which is therefore the politico-economic parallel of globalism. Marxism inhabits another matrix entirely, namely, the nurturist one (see diagram 1.2).

What of the third dimension to world affairs, the politico-social one? In the light of Wight and Gilpin's work, there would seem to be a good case for positing a parallel reading here too. This gives us nationalism (as the concomitant of realism and mercantilism), individualism (as the concomitant of internationalism and liberalism), and collectivism (as the concomitant of globalism and socialism).

It also gives us a matrix of nine analytical languages overall. These languages (and the many analytic dialects of which they are composed) constitute a large part of the modernist account of world affairs.

Human Nature as Essentially Bad: Realism, Mercantilism, Nationalism

Realism is no more real than any other politico-strategic principle. Realists do tend, though, as part of their self-promotion, to depict their competitors as singularly idealistic and utopian. This is the same ploy modernists use to depict their competitors as hidebound and old-fashioned.

The assumption behind realism is that human nature is essentially adversarial. It is a modernist doctrine, and its proponents are Rationalist. However, realists also assume (even though they are not supposed to make assumptions, since assumptions trammel reason) that as a species, we are basically bad.

As Rationalists, realists may not see this as an assumption. They may see it instead as a conclusion justified in the light of scientific findings about human behavior. This is invariably a rationalization, however. Realists rarely engage in serious discussions about the nature of human nature. If they did, they might have to concede that we are not only bad. They may have to concede that we manifest other primary qualities as well.

Consider, for example, the best known contemporary account of realism, an account Hans Morgenthau wrote at a time (the end of World War II and the beginning of the Cold War) when world affairs was dominated by struggles for big power preponderance (Morgenthau, 1972 [1948]), and it was relatively easy to depict the competition for world power as "universal in time and space," and simply "undeniable" (Morgenthau, 1972 [1948], 16–17). Morgenthau argued that human beings are basically bad, and cited the work of a University of Chicago colleague, Malcolm Sharp, in support of this argument. After reviewing the anthropological literature of his day, Sharp found only one case of a people (the Todas of India) whose conduct contradicted the hypothesis that human behavior is governed by a "universal," "innate," and "indestructible homicidal impulse . . . " (Sharp, 1947, 7). He subsequently concluded that the desire to "surpass," the "impulse to dominate," "simple hatred," and an "impulse to kill, however vicariously," work independently of "rational considerations" (Sharp, 1947, 24). Morgenthau concurred, subsequently construing the desire to dominate as "constitutive" of all human society, whether it be in the form of the family, or in the form of world affairs (Morgenthau, 1972, 17).

Though Morgenthau saw his depiction of human nature as being borne out by scientific research, thereby giving it Rationalism's highest sanction, he accepted a single article as sufficient to validate his endorsement. Morgenthau did not seriously canvass alternative accounts. He simply opted for one account by a colleague he agreed with.

Because of their pessimism, all realists tend to highlight the importance of physical force, seeing peace as only ever a lull between wars. They highlight, for example, the ungoverned and therefore anarchic character of the contemporary state system, and the prevalence there of the pursuit of national interests (Carr, 1991 [1939]). They see state-makers as promoting the bordering, centralizing, sovereign practices that they do mainly because they are part of a system of "others," who are all behaving in the same defensive/aggressive way. The result is a kill-or-be-killed, self-help milieu, that is characterized by "high political" *realpolitik*.

That people are basically bad, however, does not mean the state system has to be. Realists note emergent outcomes at the level of whole systems, for example, like the balancing of power, and how this can order world affairs, despite the malign propensities of all those involved. These patterns to whole system practice ("structures") are what are seen as preventing violence.

This leads in turn to the idea of levels-of-analysis, and the prospect of a more calculating, more abstract, *neo*realism. Thus we find Kenneth Waltz, for example, talking not in terms of bio-psychological drives, but of the structure of the state system as a whole. Realist behavior patterns repeat "endlessly," he says, with "dismaying persistence," and with "striking sameness..." (Waltz, 1979, 66). They are the result of an ongoing anarchic structure that is "generative" for the system as a whole, he argues, since it acts back upon the system's parts, thereby causing their subsequent interactions (Waltz, 1979, 72).

Waltz's version of realism is more abstract than Morgenthau's, since Waltz is a new-world Rationalist, and Morgenthau is an old-world one. At the heart of Waltz's analysis, however, is the same pessimistic assumption about our essential human nature. Because of his focus on the whole system, Waltz is seemingly unaware of this assumption, but his view of state-makers as helping themselves, and as struggling for power in an ungoverned world, vividly betrays his pessimism. Such self-help behavior would not be deemed relevant if state-makers were not deemed bad. Waltz's conclusion is only appropriate if he takes a negative view of human behavior. Though he wants to highlight the structural imperatives the whole system provides, and wants to see people as calculative (prefiguring a more liberal notion of self-help), he still thinks self-help is the only preferred strategy.

Both neorealists and classical realists see human beings as perennially bad, therefore. They see the structure of the state-system in terms of abiding imperatives that no "rational" state-maker can resist if he or she wants to survive. They remain wedded to a decidedly dire view of human affairs. If they did not, they would not see the ungoverned nature of the state system as such a dangerous one, and they would not be able to reject, as readily as they do, the legitimacy of state practices other than kill-or-be-killed ones.

Mercantilism is the concomitant politico-economic principle, since it rests on the same belief that human beings are ruthless, especially in groups (Niebuhr, 1936). Protectionism, or as it is otherwise known, economic nationalism, valorizes market self-help in the form of state self-sufficiency (List, 1966 [1885]).

At their most extreme, mercantilists are autarkic. In their more moderate guise, they tend to recommend quotas, tariffs (like import duties), and non-tariff barriers (like domestic subsidies, exclusionary regulations, targeted taxes, and the vertical integration of productive interests located abroad), as preferred ways to protect national industries and to foster state autonomy.

Nationalism is the concomitant politico-social principle, since it is the most statist doctrine in the discipline's third, politico-social dimension. As an analytic language nationalism is spoken widely by those "imagined communities" that constitute nation-states (Anderson, 1991). Since the nineteenth century, that is, state-makers have sought to legitimize their rule by fostering an atavistic sense of neotribal solidarity. In appealing to the feelings provided by a common language, a shared history, and a common culture, they have sought to inculcate neo-communalist solidarity, even where it does not exist.

Despite all we might feel about those who share "our" nation with "us," however, "our" nation is also defined in terms of "our" difference from "them." At worst, "they" are seen to be out to get "us." At best, "we" have to be pessimistic about "their" motives, regardless of how long "we" have known "them." It is human nature after all, nationalists aver, to be suspicious of foreigners and minorities, immigrants and exiles, and for international conflict always to be imminent. Locally, we may be solidarist and therefore mutually supportive. Globally, however, we must be nationalistic to meet the ever-impending foe.

The notion that each state should be a singular nation also works in reverse, prompting those who feel seized by a common national cause to seek their own state. The collapse of the great European empires gave the concept of self-determination considerable credence, though multinational states and multistate nations remain the norm. In a world where there are several thousand nations and 200 states, the fit between the two remains extremely poor.

Human Nature as Essentially Calculative: Individualism, Liberalism, Internationalism

Since Rationalism prioritizes not only reason, but also the objectifying self who is able to give reason more free rein, it is no surprise to find Rationalists valorizing that kind of self (and its global surrogate, the individual state). It is no surprise, either, to find many Rationalists assuming that human nature is essentially calculating.

The doctrine of the "sovereign self," or politico-social individualism, is a doctrine that valorizes the socially emancipated, self-realizing, self-maximizing citizen, who is relatively autonomous with regard to the society in which "it" grows up (Taylor, 1989). It is this kind of individual that underpins liberal conceptions of human rights, the rule of law, commercial contract, and representative democracy. Every society is made up of individuals, since everyone is a unique genetic experiment. Not all societies systematically promote individuated behavior on a society-wide basis, however. Those that do are the ones we denote as being individualist.

Individualism as a politico-economic principle articulates market liberalism, and the free movement of goods, labor, capital, and ideas (Smith, 1892 [1776]; Hayek, 1991). The most extreme liberals would dispense with the modernist state altogether (Godwin, 1971 [1793]; Rothbard, 1973). The more moderate liberals would not go so far, though they differ widely on how large a role the state should play. Some see as appropriate a ring-holding role (Nozick, 1974), both local and global. Others advocate a more interventionist role, one with the power to smooth out the bust and boom cycle that most markets manifest (Keynes, 1926).

Individualism as a politico-strategic doctrine promotes interstate interdependence and reciprocity, that is, the principle of internationalism. Here we find agency being conferred upon reified conceptions of "the state," which are then seen acting with sovereign determination on the world stage ("Japan" doing this and "America" doing that), despite there being considerable conceptual tension between the idea of a sovereign individual, and the idea of a sovereign state. While moderate internationalists cope with this tension by accepting the fiction that "the state" has "its" own autonomous personality and "its" own independent capacity to act (Teson, 1997, 55–61), the more extreme individualists reject this fiction, seeing the sovereign self as being superior to or more fundamental than the sovereign state, and crafting their rights claims, and their ideas about humanitarian intervention, accordingly.

Some proponents of internationalism show a keen interest in the way inter-governmental and nongovernmental institutions currently proliferate (Keohane and Nye, 1977). They may even use liberalist concerns to bring conclusions about market behavior from the politico-economic dimension into the politico-strategic one, making possible in the process a neoliberal/neorealist synthesis (Waltz, 1979; Waever, 1996).

Other, more anarchic internationalists, see the world system first in terms of calculating, inter-connected individuals, and only second in terms of states or other international institutions (Burton, 1968). This is the analytic dialect that is most consistent with liberalist individualism, though it is radically at odds with a view of the world based on state- and nation-based behavior, and tends as a consequence to get paradigm-policed.

The assumption behind all three of these theoretical principles—individualism, liberalism, and internationalism—is the assumption that human beings are essentially calculating (as opposed to base or benign). Making this assumption makes it possible to posit a concept of people without qualities. It makes it possible, that is, to posit a sense of self that subordinates gender, race, ethnic origin, sexual preference, and religious faith, while exalting a single abstract quality, namely, our common humanity. This makes possible a concept of abstract rights and responsibilities, in turn, as well as a concept of rule by law, majority rule, market behavior, international organization, and the more informal arrangement of "regimes."

Human Nature as Essentially Good: Collectivism, Socialism, Globalism

People compensate for the alienating effects of individuation not only by forming nations, but also by forming associations and social movements. This provides another theoretical principle fundamental to politico-social affairs, namely, collectivism.

This principle denotes how people come together as feminists, environmentalists, civil socialists, and so on, to further a common political interest or cause. Rather than kill-or-be-killed, or live-and-let-live, it bids us: simply "connect."

The overall effect of politico-social activity of this kind is a web of relationships now so dense that it warrants separate description in terms of a global civil society. One notion of this web would have collectivist movements creating a global civil society sufficiently robust to support global governance, and ultimately even global government. Another, more anarchistic approach, would envisage a much more diffuse, decentralized, and localized outcome.

The politico-economic form of this principle is socialism, though socialism of the sort that assumes people are essentially good enough to coordinate centralized forms of production and distribution. This is not socialism as marxists conceive of it, but rather nonrevolutionary socialism, as envisaged by those who highlight our natural capacity to care.

At the global level, most socialists would want planned production worldwide, as a way of meeting people's basic needs as equitably and as directly as possible (Burkitt, 1984). This means more than governmental or intergovernmental intervention, in the form of the World Trade Organization, for example, or the International Monetary Fund, or the World Bank. It means more than the idea of liberal ring-holders, regulating the world market to prevent bust and boom. It means having world rulers with enough power to plan production on a global basis, or some anarcho-socialist variant thereof (where production is planned to the same global purpose but in a much more decentralized way).

The politico-strategic concomitant of collectivism and socialism is globalism. Like the proponents of these other two doctrines, the proponents of globalism are Rationalists. They also, however, assume that human nature is essentially good, decent, altruistic, empathetic, and benign. Such an assumption lets "us" include most of "them" in "our" sense of who we might be. Indeed, we may not even have a choice in the matter, given the extent to which we may be biologically predisposed to be this way.

Most globalists think it not unrealistic to envisage a state-based, global (con)federation (Kant, 1963 [1795]), or even a one-world government. They imagine the regional alliances currently emerging in Europe, Asia, and the Americas, for example, coming together to make such an institution (though there are globalists who would eschew such a centralized outcome altogether in favor of one more localized).

Human Nurturing Practices

Analysts clump not only with regard to their assumptions about human nature, but also with regard to their assumptions about the essential character of our human nurturing practices. By misclassifying marxism, Gilpin alerts us to the existence of another analytic schema, one where we find those doctrines that articulate the idea that we are what we learn to be, not what we are born to be. This leads to quite another matrix.

The main difference in this second matrix is between those analysts who assume that nurturing patterns are caused materially, and those who assume they are caused mentally, though there is a third group of analysts who combine the two. Mention has already been made of the marxists, who account for world affairs in historically materialist terms and particular modes of production. There are, in addition, the Hegelians, however—currently called "constructivists"—who account for world affairs in mentalist terms. And then there are the neo-marxists, who effect a materialist/mentalist mix.

Analytical languages that articulate nurturing practices tend not to subscribe to the modernist division of mental labor between students of politics, economics, and sociology. They tend to highlight features of world affairs that cut across these concerns, like international classes, or global epistemic communities. The marxists, for example, see this disciplinary division of labor as part of the smokescreen thrown up by the owning and managing bourgeoisie. The Hegelians, on the other hand, see it as irrelevant, since we can think into being any division of disciplinary labor we like, and should not feel confined to what we inherit in this regard. Neo-marxists simply note the ubiquity of hegemony.

Human Nurture in Essentially Materialist Terms: Marxism

There are various ways of talking about world affairs in materialist terms. There is political geography, for example, which highlights the effect that physical location has upon world affairs, land-based peoples being said to face different challenges from those surrounded by sea. There is also technological determinism, which purports to explain how changes in technology effect world affairs in terms other than those of class struggle. The diverse impact of "guns, germs and steel," for example, has been used to account for the primacy of entire civilizations (Diamond, 1998). These geopolitical and technopolitical accounts of world affairs can be particularly compelling for world affairs practitioners, who must often deal at first hand with the physical vulnerability of their supply lines, or the impact of new forms of communication or transport, crop production, or disease.

The most important way of talking about world affairs in materialist terms, however, is the marxist one. As an analytic language, marxism describes world affairs in terms of historic changes in the means of production (technology), and the social relationships that characterize these changes (class struggle).

For Marx, these world affairs are fundamentally capitalist, a term he defined not only as referring to the private ownership and management of the means of production, but also as referring to the way workers are obliged to sell their labor for wages on a market like a commodity (Marx and Engels, 1971 [1848]). The theoretical principles represented by the first matrix—the naturist one—are seen as radically misleading in this light. Class formation and class struggle are seen as pre-eminent instead. State-makers are seen as being subject to bourgeois manipulation, therefore, more than they are to the ungoverned character of the state-system. Entrepreneurs and non-entrepreneurs are seen as being subject to the mechanics of capitalism, more than they are to the mechanics of the market. Moreover, those who seek to define our civic sense of ourselves are seen as being subject to ruling class indoctrination, more than they are to the autonomous attempt to define identity. (For later marxists, and particularly for those who make the doubly detached "American" mind-move, the structure of the world capitalist system itself is the key factor, with its core, its periphery, and its semi-periphery in-between (Wallerstein, 1974–80).)

Marx saw the best in human beings as only being realized under the best of human conditions. Because of the way history worked, this meant socialism first, though socialism in a very specific sense, namely, socialism as that particular mode of production that comes after capitalism, where the workers, having overthrown the owners and managers, dismantle the state and the state-system and put advanced communism in its stead. Only at the end of the entire historical sequence of dialectical change, Marx argued, do we finally get the conditions under which our "species being" can emerge (Eagleton, 1999; cf. Geras, 1983).

This nurturist view of socialism is radically at odds with the naturist view of socialism, a view already articulated above as one being redolent of an optimistic notion of human nature. Naturist socialists see marxists as dividing the global left wing and weakening its global impact. Marxists think of naturist socialists as stopping the workers from becoming self-aware, and bringing on the revolution to end all revolutions.

Human Nurture in Materialist/Mentalist Terms: Neo-marxism

Not all of those inspired by what Marx espoused are as committed as he was, however, to its materialist rationale. Many of those who follow him, while just as aware of the role productive forces play in shaping human affairs, often prefer to place the same weight he placed himself in his earlier years upon mental alienation, and upon ruling class attempts to legitimize their power by mentalist means.

These analysts subscribe to theoretical principles that are broadly called neo-marxist ones, the philosophic rationale for which is a self-conscious combination of both materialism and mentalism. Neo-marxists argue that world affairs are made not only of "stuff," but also of "ideas." Therefore they see state-makers playing a much more independent role in supporting the capitalist cause. They see them as being much more reflexive, much less "determined," and explicitly promoting private ownership, private management of the means of production, and the voluntarist extraction of surplus value on wage-based terms. While Marx highlighted the ineluctable law of historical materialism, that is, neo-marxists highlight the ongoing, conscious construction of bourgeois oppression.

Neo-marxists include the Critical Theorists of the Frankfurt School, as well as neo-Gramscians. The former argue that a proletarian revolution is not inevitable, and that ideas about social change can be relatively independent (though not wholly independent) of the material substructure that Marx identifies as the basis of all social reality (Horkheimer, 1972; Adorno, 1973; Habermas, 1978). Neo-Gramscians take a similar view, while construing human consciousness as something we can detach from its material environment in a much more thoroughgoing fashion than Marx finally did (Gramsci, 1973; Gill, 1993; Cox, 1987). All neo-marxists see liberalism, for example, as an ideological force in its own right, and as impinging independently. All note the way bourgeois doctrines get widely disseminated through the media and the schools, and how their proponents draw in the process upon the power and the institutions of the state.

Human Nurture in Essentially Mentalist Terms: Neo-Hegelianism ("Constructivism")

Marx is said to have turned Hegel on his analytic head. Hegel was turned upright again under the aegis of those who eschew the materialist assumptions Marx makes, to assert the primacy of our mentalist preoccupations instead. The analytical language that these particular modernists speak highlights ideas, norms, values, and rules, indeed, any of the cognitive practices that make world affairs mentally meaningful. The idea of the state is one such cognitive practice, as is the idea of the market, and the idea of the self. A constructivist would detach these ideas from any material context and endow them with their own causative force.

In neo-Hegelian/constructivist terms, then, to change our ideas about the state and state-system is to change world affairs. "We"—socially and individually—construct these ideas. They do not result from our essential selves. Moreover, if we can construct them, then we can deconstruct them, and reconstruct them again in some other guise.

The rationale for this kind of idealism rests upon the epistemological assumption that it is mental imagining that matters most. As such this is not a doctrine to be confused with the two supposedly "idealist" (utopian) alternatives to realism, namely, internationalism and globalism.

As non-materialists, constructivists are non-marxists. It is no surprise, therefore, to find the doctrine, at least as applied to world affairs, owing most at the moment to American liberals, who use it to help keep marxism at bay in the post–Cold War period. (They use it to keep a more radical, postmodernist threat at bay as well, since it allows them to embrace mentalist concerns without having to use non-modernist methodologies to do so.) The Soviet Union gave American analysts a ready excuse to discount the significance of marxist thought. They lost that excuse when the Soviet system collapsed, leaving them with the analytic task of thinking up a new one. The result was constructivism, the conservative forms of which—both "hard-line" and "soft-line"—are specifically designed to eschew marxist thinking (Pettman, 2000; Katzenstein et al., 1998). Being non-marxist also follows from a more revisionist form of this doctrine, as espoused by the so-called "Miami Group," whose members seek a rule-oriented theory of social behavior sufficiently comprehensive to do away with a separate discipline of world affairs altogether (Onuf, 1989).

Being non-marxist does not apply to a third form of constructivism, though, which argues the need for analysts to do world affairs research in more proximal ways. Analysis, according to this particular constructivist dialect, is about taking part personally in the subject, wherever possible and as much as possible, thereby providing access to the "commonsense" that ordinary people share in constructing world affairs in the way that they do (Pettman, 2000). This commonsense can be either emotional or phenomenological, and is accessed by first standing back to look (like conservative constructivists), then standing close to listen (like rule-oriented constructivists), and then taking part.

Human Nature and Nurture?

In world affairs practice, human beings manifest *both* essential natures *and* the ways in which they are subsequently nurtured. Nature and nurture are both determinants of what we do, the outcome being ongoing, non-additive, complex, and extremely difficult to disentangle.

Is such a dichotomy a viable one, then? Even though it is arguably the key to the way modernist analysts of world affairs do clump, should we sanction it? Should we sanction doing such violence to what actually obtains?

Evolutionary psychologists argue that "far from being a superficial issue, the nature/nurture controversy has profound evolutionary and biological roots" (Badcock, 2000, 266; Cosmides et al., 1995, 3). Plotkin says, for example, that "[t]he nature–nurture issue is not an option for social scientists; it isn't a conceptual game that we can either choose to get involved in or refuse to play. The nature–nurture problem *is* the central and essential issue that has to be settled for *every* aspect of human behaviour. . ." (Plotkin, 1998, 70).

There is a case for taking this dichotomy seriously, therefore, however fraught it might be in practice. So why is there so little interest in doing so in the study of world affairs? What might explain such resounding neglect, given how germane it is to analytic accounts of these affairs?

First, there is lack of awareness. Our assumptions are pervasive. They are like the air we breathe and the water we drink. We simply tend not to notice them.

Second, there is the Rationalist prioritization of untrammeled reason. Since any assumption compromises Rationalism, analysts of this ilk tend to ignore the assumptions they make. They tend not to want to notice them.

Third, there is the feeling that such a dichotomy restricts analysis to person-centered accounts of world affairs, or at very least, places a priority upon person-centered accounts of these affairs, at the expense of social or structural ones. This feeling is arguably an artifact of the way "[o]ne never *sees* the social except in the instance of its manifestation in 'individual' (bodily and linguistic) action" (Milbank, 1990, 71). The issue is not one of the personal taking precedence over the social or the structural, however. It is one of "antinomy. . . mediated by narration. . . ." (Milbank, 1990, 71), and of a lack of capacity to see this narration as being one about ourselves.

To sum up, then: a systematic account of the analytical languages used to describe and explain (and prescribe for) modernist world affairs reveals the ground upon which most of the arguments about them take place. This ground is made up of different assumptions about human nature and human nurturing practices. It is these preconceptions that inform all the different analytical languages, and these that turn arguments about world affairs into a kind of Punch and Judy show, where those doing the arguing whack away at each other, but the animating motives remain hidden from view.

In making such assumptions, modernist analysts are at odds with their commitment to using the intellect in an untrammeled way. Axioms like these do trammel the use of reason. They undermine Rationalism and should, strictly speaking, disqualify anyone who does such supposing from being called a modernist.

The contradiction is not as serious as it might seem, however. First, all "intelligence" depends on "lumping together things that share properties" (Pinker, 2002, 203). Second, the completely untrammeled use of reason would require a totally objective and therefore totally individuated sense of self, and that is not possible because of how socially embedded we are, and how gender-biased, ethnocentric, and embedded in language we are, and because of how much the lived-world, and practical knowledge, precedes all our theorizing.

Each analytic language, *including Rationalism itself*, speaks for an aspect of human being and human behavior. It presents part of the truth, even when it purports to present the whole. This is why such a wide range of analytical languages persists, despite the best efforts by their proponents to account for every other language in terms of their own. This is also why we find such eclectic attempts to speak several analytical languages at once, and to formulate "multiple working hypotheses" (Chamberlin, 1890). These hypotheses are not easy to formulate coherently because of the incommensurable character of the different assumptions involved but our analytic worth can be measured by how well we struggle with this incommensurability.

The analytical languages themselves are also more complex than is represented here. Much more generous accounts of all of them are available for those concerned with nuance and detail, however (Smith et al., 1996; Brown, 1997; Boucher, 1998; Burchill et al., 2001; Weber, 2001).

The point of the above was to demonstrate the pattern these analytical languages present as a whole. It was to provide a sketch of international relations theorizing as configured overall. By sketching the pattern that modernist analytical languages present, it is possible to see more clearly the limits the whole project sets, and the distortions it can cause. It demonstrates more clearly how the modernist outlook both clarifies and confounds our capacity to account for world affairs. On the one hand, for example, Rationalism makes for mental distance, freeing reason to look for explanatory patterns and causal chains using particular analytical languages. In this regard, modernist Rationalism enlightens and emancipates. On the other hand, the making of mental distance is predicated upon assumptions that constrain and skew the very project they are supposed to promote. In this regard (and at the same time) modernist Rationalism hinders and hides.

The Rationalist eschewal of the non- and the anti-Rational, in particular, precludes any kind of communal or sacral understanding. It confines our knowing exclusively to what secular, individuated reason can provide. Which is a problem, since we may well "be" the universe in ways we do not Rationally comprehend, or that the "first person" construction of modernist Rationalism occludes (Angel, 1994, 144). As indicated in the Introduction, the mental distance from the world that Rationalist individuation involves means the eschewal of social and sacral awareness, and of the knowledge that comes with individual embodiment, social embeddedness, and sacral understanding. This can seriously distort our knowledge of what being human involves, and can have a serious impact in turn upon attempts to describe, explain, predict, and control global affairs.

Getting behind the complexity of world affairs is often depicted as getting to the root of them. In the light of the above, however, this may not be the only metaphor of relevance to the study of this subject. For example, "rhizomes" may be just as appropriate as "roots," since rhizomes grow horizontally not vertically, just on or under the surface of the earth, where they connect everything to everything else (Deleuze and Guattari, 1987).

With the possibilities of a rhizomatic analysis in mind, the next section of this study looks at the modernist project from a non-modernist perspective. Since modernity is a politico-cultural project of extraordinary scope and complexity, however, a case study approach is taken here. By focusing on the world politics of world heritage, the non-modernist challenge to modernist hegemony is more readily revealed, and it is possible to see how multiple forms of modernity emerge as the modernist project becomes more de-centered, and as communalist (non-modernist) ways of "truth-saying... proving, and judging... [what is] good" come to prevail (Chan, 2001, 2). Exploring how modernists define the past, and in particular, how UNESCO (the United Nations Educational, Scientific and Cultural Organization) defines the past, makes is possible to see how modernity's basic assumptions get imposed upon other ways of knowing and living, how non-modernist cultures resist, embrace, adapt to, and innovate in the face of such impositions, and how non-modernist cultures act back upon the modernist one in the process. Those who live in any so-called non-modernist milieu will be influenced by modernist world affairs. They will not embrace these affairs without question, however. They will understand and critique them in terms of their own politico-cultural awareness, forging hybrid alternatives from which modernists themselves can and do learn. This, in turn, allows us to imagine a discipline able to articulate both modernist and non-modernist accounts of world affairs. It allows us to imagine a *world* affairs, more redolent of the majority of those in the world, and less beholden to the dominant minority there (Muzaffar, 1998).

Looking outside the modernist project also involves looking at its sacral root. It means accounting for modernist world affairs in the politico-spiritual terms that this context provides by noting, for example, the influence Christian thought forms still have on modernist world affairs. More rhizomatically, however, it means looking beyond the Christian root to consider other sacral connections. It means accounting for world affairs in the politico-spiritual terms these connections represent by noting what insights other faiths have to offer, for example, and by noting what form these world affairs might take as they further encounter these faiths. This will be the focus of the final section of this work.

CHAPTER 2

WORLD AFFAIRS—THE MOVIE

Looking outside the modernist project is done here mostly in the modernist way. This means that "other" cultural and sacral traditions will be explored below in an abstract, Rationalist fashion, that is notably universalist. For example, "world heritage" and "world religions" are discussed later, but the discussions eschew all the lived experiences involved. This is to subject these discussions to the same limits and distortions that all modernist thinking entails.

It is arguably worth pausing, then, to consider how we might compensate for modernity's shortcomings in this regard. How, for example, might we take the first step away from Rationalist orthodoxy, as described in the Introduction?

The first step would be one that stays within the modernist milieu, but deliberately subjectifies it. It is one that would involve deliberately standing close to listen to the practice of world affairs, and taking part, before standing back to look at the subject again in the orthodox Rationalist fashion. For though Rationalism is of demonstrable worth as a way to know, it is not the only way to know, or even necessarily the best way to know, particularly given what proximal research methods can do, that distal research methods cannot.

Proximal research methods foster not only participant observation but also participant understanding. They invite us to experience world affairs in a subjectifying fashion. They invite us to appreciate what objectifying is specifically designed to eschew, namely, how the facts we choose about world affairs feel.

As noted earlier, this book adopts the same objectifying mind-mode that modernists do. It does not, on the whole, attempt to step away from what is "seen" using the objectifying mind-gaze, to conduct research of a more experiential kind. Nor does it use logics less linear and less parsimonious—mosaic logics, for example, logics that proceed in parallel and in multiple streams, logics that converge from different points of awareness, or logics that spiral in toward their conclusions rather than proceed straight away toward them (Kaplan, 1966b, 10).

Except for what follows. Though the step toward experience is a contentious one (Gupta and Ferguson, 1997), the participant understanding it provides is as compelling as the knowledge that objectifying Rationalism provides. This can be readily demonstrated by considering, for example, what American state-makers might have learned about the durability of their Soviet adversary by sending drunk poets around the Soviet Union disguised as vodka sellers, to talk to ordinary citizens in their kitchens, rather than by relying on satellite measurements of the wheat crop in the Ukraine, and spy reports of elite Soviet conversations. In terms of a capacity to anticipate the communist regime's collapse, the latter proved to be woefully inadequate. American epistemological preferences precluded any sustained attempt to get closer to listen to Soviet accounts of their own predicament, however, ultimately to the detriment of the political understanding of the American policy-makers concerned.

What follows is an attempt to provide the reader with a more proximal experience of how world affairs feel. In a book, this can only be done vicariously, but it can be done. To repeat: this does not mean shunning the Rationalist outlook. Rather, it means using this outlook to provide distal accounts of world affairs, then subjecting these accounts to the more proximal sorts of scrutiny, then reassessing the results. The reassessment part of this cycle of knowing is left here to the reader. Meanwhile, enter right . . .

    . . . our *Narrator*:

    I'm standing on the roof of a mid-city skyscraper. I'm holding a suitcase and it's full of rocks so it's pretty heavy. I'm just about to drop it over the edge here, onto the side-walk. It's lunch-time and the pavement is pretty crowded, so I'm very likely to hit one of the pedestrians below.

    Before I let go I want to ask you what chance you think I have of hitting a good person. 70%? 50% 30%?

[The narrator drops the suitcase. The camera tracks its descent but the frame freezes just over the heads of the people in the street. The image rotates through 360 degrees, as our attention is returned to the . . .]

Narrator (voice over):

    If you think I've got 70% chance of hitting a good person, you're probably optimistic about human nature. You probably think that we're essentially good.

    If you think I've got 30% chance of hitting a good person, you're probably a pessimist. You probably think that we're basically bad.

    If you think I've got 50% chance, or you want to know more about what the pedestrians are like, then you probably see people as something else, probably something more like what you're doing by asking this question. You probably think that we're basically calculating.

[The suitcase completes its fall, narrowly missing two startled pedestrians, before smashing into the pavement.]

Narrator (standing by the suitcase, as pedestrians pass in profusion, sometimes bumping into one another in a rather aggressive way):

    Feelings about how good or bad we happen to be, just like ideas about what it means to grow up in different places, or what it means to be a particular gender, are fundamental to all our ideas about international affairs.

Narrator (takes out of his coat pocket a folded map of the world and unfolds it, holding it toward the camera. He starts to walk forwards. The pedestrians walking by tend to collide with him as they pass . . .):

    Take this map of the world. It's the usual sort of map. It shows all the world's countries, their territories, their borders, their capital cities, that sort of thing. What's most interesting about this map is what it doesn't show, though. To the pessimist, for example, this is a Wild West world . . .

[Fade in images of cowboys and (Amer)indians charging to and fro.]

Narrator (voice over):

. . . where international peace is only a lull between wars. Pessimists see this world as predicated upon self-help. As it's ungoverned, they see world affairs as anarchic. They see it as full of potential enemies. They see it as only ever ordered temporarily, and only then as the result of some kind of armed truce.

[Interview with a notable state-maker, discussing the vulnerability of the contemporary state in an ungoverned, and therefore anarchic world, and the necessity for constant vigilance and eternal suspicion.]

Narrator (sets fire to the map with a lighter. He drops the blazing map and takes out another, unfolding it and holding it up. It's a map of major transnational corporations, showing their global subsidiaries. He continues walking along the street towards the camera. The pedestrians continue to bump into him . . .):

Behind the most common kind of map is another one. This map's a map of the world's markets. It's a map of multinational corporations, global production systems, and international labour flows. It's a map of trade and investment, commercial wheeling and dealing, manufacturing patterns, and patterns that show where the world's work gets done. Pessimists see this map as a dog-eat-dog one too.

[Excerpt from Bruce Petty's short film for the Australian Broadcasting Commission, *The Money Game* (n.d.).]

Narrator (voice over):

If people are basically bad, then what "they" win, "we" lose, and what "we" win, "they" lose. Any country that wants to be well-off has to protect itself from economic exploitation by outsiders. It has to control the way the world market crosses its economic borders. It has to make sure that what crosses these borders is done on its terms, and not those of others.

[Interview with another notable state-maker, discussing the vulnerability of the contemporary state economy in a world one that's unregulated, and the necessity for protectionist measures that control short-term capital in- and out-flows.]

Narrator (sets fire to second map. He drops it and takes out another one. He continues to walk along the street towards camera. The pedestrians continue to be relatively aggressive in how they pass . . .):

Behind the map of the international political economy is another one again. This map's a map of the global civil society. It shows people's social identities on a world scale. It shows how, in global terms, people think about themselves and their societies. It shows what kinds of patterns these identities make.

[Fade in an image of a European soccer crowd, chanting in unison.]

Narrator (voice over):

Not surprisingly, those pessimistic about human nature see this map as a kill-or-be-killed one too. While "we" might trust those who share our language, our culture, our history, our common identity, "they" are not to be trusted. "They" are "other" people, to be frowned upon or feared.

[Interview with an English soccer lout, articulating the kind of patriotism associated with highly emotive forms of national loyalty, and expressing the lout's radical aversion to non-nationals.]

Narrator (continuing to walk along the street. This time the pedestrians are less aggressive, occasionally making polite comments as they pass . . .):

What if you're not a pessimist, though? What if you think people are neither good nor bad, but something else? What if you see people as essentially calculating, for example? Maybe you think we can do better than these dog-eat-dog, kill-or-be-killed, Wild West types believe we can. Maybe you think that by thinking and talking we can cooperate, instead of having to compete all the time.

[Fade in images of world leaders meeting, shaking hands, etc.]

Narrator (voice over):

After all, we do manage to make international laws and international organizations. Post a letter at one end of the world, and there's a fair chance it'll reach the other. There are thousands of inter-state organizations that work all the time to mutually beneficial effect. Leaders meet globally, and against all the odds, they do make international rules, and some of these rules even get obeyed. We don't resort to war all the time. We don't always conflict. We often choose to live-and-let-live, thinking of each other more as rivals, with interests in common, than enemies, always at odds.

[Interview with a United Nations official, talking about the kinds of things that international laws and organizations make possible, as well as the international courts, and the willingness to endorse more cooperative ways of behaving in the world.]

Narrator (continuing to walk along the street, still among more sociable pedestrians . . .):

How does an assumption like this apply to the world market? Seeing human nature as calculating rather than bad allows us to imagine a world where individuals make decisions for themselves about what to produce and what to consume, where to invest and when to work.

[Fade in images of a local vegetable market, goods being shipped, stock exchange deals, etc.]

Narrator (voice over):

This is the liberal market, with all the supply-and-demand puzzles that its shoppers set . . .

[Fade in images of stock exchange floor trading. Then images of a parliamentary debate on economic regulation.]

Narrator (voice over):

. . . like the state controls that local markets may need to stop monopolies destroying them, or to cope with the things marketeer's don't want to be bothered with, like cleaning up, or funding dispute settlement institutions, or building airports. World markets may need a hegemonic power to hold the ring for them like this, so that they don't self-destruct.

[Images of parliamentary debate becoming images of sideshow sprewkers shouting: "Roll up, roll up. Everyone's a winner. Everyone gets a prize. You, ma'am? You, sir!"]

Narrator (voice over):

A liberal market is one where harmony is supposed to happen of its own accord. The pursuit of private interest is assumed to provide for the public good at the same time. This simple social equation, *private gain* equals *public good*, has proved to be a very powerful one. It's had more of an effect than Einstein's *e* equals *mc* (squared).

[Interview with a notable business person extolling the virtues of a deregulated and privatized market in terms of efficiency and effectiveness, explaining how under such circumstances the weak get weeded out, information flows more freely, prices are driven down, and service improves. He or she recommends individual incentives as the best way to maximize labor productivity, reward entrepreneurial flair, and make new jobs.]

Narrator (continuing to walk along the street among more sociable pedestrians):

How does a more calculative view of human nature apply to how people feel about the society rather than the market? What kind of global individual does it imply?

Well, basically it's one where personal freedom is paramount . . .

[Fade in images of democratic behaviour, voters going to the polls, etc.]

Narrator (voice over):

. . . a world of independent selves, who each have to think who to vote for, what values to believe in, what job to do, and how to answer the big questions about the meaning of it all.

A global society of constantly calculating individuals is one where people behave tit-for-tat. It's one where people relate to each other as autonomous beings, where they build sets of rules that promote democracy, human rights, and written constitutions.

[Interview with an "ordinary citizen" about being an individual in a world where autonomy is prioritized; the interviewer seeks to find out how, for example, it felt being brought home as a baby, stuck in a cot in a room alone, being obliged to scream for help which did not always come; how it felt having to decide as a child what to be once grown up; how it felt to be given pocket money as a form of apprentice wages; how it felt to have a premium placed on the personal capacity to decide what was good or bad in the world, and what the whole of life—and death—might mean.]

Narrator (turning off the street into a park, where people are picnicking on the lawns and playing together. The narrator takes out a blow-up, plastic globe of the world and a small air-pump. He starts inflating the globe):

What if you're not a pessimist, though? What if you're not someone who thinks we're basically calculating? What if you're an optimist instead—one of those people who think we're essentially good? Then you probably think we can do better than this. You probably think we can have a world that's neither kill-or-be-killed, nor tit-for-tat, a world where our best hope lies in our capacity to inter-connect, and where sympathy and empathy and altruism prevail. There's no reason, you might think, why a world of people like these could not be governed globally as well as locally, or at very least, why it could not have more comprehensive global peace-keeping and judicial structures that the ones we have at the moment . . .

[A sedate progression of images of globalist practices, e.g. United Nations peace-keepers at work, etc.]

Narrator (voice over):

. . . structures that would bring together state-makers as potential friends, not cunning rivals, or dangerous enemies. Optimists want a cosmopolitan planet. They want order and justice for all. And they think we're good enough to get it.

[Interview with an academic advocate of a one-world solution to international conflict, articulating the various options in this regard, and the means whereby the most likely of these options, namely, a global confederation of regional confederations, might be achieved.]

Narrator (still in the park, still with people in the background playing games, etc., and having a bit of difficulty getting the plastic globe to stay inflated):

How does the optimist see the world market? What would they do with the global political economy? They'd certainly try and do better than economic nationalism. They'd certainly try to do better than endless interpersonal competition as well. If, like they say, we're basically benevolent . . .

[Fade in images of socialistic practices, e.g. a commune or coop shop.]

Narrator (voice over):

. . . then there's no reason not to think we can plan the world market to meet everybody's needs. There's no reason not to think that we can bring the benefits of the industrial revolution to everyone on the planet. Why not alleviate poverty world-wide? We certainly have the industrial means to do so. Why not feed, clothe, and house everyone? We just need to plan global production systems that are socialistic and cosmopolitan, rather than liberal and competitive, or protectionist and defensive. And for that, we just need to exploit our capacity for sympathy and altruism.

[Interview with a notable representative of the world's poor, extolling the advantages of a world market organised for the good of all, rather than for the singular benefit of a few; advocating production planned by a central authority, that is beneficent enough not to divert resources to itself, but to devise production practices that meet basic needs on an equitable basis.]

Narrator (The plastic globe finally inflates. He starts dribbling it around the park with his foot):

What does optimism do for ideas about world society? What sort of world citizen does assuming we're basically good make for? If we're not huddling together, looking for communal solidarity, the way nationalists do; if we're not celebrating our personal independence, the way individualists do; what are we going to do? Well, maybe we could come together for a common interest or a collective cause.

[Fade in images of social movements, going about their work, e.g. anti–free trade demonstrators.]

Narrator (voice over):

Social movements bring people together, not in a backward-looking way, like a nation, but in a more forward-looking way. There are thousands of these in the world today. They oppose the global free trade regime. They save animals threatened with extinction. They expose child labour. They publicize the plight of political prisoners or minority peoples. Collective associations like these are made up of ordinary people using their better feelings to try and improve the lot of other people all around the world.

[Interview with a member of a social movement, discussing the work of that movement, how it is organized, who belongs to it, and what it feels like to act altruistically on a local and global scale.]

Narrator (sitting on a bench in the park):

So: there it is. Three different assumptions about human nature. Good. Bad. Calculating. And a whole range of ways of talking about world affairs, depending on whether we're talking about states or markets or ourselves.

And that's just for starters.

Because there are lots of people who don't think we're basically anything. These people think we behave the way we do because of how we're brought up. They think it's society that makes us what we are, and that it doesn't matter if we're basically good or bad or calculating or anything else. Good societies make good people. Bad societies make bad ones. Smart societies make smart people. Joyous societies make . . . well, you get the picture.

[Fade in advertising images of industrial progress, with happy, smiling consumers doing satisfying things. Cut to Charlie Chaplin, in *Modern Times* (1978 [1936]), having just left the assembly line, continuing to tighten nuts on bolts in mid-air . . .]

Narrator (voice over):

What makes for differences like these, though? Some people think societies are determined by their technology . . .

[Cut to a rapid succession of images of historically significant machinery, like the plow, the sail, the clock, etc.]

Narrator (voice over):

. . . while some people think it's not only technology. They think we also get taught to decide what kind of society we want . . .

[Cut to a succession of images of extolling production, military recruitment, etc., plus headlines from the TV and press news.]

Narrator (voice over):

. . . while some people think we're the ones who ultimately decide, and that's it. There's nothing else that makes societies the way they are. We are the ones who think up what we want. States and markets and ideas about ourselves are what we make of them.

Narrator (outside the Museum of the Communist Party in Beijing):

I'm standing in front of the Museum of the Communist Party of China, in Tienanmen Square, Beijing. Down there [camera pans left] is the Forbidden Palace of the ancient Chinese emperors. Over there [camera pans the other way] is the tomb of Mao Tse-tung. In here is the story of humankind.

[The camera, hand-held, tracks into the museum, and pans slowly over the cabinets that constitute the part that tells the story of human history, moving around Chinese spectators as it goes.]

Narrator (voice over):

Inside this museum is the story of humankind told in a materialistic way. Like all Marxist parties, China's Communist Party highlights the basics of human life and how they get provided. So they start by describing the primitive technologies we once used to make a living. They talk about the invention of agriculture and how this made for settled society. They talk about slave-owing societies where the surplus was generated by force. They talk about the feudal societies that followed, and how the serfs fed and housed and clothed the aristocrats because they believed it was their duty to do so. They talk about contemporary society as being capitalist, where those who do the work sell their labour for wages, and where declining rates of profit end in revolt. At which point the workers are supposed to dismantle the state system and put a communist one in its place. As communists, people are then supposed to produce what they're best at, and get what they basically need, in a world where they're free to work in the morning, go fishing in the afternoon, and talk philosophy until the early hours of the morn.

[Interview with an academic professor discussing the materialist, and especially the marxist, conception of world politics, contrasting it with neo-marxist alternatives that point out how ideological hegemony plays a more prominent role, and with neo-Hegelian alternatives that argue for a constructivist view of world affairs, where "anarchy is what we make of it," and "free markets are what we make of them" and "we are what we make of ourselves."]

Narrator (back on the original street, standing at an intersection):

Then again, some say the whole question of what we're like has to do with the battle of the sexes, and the way our biology works. Some say it's to do with what we learn about how to be masculine or feminine as we grow up.

[Fade in an image of masculine and feminine behaviour that is stereo-typically Western and urban in character, circa 1950 AD, e.g. a man digging in the back garden stopping to wave to a woman at the sink.]

Narrator (voice over):

The gender fault-line certainly runs through every society and culture. It's so basic it often doesn't get noticed. And even when it is, we often fail to see how important it can be.

[Fade in images of the Greenham Common demonstration, and of the anti-nuclear protesters there, pinning tea-sets to the missile base fence, etc.]

Narrator (voice over):

Here we see some of the women who for decades protested at Greenham Common in the U.K. Greenham Common was a nuclear missile base. A number of local women, plus a few men, didn't want nuclear missiles down the road. The nuclear deterrence doctrine said that missiles down the road made them more secure. They said they felt very insecure. They begged to differ and they tried to say so in a number of innovative ways. They didn't manage to get the base closed, but for years they made a very important point.

[Interview with one of the Greenham Common women, discussing what was attempted, what was achieved, and what was not.]

Narrator (at the intersection again):

Industrial capitalists are able to make highly destructive weapons—big, small, and insidious. They do so in very large amounts.

[An armored personnel carrier trundles by. The camera goes inside. Soldiers are driving it, talking on radio communications equipment, etc. Looking outside, we see that the carrier is arriving at a large demonstration.]

Narrator (voice over):

Industrially produced weapons were used by Europeans to build huge global empires. We live in the rubble of these empires. The last of them, the Soviet one, collapsed in 1989. As a consequence we live in two hundred or so European-style states. Or in some cases, we fail to.

The imperial lands are largely gone now but the global power of the imperialists hasn't. This power is less likely to be used to hold territory these days, but it's still used to make sure that world affairs work to the benefit of those who got in on the ground floor. The great Asian come-back challenge is underway, but the men who run world affairs are still mostly white, and they still mostly come from Europe or the United States.

[Interview with an African official on the partition of Africa, followed by an interview with an Australian aboriginal about the slaughter of her ancestors for being unwanted "animals" inhabiting an "empty land," followed by an interview with a Chinese academic about the Opium Wars and the importance of non-intervention.]

Narrator (still on the street corner):

All of which may be academic, as they say.

[A large garbage truck passes. The camera picks up the truck and tracks its progress through the streets until it arrives at a large dump, where it discharges its load onto the shore of a vast sea of rubbish.]

Narrator (voice over):

Humankind's capacity to pollute the planet is unprecedented. It's not that we can't control planet-wide pollution. We can. The problem is that we may not be convinced enough of the need to do so until it's too late. By which stage we may have made our own habitat uninhabitable.

We don't actually know how robust the earth's eco-systems are. We're assuming they're robust enough to cope with what we're currently doing to them. This is a large assumption, though, because if it's wrong, then what we're currently doing to our environment could be making life on earth unsustainable. This means we could be currently in the process of ceasing to survive. And if this happens, then the human race on earth will be run, and so will world affairs. A few might make it off-planet, but there wouldn't be much to come home to, not for a while anyway.

[Interview with an environmentalist, pointing out that all human endeavor is predicated on a viable planetary habitat, and that what we are doing at the present not only has eco-costs in terms of pollution, resource depletion, and the loss of biological diversity, but may carry an absolute eco-cost in terms of the earth's capacity to sustain human life.]

Narrator (still standing at the crowded intersection):

With such a wide range of ways in which to see people, and such a wide range of ways in which to see world affairs, it's no wonder people argue. It's no wonder they find it hard to agree, and why the arguments about world affairs never end. Mostly we talk passed each other, because we don't talk about what really divides us, which is the different assumptions we make about who and what we are really like.

[Fade in animated images of heads talking passed each other as in a Punch-and-Judy show.]

Narrator (voice over):

Imagine you're the leader of a poor country with a large international debt. Imagine that the interest repayments on this debt are crippling your country. Imagine you've got too little to build roads with, or to buy the health services your people need. What do you do?

Narrator (standing at the intersection):

Do you default and declare yourself bankrupt? But then no-one's going to give you any help at all. Do you try and get the debt reduced, while trying to trade your way out of trouble, maybe lifting restrictions on the money and goods that cross your borders, or selling off your country's assets? But then you're only helping to keep the whole system going—the system that got you into debt in the first place—while opening yourself wider to exploitation by people who don't care how you live, people who only want profits. Do you attack those who got you into debt into first place, the international banks and fund managers? But capitalists are powerful. They are likely to fight back. Do you confront the male-made character of the plight your in? Would women do better running things, even though the system is one that women didn't make?

[Fade in images of Russian citizens in 1991 selling their goods on the side of the street.]

Narrator (voice over):

You could be a kleptocrat, of course, and just go on robbing your country blind. That would make you part of the problem, though. If you're a more honest leader, and you really want to help, do you pin your hopes on one of the alternatives just mentioned, like the "free trade and sell the family silver" one? Perhaps you might go for a combination of policies, using every ploy you can think of to help your people out.

Narrator (standing at the intersection, the camera rising to take in his urban context):

All this is important. It's the nitty-gritty of world affairs. One thing we tend not to notice, down here in the thick of it, though, is the context in which people live. Get above the buildings, get a bit of distance, and what do you see? A vast human construct that houses millions.

[The camera slowly becomes more distant. The narrator peers upwards as it gradually passes out of sight. The perspective is that from the camera.]

Narrator (eventually voice over):

This one's a modernist city, so most of it's industrially made. To have modernist industry you have to have modernist technology, and for that you need modernist science, and the modernist modes of thinking that make modernist science possible—objectifying ways to thinking that work the way this camera does.

The camera is currently putting distance between itself and me. As it does so, it sees more. Our minds are similar. If we're taught to put distance between our minds and the world, our minds see more. We think more freely, because we're not so caught up in what the world's doing.

Putting distance between the mind and the world also means becoming a particular kind of person. It means becoming an objectifier. It means becoming more individuated, more independent, less conformist. It means thinking more for yourself, and using that thinking to look for patterns in the world with. It means power, big power, which is why lots of people want it.

[Interview with an old gardener, saying something like: ". . . and it's all an illusion. Knowing stuff is not about having a good view. It's more like gardening. It's more like digging in, fertilising and planting, watering and weeding. You look after the ideas that seem the most promising, and you hope they bloom. They die. You dig them back in and start again. That's what's important. Not trying to see everything or know everything."]

Narrator (standing at the intersection, takes out a palmtop computer and types in a website address. The camera moves in to see the screen until it's completely filled with an image of the world at night: http://antwrp.gsfc. nasa.gov/apod/image/0011/earthlights_dmsp_big.jpg. The sun subsequently rises over the earth's horizon, and the image of the world by night is replaced with one of the earth by day):

Narrator (voice over):

For the first time in human history we do have eyes in the skies. What do they see?

This is the world at night, as space satellites and space travellers see it. From space you can see the lights of human habitation around the whole world.

And this is the world by day, as astronauts see it. There's few signs of people. There's no sign of world politics.

At this height we can see beyond the international world, to the interplanetary one. It's a magnificent sight, astronauts say. Looking out into space, you're looking into the cosmic void, and no-one who has done that has not been awed.

[More of the interview with the old gardener again, who is saying something like: "I'm an astronaut. You're an astronaut. Here's the planet. Look at this leaf. Look at this lady-bird . . ."]

Narrator (standing at the intersection. He points across to the opposite corner. The camera follows the gesture to take in the new aspect):

Narrator (voice over):

Over there is a Christian church. It's an important reminder that the modernist way of using the mind arose in the context of Christianity.

[The camera enters the church and pans along its stained glass windows.]

Narrator (voice over):

The modernist project was first proposed in Europe at a time when Christians were fighting amongst themselves about how best to know god. One part of that project was to take religion out of the public domain, and to put it in the private one. So one consequence of the modernist revolution was to dichotomise the Church and the State, and to put the Church at a political distance.

[The camera focuses on an image of the Cross. It fades to a similar image being carried by a parade in Northern Ireland, followed by footage of clashes between Northern Irish Catholics and Protestants.]

Narrator (voice over):

The traces of that Christian context are still evident in world affairs. They're not just evident in something like the conflict in Northern Ireland, where religion has long been an important source of hate and strife . . .

[Fade in images of footage of the conflict in Vietnam between the U.S. and the Vietcong . . .]

Narrator (voice over):

. . . or in Cold War conflicts like Vietnam, where Christian American Presidents vowed to stop the advance of what they called "godless communism."

[. . . then footage of a choir singing "Onward Christian Soldiers."]

Narrator (voice over):

The traces of modernity's Christian context are to be found in the idea that wars can be just . . .

[It becomes clear that the choir is singing in the Church on the street intersection. The narrator is standing at the back of the choir. The camera gradually focuses on him.]

. . . They're to be found in the value we place upon international peace-making. In the idea that free markets are naturally harmonious. And in the concept that we're all equal and we're all entitled to human rights.

Some credit Christianity with helping perpetuate patriarchy, too. It's because Christians go on so much about the Holy Father and His Son.

Narrator (walks out of the Church back onto the street intersection. The camera backs out):

By being objective, we put religion at a mental distance too. Once at a distance, though, we may not be content to solve the puzzles a religion like Christianity sets. We may want to look for more immediate puzzles to solve. Like how to get customers to pay more.

[A group of Buddhist monks goes passed. The camera follows them to a nearby automatic teller machine, where they stop so one of them can withdraw money.]

Narrator (voice over):

All this thinking is what makes us modernist. It is why we have so much science and technology, and it is how we make our lives more comfortable and healthy and entertaining.

[The monk with the money distributes it to those with him.]

Narrator (voice over):

All this stuff is not working out the same way in other cultures, though. In places that have other ideas about human being, all this emphasis on individual objectivity just doesn't wash.

[Interview with an academic on the issue of contested senses of the self, and the issue of "multiple modernities."]

[The camera continues to track the monks walking down the street. The monks pass an advertising poster for a holiday in Japan, featuring a photo of a bullet train. This becomes footage of a moving bullet train, followed by footage from the train of industrial landscapes.]

Narrator (voice over):

The Japanese were able to select from the West what they needed to make an industrial revolution for themselves. They reproduced the power that scientific technology provides. They built a social form of capitalism second only to that of the liberal capitalists in the United States.

[From the train, the camera takes in the staff of a Japanese firm, on the roof of their factory, doing exercises together.]

It is taking the Japanese much longer to come to terms with the intellectual revolution that's the basis of modern science and scientific industry, though. Japanese culture is relatively conformist. It doesn't teach for the kind of mental autonomy that modernist thinking relies on. As a consequence, modernity is being worked through there in a way that combines the old and the new. The Japanese call this *wakon yosei*, or "Western knowledge, Japanese spirit." It used to be "Chinese knowledge, Japanese spirit." Times change and so do the Japanese, but not as fast as their technology and their industry do.

Narrator (back on the roof of the skyscraper):

I'm back here for a second try. I missed the first time, so I'm going to have another go. I'm getting to enjoy this presenting business. Particularly when you can play at being god.

[The narrator stands at the parapet and gets ready to drop the suitcase. He is unaware that a huge suitcase is falling out of the sky toward his head. The frame freezes just before this second suitcase squashes him flat.]

End

Part II

Community

What is the difference between modernity, and more communalist ways of living and knowing? How do modernists exercise their hegemony, and how do communalists seek to compensate for the limits and distortions of the modernist worldview? And what does this mean for contemporary world affairs?

Modernity is seen here, as discussed already, as a whole cultural project that prioritizes reason as an end itself. Such a project is predicated upon very particular assumptions, like the epistemological primacy accorded the objectifying mind-gaze, and the individuated sense of the self necessary to make such a mind-gaze possible and to give reason untrammeled reign.

A modernist study of the assumptions that make modernity possible will remain within the epistemological rubric set by these assumptions, however. This is why communalists argue that it is necessary to contextualize these premises if we are to understand how modernity is constructed, how we might transgress its limits, and compensate for the distortions it causes. This is not so much a second story about the modernist account of world affairs, however, as the beginnings of a very different story. This is about modernists beginning to listen and learn from non-modernist truth sayers, rather than presuming the right always to talk and to teach.

CHAPTER 3

THE WORLD POLITICS OF WORLD HERITAGE

What follows is a case study of a single concept, world heritage. It looks at the construction of modernist heritage politics on a global scale, and at attempts to critique and countercolonize these efforts in communalist terms. It could have been a case study of any number of issue-areas. It could also have been more materialist and less mentalist (and given the contemporary significance of the capitalist mode of production, should arguably have been so). Because of the relative neglect of world heritage as a politico-cultural concept, however, and the clarity with which modernist/non-modernist concerns are manifest in such terms, it was this issue that was chosen to exemplify the way modernity works.

What follows examines how ideas of world heritage are crafted world-wide, first, in terms of the difference between modernist and communalist ones, second, in terms of the global dominance of the modernist project, and third, in terms of the way communalist projects transgress the limits modernity sets, and compensate for the distortions in understanding it creates. The world politics of world heritage will be interrogated, that is, to see how they define the heritage concept, how they privilege modernity in global practice, and how communalists have successfully challenged this particular piece of modernist hegemony over world affairs (Eisenstadt, 2000).

Modernist Conceptions of World Heritage

The OED defines heritage in terms of the "fact" of "hereditary succession" and the "condition or state transmitted from ancestors." This is the most general of its meanings, since it refers to no more than the "circumstances" of our "birth."

The OED also defines heritage in terms of "any property, esp. land, which devolves by . . . inheritance . . . ," however, "[a]s distinguished from conquest . . . [or] purchase[ ]" (OED). In doing so, the editors highlight one very particular kind of trans-generational bequest, namely, land or "similar property."

Not all societies pass on land or property from one generation to the next, and of those that do, not all bequeath it in the commodified form implied by the editors of the OED. Theirs is clearly not a neutral definition, therefore. It is skewed, and in a very distinctive way. In choosing to highlight one aspect of inheritance, that is, the transmission from one generation to the next of commodified forms of "property, esp. land," the OED's editors are making a sociocultural decision not to highlight other definitions of this concept. Which is a problem, since sustaining human cultures over time involves bequests of many kinds, not only those that the editors of the OED are happy to specify.

Can we be more specific about what the OED does not include? There are many non-propertarian practices that "condition" or "state" what we inherit from our ancestors, and that surround the circumstances of our birth. Adults bequeath a wide range of goods, skills, attributes, ideologies, and memories (both good and bad). There is language itself, for example, or particular forms of knowledge, or particular forms of religion or faith. There are also those societies where property is not something people own in any personal sense—where it is held in common, for example, and is passed on communally. Can the latter seriously be said to bequeath lesser forms of heritage? Can we say that they are impoverished by not having commodified forms of property, without being culturally neo-imperialist on behalf of a worldview where one generation's legacy gets parceled up and passed on in the form of pieces of territory sufficiently discrete to allow of conquest, purchase, or inheritance, that is, a worldview where property is some-*thing*, to be had by capture, exchange, or right of birth?

The commodified view of property that the OED promotes long predates modernity. In the English-speaking world, for example, being able to define property clearly has, for more than a millennium, been an important part of providing for property succession in wills, or for granting property by charter. Heritage defined as property is not a new thing (Lacey and Danziger, 1999, 198).

In highlighting such a definition, however, the editors of the OED, wittingly or unwittingly, also promote an objectifying mind-gaze. In choosing to define heritage in the reified way they do, they are not only perpetuating a historical preoccupation with property as bequest, but they also promote a mental perspective (objectification) of a kind the modernist project requires.

Such a worldview is very particular. It emancipates, since it eschews sacral wisdom (religion) and received wisdom (tradition). It also limits our knowing, however, to what can be found out by individuated individuals, using an objectifying form of reason. By narrowing our mental perspective like this, such a worldview intensifies the Rationalist mind-gaze. It also occludes other ways of knowing, however. Transgressing the limits this sets, and compensating for its distortions, means using the mind in other ways, then. It means looking in other ways, and ultimately, being prepared to be other kinds of human being. It means acknowledging that there might be nonobjectifying accounts of the world that contribute to what we know, as well as non-individuated ways of living in the world that make such accounts meaningful.

Turned upon the Past, such a worldview "sees" an objectified, reified entity, or place. It sees some-thing separate from and conceptually equal to two cognate places, the Present and the Future. Having construed the Past as a place, it then proceeds to find other "things" there, like valued monuments (if they are not movable), or museum pieces (if they are), or particular landscapes.

The most conspicuous global form the modernist mind-gaze takes with regard to "the past" is the *Convention Concerning the Protection of the World Cultural and Natural Heritage* (Titchen, 1995). This particular piece of international law was adopted by the United Nations Educational, Scientific and Cultural Organization (UNESCO) in 1972, in the context of a worldwide attempt to protect a major Nubian monument (Abu Simbel) from inundation.

The *Convention* invites those state-makers who are party to it to nominate cultural and natural sites for inclusion on a World Heritage List. From these nominations a 21-member World Heritage Committee, advised by a seven-member Executive Bureau, regularly chooses (with the help of a couple of nongovernmental organizations) those sites deemed to be of "outstanding" and "universal" significance (UNESCO *Operational Guidelines*, 1999a, para. 6 (i)). The international status of a list item is confirmed, therefore, when the Committee judges it to be of "outstanding," "universal" significance. Inclusion means United Nations recognition as a world wonder. It means recognition as an item of relevance to all humanity. It means becoming the notional possession of all the peoples of world, regardless of where they live. To quote the UNESCO formulation, these are "our touchstones, our points of reference, our identity," and the "irreplaceable sources of [our] life and inspiration" (UNESCO, 2000b). For those who will succeed us, they are deemed to be our most valued properties and lands. They are our ultimate global bequest (*Convention*, 1972, Article 12).

Over time, the *Convention*'s focus has broadened. It now includes "complex, multidimensional cultural ensembles," and the context in which monuments and parks are found, as well as the monuments and natural features themselves (Levi-Strauss, 2000, 155). The definition of a world wonder has also been extended to cover what UNESCO deems to be the human project as a whole (Levi-Strauss, 2000, 158).

The Committee remains focused, however, on an objectified, reified concept of world heritage. It remains focused on cultural and natural heritage items, and on sites that come under both categories, and are therefore said to be mixed. The World Heritage List has several hundred entries now, most of them cultural. Cultural heritage items are those made by people. They include such things as the Acropolis in Athens, or the Taj Mahal in Agra. Though the *Convention* makes no mention of the need for one, the Committee applies an "authenticity" test with regard to design, material, workmanship, and setting (UNESCO *Operational Guidelines*, 1999a, para. 24(b)(i)(ii)). Natural heritage items, on the other hand, are naturally made things, like the Grand Canyon in the United States or Iguazu Falls in Brazil. Mixed items are a combination of both.

More recently a subcategory of the mixed category has emerged called "cultural landscapes," where the culture and the land are seen to be mutually constitutive of each other (von Droste et al., 1995; Titchen and Roessler, 1995, 423). The Committee's *Operating Guidelines* make extended reference to cultural landscapes now, in part in the attempt to narrow down what is a very broad notion (UNESCO *Operational Guidelines*, 1999a, para. 36). There are said to be three main types: designed, organically evolved, and associative. The last is the most problematic. Here the natural element is supposed to be one charged with "powerful religious, artistic or cultural associations" (UNESCO *Operational Guidelines*, 1999a, para. 39). Demonstrating a tangible and direct link between the property and the "events or living traditions . . . ideas . . . beliefs . . . [or] artistic and literary works" that are said to provide it with a universally significant charge is not easy, however, which is why the Committee only applies this category under exceptional circumstances (UNESCO *Operational Guidelines*, 1999a, para. 24(a)(vi)). In general, the Committee tries to keep to the modernist spirit of UNESCO's founding Constitution, Article I of which obliges UNESCO to conserve "things" like "books, works of art and monuments of history and science." The World Heritage List has already been opened to sites like Auschwitz, which was inscribed in 1979, or the Genbaku dome at Hiroshima, which was inscribed in 1996. Since such "bad memory" places are legion, it would be very easy for the World Heritage List to be swamped by them. Note in this regard the operative section in the *Operational Guidelines*, namely, cultural criterion six, the wording of which has been changed seven times since 1977 (UNESCO,WHC-2001/CONF.205/INF.8, 4), and the way debate continues to this day about what counts as exceptional circumstances, and whether this type of site should stand alone (UNESCO, WHC-2001/CONF.205/10).

It is the concept of "cultural landscapes" that demonstrates most clearly the controversial character of the current UNESCO construction of world heritage. Where a people, over an extended period of time, has utterly transformed the landscape, it is easy to see that a "cultural landscape" has been created that might deserve designation as part of the heritage of the world. What, however, of a place that has outstanding universal significance only because of how it has been painted by famous artists? (Pressouyre, 1996, 30). Is there a case, for example, for adding cultural criterion six to the other reasons for listing Toledo, in Spain, because of its association with the famous painter, El Greco? Are Constable's canvases reason enough to put the landscape round Flatford Mill in the United Kingdom on the World Heritage List? Are Wordsworth's poems about the English Lake District enough of a reason to inscribe this site too? (Cleere, 1995, 56).

Given that the cultural associations of a particular place must be exceptional, and the landscape concerned must have listworthy merits of other kinds, no such site has been accepted to date because of a local people's commitment to that site alone. It is "value added" to have a place recognized as one of outstanding universal significance because of its local cultural importance, however. Much greater status is conferred upon cultural "events," "living traditions," "ideas," "beliefs," or "artistic and literary works" if its promoters can win global acknowledgment for it in this way (UNESCO *Operational Guidelines*, 1999a, para. 24(a)(vi)). It gives the culture concerned international prominence of a kind that its promoters would not have otherwise received. It is therefore a prize that many peoples want to win.

Drawing the line is problematic, however. Given that nearly all peoples invest the place where they live with some degree of significance, perhaps no such line exists? Most peoples would extol their physical environment. Presumably, most would also like to have the particular relationship they have with "their" place given the cachet of formal UNESCO acknowledgment. Are we, therefore, to accept every claim of this kind? Alternatively, does a cull have to be made? And if so, on what grounds?

Consider a festival, like the Carnival in Rio de Janeiro. This would surely qualify, under the current criteria given in the *Guidelines*, as an "event." In principle, therefore, it should be on the World Heritage List. And what about the site of a great celebration, like the fourth of July, which is honored throughout the United States? As a "living tradition" the "fourth of July" certainly meets the *Guidelines'* criteria. It ought, therefore, to be on the List as well. Alternatively, we might consider the site of the formulation of a great concept, like that of state sovereignty, which was part of the treaty of Westphalia signed at Muenster, in Germany. State sovereignty would clearly, in the light of the *Guidelines'* criteria, be a globally significant "idea." Why not list Muenster, then? Or consider the site of a great spiritual event, like the gathering that takes place in India every 12 years at the confluence of the Ganga, the Yamuna, and a mythical third river, the Saraswati. This event is surely, in terms of the *Guidelines*, an outstanding example of "belief." Should this confluence not be listed? And what about the site of a great feat of the human imagination, like the film competition at Cannes, which regularly brings together so many of the world's great "artistic works," or the site of a great writers' competition, like the Booker Prize, awarded every year in London to celebrate "literary works." Should Cannes and London not be on the World Heritage List? Every one of these sites is demonstrably an "associative" cultural landscape. All of them bear "exceptional testimony to a cultural tradition" (UNESCO *Operational Guidelines*, 1999a, para. 24(a)(iii)).

Any state party that was sufficiently determined to test UNESCO's wording could use the current criteria to open up the world heritage project, as defined by the World Heritage Convention, to a whole swathe of more intangible concerns. And yet state parties do not, in part because of the unwillingness of state-makers to entertain them, and in part because cordoning off a site on terms that depend so much for their significance on the eyes of local beholders means maintaining the integrity of the culture of those peoples doing the beholding. It means actively conserving that group's cultural beliefs, and therefore, that group. And this has political implications that can be very difficult to address.

Communalist Conceptions of World Heritage

What is it that most of the peoples of the world want to pass on to those who will come after them? If we are to believe the framers of the *Convention*, these questions are best answered by having a World Heritage List. We are well satisfied having an inventory of preferred cultural and natural sites. Yet the UNESCO List is radically skewed in favor of its modernist proponents. It is neither balanced nor comprehensive, there being important gaps in the current collection with regard to "regions of the world" (Europe is over-represented), and with regard to "types of properties" (cultural) and "periods" (the twentieth century and the prehistorical era) (von Droste, 1995, 21; Roessler, 1995, 47). "Living cultures," particularly those of "traditional" societies, are radically underrepresented (von Droste, 1995, 21), and "movable" heritage is not represented at all (Pressouyre, 1996, 30–1).

Viewed globally, people bequeath a wide range of ways of doing things, not just things themselves. UNESCO's bias toward the latter is very evident, however, in calls for a more anthropological or global approach to world heritage, and in the attacks on UNESCO for failing adequately to recognize the cultural significance of living cultures. The general point being that every generation leaves a rich array of culturally charged properties *and* practices to those that succeed them. Indeed, one could argue that most of the world's heritage is passed on in non-tangible form. It is not made of concrete artifacts, cultural or natural. Indeed, many cultures do not even recognize this distinction.

Which leads us at once to the concept of intangible heritage, which is the dimension to the subject that has been historically shortchanged. And while UNESCO cannot be accused of completely ignoring the limits the *Convention* sets in this regard, UNESCO has only relatively recently confronted what is the main non-modernist component of the heritage concept in a meaningful way. It is only relatively recently, for example, that UNESCO has given the broad debate about intangible heritage serious consideration, or directly addressed the universalist reading of Western values that this debate problematizes.

What are "intangible practices"? Why is it that the Norse sagas, for example, are currently considered less of a monument to world heritage than the Taj Mahal?

One way to show what is meant here is to make a two-by-two matrix of the key concepts involved. This is no more than an analytic ploy, but it does help clarify the issues involved.

The first step in making such a matrix is to dichotomize products and practices. The analytic cogency of such a distinction is arguable. It is rejected outright by those communalists who see cultural practices as all pervasive. This is a dichotomy that recurs throughout the world heritage literature, however, and though it may be inappropriate in principle, it has considerable utility in practice.

The second step in making such a matrix is to distinguish what is culturally tangible from what is culturally intangible. The cogency of this distinction is also contested. It is equally pervasive in the world heritage literature, however, and has a similar role to play in highlighting the character of the politico-cultural lacunae that are evident here.

By comparing the first dichotomy with the second, we get four categories, namely, tangible products, tangible practices, intangible products, and intangible practices.

	Tangible (material)	Intangible (nonmaterial)
Products (artifacts)	*Victoria falls/Cologne Cathedral*	*Aboriginal Dreaming*
Practices (processes)	*Rio's Carnival*	*Modernity/Custom*

The *tangible products* component of this matrix (top left) is the one that modernists find easiest to understand, since it is the one most readily cast in objectifying, reifying terms. The World Heritage List is full of tangible products. Natural sites like the great waterfall on the Zambia/Zimbabwe border, and cultural sites like Cologne Cathedral in Germany, are obvious examples. The modernists who currently dominate the global cultural construction process find this aspect of world heritage the easiest to comprehend. It is the one most compatible with their preferred approach, and it continues to predominate in world heritage politics.

The *tangible practices* component (bottom left) is more problematic for modernists since practices are harder to objectify and reify than architectural monuments or natural parks. In heritage terms, tangible practices are those that have visible manifestations. They are practices that have some aspect that can still be put at a mental distance. Their material concomitants still give modernists something to objectify, that is, even if what they objectify is not ultimately the point of the heritage enterprise. The annual Carnival in Rio de Janiero is a good example. It is a festival, and a festival is a complex set of cultural practices. And while groups of revelers do physically reproduce the events that constitute the Carnival, providing spectacular manifestations of the practices involved, and giving modernists something physically to look at, the Rio Carnival is not likely to be allowed onto the World Heritage List. It is not enough of a thing. And while the "cultural landscapes" criteria would technically allow Rio's Carnival onto to the List, the non-modernist (communalist) character of this Carnival militates against its Listing.

The *intangible products* component (top right) of this matrix is also more problematic than the first one. Again, it is its non-material features that make this category less easy to objectify, giving modernists less to latch on to. Take, for example, the Dreamtime sites of Australian Aboriginal lore.

There are specific places, to be sure, which the custodians of Aboriginal beliefs can point to, places that during the Time of Law were significant for the epic entities that moved over the landscape, fighting, and foraging there. The most important of these places are said to be those where they entered the ground. Here "their fecundity is concentrated," and can be released (Layton and Titchen, 1995, 177). Their heritage significance, however, comes mostly, if not wholly, from their cultural meaning, not their physical manifestation. Their heritage relevance is entirely non-material. Indeed, it is spiritual. And while the "cultural landscapes" clause can be applied, as it was in the case of Ayer's Rock/Uluru, to list such sites, the cultural aspect of that bequest makes them hard for modernists to fathom.

The most problematic quadrant of all from the modernist perspective is the fourth one, however, the *intangible practices* one (bottom right). This particular combination of concepts includes modes of behavior that have no immediate material referents. It refers to cultural processes that have no obvious substantive referent. Such a category is difficult for heritage modernists to objectify, hence their reluctance to entertain examples of it, or to recognize their possible heritage significance. Yet, in the heritage terms most people in the world would consider the most meaningful, this quadrant is arguably the most important one. Paradoxically, modernity itself is a prime example. Here is a bequest that can only be grasped in the form of the mental practices involved. Here is a legacy that is of outstanding, universal significance, that gets handed on to the young in the form of cultural teachings designed to define their most fundamental sense of self and their primary mental commitment. Yet, none of this is Listable, even though it results in more "things" than we know what to do with, including the idea of a List of valued things itself. Modernity itself entails living practices, not dead sites, which is why it is so patronizing to stigmatize the so-called traditional and indigenous cultures of the Pacific, Africa, Latin America, and the Caribbean as such (Aikawa, 1999a, 114).

Debates about the significance of intangible practices have been conducted in UNESCO since the mid-sixties. If we include in these debates the various discussions UNESCO has had on the relationship between copyright and folklore, we can say that it has been thinking about intangible world heritage since the adoption of the *Universal Copyright Convention* in 1952 (Sherkin, 1999, 3). Debates about copyright directly confront the question of how to put the more intangible aspects of world heritage within the framework of international law, a modernist project that goes back to the *Berne Convention* of 1886.

The *World Heritage Convention*, however, in the form in which it was passed in 1972, completely ignores intangible cultural practices. The previous year UNESCO did consider something of the sort to strengthen folklore protection, but these deliberations had no effect upon the subsequent *Convention* (Sherkin, 1999, 7). The following year Bolivia asked for a Protocol to be added to the *Universal Copyright Convention* to protect the "popular arts and cultural patrimony of all nations" (Sherkin, 1999, 7), in part as a response to the commercial success of the Andean folk song, *El Condor Pasa*, which had been used to considerable profit without any attempt to remunerate the song's traditional owners (Sherkin, 1999, 7, fn. 13). The various international copyright organizations involved, and the World Intellectual Property Organization (WIPO) in particular, felt that the issue was cultural, not legal, however. At their request UNESCO asked member states to complete a questionnaire on folklore protection that was designed to "evaluate the present situation of intangible cultural heritage," and to allow "additional measures" to be developed to protect against "distortion" (Sherkin, 1999, 9–10). Nothing came of it. It was not until 1982 that UNESCO first created a separate section for dealing with what it called at that time nonphysical heritage, and convened a meeting of experts to draw up a program to study this issue and to plan some relevant pilot projects (UNESCO, 1984, CLT-84/CONF.603/ COL.2).

By 1985, UNESCO had decided to establish an international instrument to address the "folklore issue," as it was still formally known. Another questionnaire was sent out, and another meeting of experts was convened to prepare a plan of action (UNESCO, 1987, CC-87/CONF.609/COL.1).

The outcome was ultimately the *Recommendation on the Safeguarding of Traditional Culture and Folklore* (1989), though the *Recommendation* was a singularly modernist document, that drew attention to the intellectual property issues involved (Section F), and defined folklore in the fixed fashion most suitable for classifying, archiving, and putting it in museums (Section C). It dealt with folklore in an objectifying, reifying way, as products and as property rather than as practices in living cultural contexts.

The modernist state-makers of Central and Eastern Europe were formally supportive of the *Recommendation*. In large part, this was due to their socialist commitment to ordinary working people. The representatives of a range of non-modernist countries, in Africa, Latin America, Asia, and the Pacific, also backed the new initiative. It was, after all, the first attempt to establish an international standard-setting instrument for practices they valued more highly than the tangible products the *Convention* covered. The year of the *Recommendation* (1989) was also the year the Berlin Wall came down, and the Soviet Union collapsed, however, bringing with them an end to the Cold War, and making it possible for local peoples, heretofore stymied by the global rivalry between communists and democrats, to affirm their cultural identity. Growing awareness that successful economic development required much greater sensitivity to issues of social and cultural context reinforced these initiatives, as did recognition of the way globalization not only erodes cultural self-consciousness, but also stimulates it.

UNESCO's response was to declare support for the maintenance of cultural diversity a prerequisite for the development of a more multicultural system and for winning world peace (Aikawa, 1999a, 115). The first conclusion requires little justification since multiculturalism is clearly not possible without cultural diversity. The second conclusion is not so self-evident, however, since valuing cultural variety is not necessarily a greater guarantee of world peace than cultural homogeneity or cultural unity-in-diversity. Declarations of cultural diversity are popular rhetorical alternatives to the spread of modernity. They claim to counter its homogenizing effects. They respond to fears of the spread of international sameness, and they prompt policies of cultural protection as member states turn to their "traditional popular cultures" to defend local spiritual values and local symbols of cultural identity. It is not self-evident, however, whether this heightens world conflict or mitigates it.

Despite the kind of member state interest evinced above, the *Recommendation* failed to inspire much of a response. This was due in part to it not being a *Convention*. It did not oblige either UNESCO itself, or member states, to act. As such it was yet another Cinderella instrument— one that looked for a reaction from member states that was not forthcoming. Following the adoption of this *Recommendation*, for example, UNESCO member states were supposed to report on what they would do to implement it. In 1990 member states were asked to provide reports, but despite a reminder in 1991, only six countries responded.

In 1992 UNESCO sought a technical appraisal of what had been achieved to that date. This, the Gruzinski report, was a wide-ranging survey of UNESCO's achievements and initiatives in the whole area.

Most radically, the Gruzinski report expressed clear reservations about the way the world heritage project objectified human culture, and created highly abstract categories in order to do so. It saw the whole attempt to isolate abstract universals as peculiar to the Western scientific tradition, and as a particular cultural predilection writ large (Gruzinski, 1993, 11). This observation was directly in line with many non-modernist accounts of such efforts as neo-imperial (Simon, 1999, 5–6).

The Gruzinski report also concluded that what UNESCO was doing militated against the relatively new, highly dynamic, often hybrid innovations that were occurring in world culture because of widespread migration into the world's great cities. In choosing to ignore these developments, UNESCO was said to be favoring the rural, the preindustrial, the supposedly unadulterated, and the ostensibly old (Gruzinski, 1993, 21; UNESCO, 2000a).

The lack of "all reference" to religion was also seen to pose a problem. This lack, the report concluded, was bound up with the "liberal and/or materialistic Western scientific tradition" (Gruzinski, 1993, 12). It was deemed to be of growing significance, as modernists and non-modernists alike seek to come to terms with the politico-spiritual consequences of this hegemonic tradition.

More particularly, the Gruzinski report saw all UNESCO's terminology as contentious. The report saw the use of "culture," for example, as legitimating a portmanteau term that contains many different meanings. It also saw reference to the "traditional" as affirming a particularly static conception of culture, one that presupposes a past "which is, or should be, the subject of faithful, unchanged and undistorted reproduction . . . ." This obscured in turn, it said, how dynamic a tradition can be, and how "every living culture evolves and constantly integrates new elements into its fabric" (Gruzinski, 1993, 10–11). "Traditional," the report said, implies a dichotomy between a popular culture that abides on the one hand, and "national . . . or 'official'" cultures which are more modernist and therefore, more relevant, on the other. This dichotomy is highly suspect, however, since the traditional and the modern are two sides of the same coin, and any consideration of the one divorced from the other distorts both (Gruzinski, 1993, 10). The term "folklore" was seen to imply the same sort of dichotomy, folk culture being represented (as in the *Recommendation*) as the same as traditional or popular culture, and therefore as the opposite of the kind of high culture that is national and official. And yet, this dichotomy is also highly suspect, the report maintained, particularly considering the way local, traditional, popular, and folklore materials are incorporated into national dance and theater productions (Goody, 1993, 4). (Indigenous peoples tend to eschew the term altogether. They see it as inappropriate, inaccurate, and patronizing, preferring to talk instead about cultural heritage as a whole, or intellectual and property rights, or indigenous knowledge, or sacred norms (Simon, 1999, 4–5; the *Mataatua Declaration*, 1993; the *Suva Declaration*, 1995; Blake, 2001, 7, fn. 30). Even those modernist Rationalists who study "folklore" in an objectifying way no longer reify their subject in terms of songs, stories, designs, beliefs, or medicines alone, tending to see these things in the context of the knowledge that makes "folklore" practices possible.)

By 1995, the Czech Republic had put a resolution to the UNESCO General Conference calling for a worldwide assessment of traditional and folk heritage safeguards. UNESCO responded by holding eight regional seminars over the next four years (1995–99). All of these seminars agreed that UNESCO needed to disseminate and apply the *Recommendation* more assiduously (Seeger, 1999, 2–3). Every regional seminar expressed concern over the paucity of legal protection for the producers of traditional and popular culture, and for the products of their knowledge (Seeger, 1999, 4). The copyright and intellectual property issue was clearly alive and well, though there were distinct differences between the conclusions drawn at the regional seminars. The Latin American seminar, for example, highlighted the significance of multiculturalism and hybrid cultures. The Pacific states stressed that in their case the distinction between intangible and tangible heritage was a distinction without a difference. They also stressed the importance of customary law, and the need to include members of local communities in the relevant decision-making processes. The Asian seminar emphasized the importance of traditional high (or court) culture, and the way folklore festivals distort traditional cultural expression. The seminar for Central Asia and the Caucasus underlined the importance of traditional and popular culture in the process of nation making. The African seminar emphasized the importance of the family, the clan, the ethnie, and the region, and not just that of the nation. The Arab seminar talked of globalization as a threat, rather than as an opportunity. The Central and Eastern European seminar complained of lack of money. While the Western European one called for the protection of the intangible heritage of minority groups (Seeger, 1999).

In 1999 UNESCO convened a global conference in Washington to revisit the *Recommendation*, and to review all of the above (UNESCO, 1999b,c). The result was an agreement, made at its thirty-first General Conference (in 2001), to proceed with the development of a new *International Convention for the Safeguarding of Intangible Cultural Heritage*. Intangible heritage was finally to be put on a similar footing to tangible heritage, at least as far as the international legislation goes.

One result of this conference was the commissioning of another expert report to look at the feasibility of adopting a new normative instrument, one better able to protect traditional culture and folklore. This report was prefigured by a study presented to the 1999 Washington conference, in which it was argued that intangible heritage was undervalued in the West, despite it being the main form of global cultural heritage (Blake, 1999, 3, fn. 8). This study also argued that the 1989 *Recommendation* was "heavily weighted toward the needs of scientific researchers and government officials," and was not cognizant of the role played by culture creators (Blake, 1999, 7; 2000).

The post-Washington report covered a wide range of issues. It looked at intellectual property rights as they applied to intangible heritage, and it looked at the 1989 *Recommendation*, the protection of traditional knowledge, the cultural heritage of indigenous peoples, and the 1972 *Convention* and *Recommendation*. It concluded by suggesting that UNESCO develop a new standard-setting instrument to protect intangible cultural heritage (Blake, 2001, 91), a suggestion UNESCO took up the following year (Blake, 2001, 78).

The post-Washington report also highlighted some key administrative concerns. Should or could the World Heritage Centre, for example, a body completely dedicated to protecting the more tangible forms of world heritage (under the terms of the 1972 *Convention*) oversee the operation of a new *Convention* on the more intangible forms of world heritage? (Blake, 2001, 75). The World Heritage Centre is a large, relatively free standing part of UNESCO's Culture Sector (one of the five Sectors that constitute the main bureaucratic body of UNESCO). The Centre is housed in a separate building that is within the grounds of UNESCO's own headquarters, opposite its front door. It is not geared to the issue of intangible world heritage in any way, with the limited exception of its "cultural landscape" concerns. UNESCO's Culture Sector does have a Division of Cultural Heritage, but this has little to do with the World Heritage Centre. It is housed in a separate building at some physical distance from the headquarters one. This Division has its own section for dealing with tangible world heritage issues, though this section only works to safeguard sites and to restore them. It also has an intangible world heritage section, which in the light of the story just told one would expect to be relatively large. It is very small, however, and is largely staffed by non-permanent personnel. As it currently stands it would not be capable of administering a new *Convention*. Since the World Heritage Centre is focused on tangible things only, and would be difficult to augment or reorient to include intangible practices, another Centre, a World Intangible Heritage Centre, would presumably have to be built for the purpose. That would involve establishing a World Intangible Heritage Fund, however, commensurate with the fund that underwrites the activities of the World Heritage Centre, and whether sufficient money for such a fund would be forthcoming from member states is far from self-evident. Japan and Italy would likely contribute, but how much, and who else might contribute, remains to be seen.

The post-Washington report was discussed in-house at a meeting of international experts, convened by UNESCO in Turin in March 2001, where the conclusion to adopt a new normative international instrument was subsequently endorsed. A meeting of experts, in Paris in June 2002, devised a comprehensive definition of intangible heritage, and it was this definition that was offered as the basis for a new *Convention*. It is notable, therefore, that this definition talks not only of "practices" but also of "representations." Thus while it talks of the "knowledge . . . [and] skills" that pertain to the oral expression of intangible heritage, and the performing arts, rituals, festivals, and other practices this entails, it also talks about the "instruments, objects, artefacts and places" involved. In doing so it is clearly hedging its modernist bets (UNESCO, 2002a, 4–5), as well as clearly manifesting UNESCO's reluctance to relinquish the objectified, reified concept of heritage so evident in its approach overall.

Despite the conclusions the post-Washington report comes to, difficult questions remain. For example, are the interests of those concerned likely to be met by formulating another international legal instrument? Can local knowledge be preserved in this way, and with it, cultural diversity? How important is cultural diversity, particularly with regard to global social cohesion? Would a strategy that promotes homogeneity, or unity-in-diversity, be preferable?

There are political economy questions too. The report refers to intangible cultural capital giving rise to a flow of services that can create economic value, like the craft industries that grow up in response to tourism. It also refers to the role traditional knowledge plays in protecting the resources a community needs to survive, like the traditional medicinal knowledge that an estimated 70–80 percent of the African population still rely on for their primary healthcare. However, these are only the start of an argument for culture as a basis for sustainable economic development (Blake, 2001, 4, 6, 47).

The report also says that "generally accepting and increasing the profile of local cultural traditions is more positive for the State than not"

(Blake, 2001, 3). This is highly debatable. Who are these "cultural rights" for? Proclaiming a universal interest in intangible global heritage is not a way to put this heritage in the hands of its holders, controllers, and creators. It is a way to put it in the hands of UNESCO, and thereby, in the hands of the state parties to UNESCO, many of whom are no answer to these questions, since they are themselves the main cause for concern (Blake, 2001, 13).

Within UNESCO itself, there are skeptics. These include Lyndel Prott, who at the time was head of UNESCO's key Division of Cultural Heritage. Prott talks of the whole project as premature. She is not convinced that a new *Convention* is able to provide one size that can fit all, and she draws attention to the need for greater discrimination in the choice of the means used to safeguard the cultural practices deemed to be at risk. She highlights, that is, the need for a more *sui generis* regime, one able to accommodate the "specificities" of this particular type of heritage (Prott, 1999, 8; 2001). She recommends looking at several kinds of intangible global heritage and how they might be protected (while noting herself that such a particularistic approach militates against the holism definitive of non-modernist conceptions of life and nature). And she highlights a wide range of potential protection practices, and what might be done to implement them (Prott, 1999). To preserve a threatened language, for example, it might be necessary for those speaking something else to help maintain a viable language community, which might mean ensuring the survival of a minimum number of those speaking the language, as well as international and national legal intervention, educational and archival programs, and programs to honor those using the language in traditional ways (those who tell epic oral poems or stories, for example). A picture just as diverse, she thinks, emerges from consideration of other aspects of intangible global heritage, such as the performance of religious rituals, the making of handicrafts, the performance of traditional music and dance, the practice of traditional cuisine and medicine, and the practice of those skills used to hunt and track, sustain the environment, resolve conflict, and show respect for age. No UNESCO convention could be said to be ready to do all this, she concludes. No UNESCO convention could ever be so comprehensive (Prott, 1999, 2–6).

Prott is very conscious of the clash of worldviews that underpin this whole issue-area. Thus while she supports the way a modernist doctrine like human rights proscribes practices like genital mutilation (Prott, 1999, 7), she is also aware of the way modernity, however well-meaning, endangers non-modernist ways of thinking and living. The language of human rights and human responsibilities is an individualist, and at most a collectivist language. As such it is very different from the language of communal privilege, or traditional gift, or divine grace. As such it directly impinges upon non-modernist communalist societies and cultures, and in negative ways.

She is conscious, too, of what all that this might mean, not just for those who still live in communities, but for all of us. "These lodes of traditional wisdom," she says, "these other ways of looking at the world, these alternatives may one day, we cannot tell, become critically important." Indeed, they might be critically important already, particularly given the growing contemporary awareness of the need for environmental sustainability (Prott, 2001, 662). Might it not be prudent, she argues, to promote and protect, what communalist non-modernists know and do?

She also points to the power of international corporations, and wonders how relevant such debates might be when public control over private bodies like these has become so circumscribed. "[W]inning the theoretical argument," as she puts it, does not "guarantee protection." Having an intellectual property rights scheme, for example, that protects the lifestyle that makes traditional knowledge possible, does not necessarily prevent global capitalism making such a scheme redundant. Hence her avowed interest in education, and her argument that it is by these means, rather than by proffering yet another *Convention*, that we are most likely to empower non-modernists in their bid to preserve alternative forms of life practice, and to protect the "different criteria of 'success' " that these practices represent (Prott, 2001, 686).

Despite such misgivings, it is the conclusions of the post-Washington report that were put to the thirty-first session of UNESCO's General Conference in November 2001, as part of the proposal for a preliminary draft of a new international convention, and were endorsed there as one of the "main lines" of an action plan to implement UNESCO's Universal Declaration on Cultural Diversity, a declaration that specifically obliges member states to formulate policies to preserve world heritage in general, and intangible heritage in particular (UNESCO, 2001, 31C/Resolution 30, Annex II, art. 13). The Prott critique did not prevail.

As it moved toward the drafting of a new *Convention*, UNESCO continued with its "watering can" approach, funding two other major programs, plus a number of minor ones. Hence we have the Living Human Treasures project, and the Masterpieces of the Oral and Intangible Heritage of Humanity project, as well as adjunct projects like the Red Book of Endangered Languages (Wurm, 2001), other specialized publications, the ongoing development of networks of expert institutions, the organization of intergovernmental conferences, the UNESCO Collection of Traditional Music of the World, and contributions to various festivals. Other cognate projects include ongoing work with WIPO on the copyright and intellectual property aspects of heritage protection, work that has already involved a world forum in Phuket (in 1997), four regional meetings (Blake, 2001, 13–30), and ongoing consultations with indigenous people's organizations (UNESCO, 2001, 162 EX/17; UNESCO, 2001, WHC-2001/CONF.205/WEB.3; Blake, 2001, 47–69).

The Living Human Treasures project came into being in 1993. Though proposed by Korea, it was an attempt to replicate globally the *ningen kokuho* program that Japan initiated domestically in 1950 (see next chapter).

The idea of this project is for state parties to give official recognition to, and support for, the work of individuals and groups who have outstanding mastery of particular arts and skills deemed basic to a country's identity. The point is to make it possible for these skills to be passed on. In 1996, after a review of programs of this sort in Japan, Korea, Thailand, and the Philippines, UNESCO drew up guidelines for member states seeking to establish a Living Human Treasures system for themselves. It began holding regular training workshops. It also offered to provide preparatory assistance in the form of consultant services and training to those member states wanting to set up such a system. Few states have done as much so far, though nearly 50 member states are said to have expressed an interest in doing so (Aikawa, 1999b, 4).

This project is a direct expression of a respect for intangible global heritage, since it deliberately endorses the value of what particular people do, rather than the value of the products they produce. As such it is the most radical attempt by UNESCO to date to acknowledge the force of the non-modernist argument that world heritage entails living practices, not dead things. Its footnote significance within UNESCO speaks volumes about UNESCO's primary commitment. The Japanese themselves are known to express reservations about a project with such a particular national root, being used to create such a universal plant, though they have expressed considerable willingness to share their own experience with others who want to replicate their program.

The Masterpieces of the Oral and Intangible Heritage of Humanity project was initiated in 1997–98. It allows UNESCO to proclaim, on a biennial basis, and after consideration by an international jury, outstanding examples of intangible world heritage. It also provides an implementation guide that explains the procedure for submitting candidates, as well as the selection criteria, the evaluative procedure, the monitoring process, and the assistance that UNESCO can provide. This project was first proposed to complement the World Heritage List. It was meant to make it possible to acknowledge the outstanding and universal significance of those cultural practices that could not be included on the List because they had no site. It grew out of the sense that there were oral traditions, languages, cultural spaces, and modes of cultural expression that deserved to be part of the memory of all the peoples of the world, and deserved therefore to survive (because of their distinctive cultural features), even though they were not internationally recognized parts of the physical makeup of the planet, or recognizable as being among its high-profile architectural treasures. This project would presumably be incorporated into, or replaced by, the new *Convention*.

The Masterpieces inventory has a distinctively modernist cast to it, nonetheless, in that the language in which it is couched talks of master-*pieces*, that is, intangible *products* and *tangible* practices. It does not really encompass *intangible practices*. Thus while the inaugural list of putative masterpieces, proclaimed in March 2001, includes some (relatively intangible) forms of dance, music, ancestral ritual, and oral tradition, as well as some (relatively tangible) cultural practice spaces and theatrical performances, it has yet to grapple with the sort of practices that constitute most of the world's intangible heritage, and hence, most of the world's heritage.

The Masterpieces initiative also flies in the face of UNESCO's aim not to "crystallize" cultural processes, or remove them from their original context (Aikawa, 1999b, 3). It is supposed to be a "bottom up" approach, even though the selection process requires scrutiny by an international jury, and as such, dissuades potential participants from putting forward candidates. Nor does this show much confidence in the capacity of participants to make legitimate nominations, keeping control in the hands of state-makers, many of whom are the ultimate cause of the ongoing grief most of those involved suffer.

To sum up then: heritage is a multidimensional concept whose definition to date has been dominated, in the global arena, by sovereign state-makers with national identities to consolidate and coffers to fill. Security cast in terms of a state-made world, prosperity cast in terms of liberal marketeering, and identity cast in terms of personal freedom, are arguably the most characteristic forms of contemporary world affairs. As such they impinge directly upon the world heritage debate, and the attempt to determine what should be bequeathed to the next generation. As a consequence, global heritage is now a matter of gross national product (to say nothing of gross national pride).

Fundamental to world heritage politics is the modernist project itself, since it is this project that sets the context in which contemporary world affairs are forged. It is this project, defined by the use of reason as an end in itself, that has created non-modernist peripheries. All those cultures that modernists call traditional are on these peripheries.

The attempt by modernists to define global heritage in terms congenial to themselves is a revealing issue in world affairs. It is one way in which modernists assert their hegemony, and assert the Rationalist approach to truth they believe is paramount. It is this hegemony that so-called non-modernists contest, whether as "pre-modernist indigenes," or as "traditionalists" (both of which are modernist labels). This contest highlights in turn the limits and constraints set by the Rationalist construction of the truth, and the possibility of Rationalist falsity, as well as the existence of non-Rationalist truth (and the possibility of non-Rationalist falsity).

UNESCO's attempts to account for world heritage in terms of intangible practices bears witness to a degree of success on the part of non-modernists in getting their views considered. The relatively limited character of this success, however, especially when compared to UNESCO's formal efforts to promote and protect tangible property, shows how limited international awareness still is of the significance of intangible alternatives to the tangible view of heritage that still dominates the Western worldview. This demonstrates the power modernists continue to have to set global agendas. And it demonstrates the key problem hegemony poses, namely, the extent to which it means analytic bias, and policy bias too.

CHAPTER 4

THE WORLD POLITICS OF WORLD HERITAGE—JAPAN

To the modernists who dominate contemporary world affairs, heritage is defined in objectifying, reifying terms that highlight tangible products. This definition is manifest in terms of a hegemonic preference for protecting cultural monuments, for building museums, and for designating natural parks.

As modernists, the Japanese define heritage in these particular terms. They are also non-modernists, however, and as such they promote and protect what heritage involves in more communalist terms. Hence the emphasis they place on a range of culturally valued, albeit relatively intangible practices, such as the skills they deem to be of cultural significance that might be lost without governmental support. Japan's capacity to maintain both modernist and non-modernist heritage strategies has become an example to the world of what is possible in this regard. Current global heritage debates owe more than is generally realized to the inspiration they provide.

The Japanese embraced modernity as a whole-cultural project after a long period of self-imposed isolation. The contrast is uncommonly clear, therefore, between the character of the communalist ("pre-modernist") society that they continued to be, and the more modernist one they sought to become in their bid to replicate the industrial and military might of the Europeans and the Americans. Communalist conceptions of heritage, for example, were not replaced in Japan by modernist ones. Rather they continued to promote and protect these concerns, ultimately playing their part in the global practice of multiple modernities (Eisenstadt, 2000). In due course, that is, the Japanese were able to present alternatives to the modernist conception of heritage, their own practices becoming examples, and sometimes compelling examples, of what the rest of the world might do.

Having staged their own version of the industrial, technological, and scientific revolutions, the Japanese are now engaged in realizing social and intellectual ones. They are not necessarily doing so, however, in the same way that these were realized in the West. Their heritage politics manifest a combination of both modernist reification and non-modernist process thinking. Both are embraced, and with seemingly equal fervor.

In making the past into a thing in itself, modernists find things in it that they then call natural parks, cultural monuments, or museum pieces. In this respect, the nature conservation and museum movements are modernist ones. They spread as modernity did, and are symbolic of the modernist way to live.

In copying how the West made modernity, the leaders of post-Meiji Japan copied the modernist practice of making museums and natural parks. Thus the public collection of old things deemed to be of high cultural value, as well as the identification of swathes of countryside deemed naturally special in some way, became important symbols of Japan's membership of the modernist club.

Consider museums. Horne talks of the museum in terms of its "encyclopaedic vision, its aims of edification, its categorisations, and its precise concentration on *the object . . . .*" In museums, objects are made of *"matter,"* he says, so that there is no denying the "truth" of them. In his view, a trip to a museum is a reaffirmation of the "values of the industrial world, values reflected in the organised tour with its imposed order, its planned movement of bodies, [and] its concern with time-tabling" (Horne, 1984, 116; Anderson, 1991, ch. 10; Macdonald and Fyfe, 1996; Bennett, 1995; Hooper-Greenhill, 1995; Pearce, 1992; Hudson, 1975; Walsh, 1992).

The story of the Japanese museum movement can be told in precisely these terms. It is the story of a modernist institution, constructed in a cultural context very different from that in which it originated. Japanese museums are replicas of Anglo-European originals, providing diverse objects for public display. Detailed analysis of the character of the replication betrays telling differences, but the impetus remains the same.

The story of the Japanese natural parks movement is similar. It, too, documents Japan's modernist aspirations.

The *World Heritage Convention* plays an important role in certifying the authenticity of all such movements. The World Heritage Committee's listing process was the first attempt in human history to create a formal, global inventory of all those things deemed to be truly outstanding, and therefore, universally worth preserving, on behalf of all humankind. The judgments that the World Heritage List represents are consciously made for the entire planetary population. They are meant to articulate global agreement on what the wonders of the world might be for all of us, specifying what these wonders are, and why it is that they should be passed on to the next generation.

To do this the Committee must assume that humankind is a singular entity, and not a plural one. It must assume that it is state-makers who speak most authoritatively in this regard, and who have the prime commitment to passing on, in as pristine condition as possible, the most wondrous things their territories contain.

Japan signed the *World Heritage Convention* in 1992, 20 years after it was first established. Japan then nominated *Horyuji* temple and *Himeji* castle for immediate inclusion. These were put on the List the following year, while shrines and temples in Kyoto, Uji, and Otsu, and historic villages in Gifu and Toyama, were added soon after.

Signing the *Convention* was a key symbol of Japan's acceptance of the modernist project. It was not the first such symbol, however. Since the time of the Meiji restoration the Japanese have been objectifying their past and selecting things from it for conservation and preservation. As a response to the social unrest that attended the Meiji restoration, for example, the government formulated an Imperial Decree for the Preservation of Ancient Objects (1871). This was followed by a Law for the Preservation of Ancient Temples and Shrines (1897), a Law for the Preservation of Historic Sites, Places of Scenic Beauty, and Natural Monuments (1919), a Law for the Preservation of National Treasures (1929), and a Law Concerning the Preservation of Important Objects of Art (1933).

This is not all the Japanese have done, though. The Japanese concept of heritage has another aspect that is notably less modernistic, an aspect prefigured by the word for heritage in the Japanese language itself: *isan*. This word means not only the inheritance of family assets (which once included a family's debts), but also the inheritance of one's ancestors' achievements and cultural assets (Kindaichi et al., 1984, 51). The word itself is conceptualized not only in propertarian terms, but also in terms of particular achievements. It implies a concept of heritage that involves intangible practices as well as tangible products.

The Japanese honor two different meanings of heritage, therefore, an objectified (modernist) and a communalist (non-modernist) one. They certainly revere particular artifacts and places, like old monuments and natural parks. They also, however, revere ongoing cultural practices like those that characterize particular festivals, ceremonies, and skills. In the latter case the reverence exists in part because of the sense of cultural continuity these traditions represent, the sense a modernist state-maker might encourage to consolidate national identity (Terada, 2000, 55). They also serve a communalist purpose, however, since they represent ways for the Japanese to practice a culture distinctly their own.

The Japanese are not the only ones to conceptualize heritage in communalist as well as modernist terms. In Japanese society, however, the coexistence of modernity and non-modernity is unmistakable. Because they came to modernity later than most Westerners did, or because of their history of isolationism and separate development, the Japanese are notably both modernist and non-modernist. The difference between Japan and other societies is only relative in this regard, but the difference is marked nonetheless.

In 1950, for example, 40 years *before* it signed the *World Heritage Convention*, the government passed a Law for the Protection of Cultural Properties. This law was prompted by the impact of the many changes that attended the end of World War II, though it was precipitated by a fire that destroyed the murals in the Golden Hall of *Horyuji* temple in Nara.

The Law for the Protection of Cultural Properties covers not only tangible cultural properties, like architectural structures, paintings, sculptures, books and documents, historic sites and beauty spots, and groups of historic buildings. It also covers intangible cultural properties. Indeed, in 1954 it was extended to make possible state protection of any skill used in "drama, music and applied arts," or any other intangible cultural practice said to have "high historical and/or artistic value in and for Japan" (Agency for Cultural Affairs, 2001, 4).

In 1975, this Law was amended to recognize the need to protect the conservation abilities of those who keep traditional buildings, costumes, instruments, paintings, furnishings, masks, and stage props in good repair. These amendments introduced a new category, that of folk-cultural properties, in their tangible and intangible forms (Agency for Cultural Affairs, 2001, 18).

It is under the auspices of this Law that the Agency for Cultural Affairs of the Japanese Ministry of Education, Science, Sport, and Culture identifies, records, and otherwise gives support to those individuals and groups who practice traditional crafts. The list includes pottery, textile weaving, lacquer work, metal work, woodwork, doll making, ivory engraving, and papermaking. It is under this Law that the Agency is also able to support the work of those who perform such theater arts as *Gagaku*, *Nohgaku*, *Bunraku*, and *Kabuki*.

This support program is formally known as the *juyo mukei bunkazai hojisha* [important intangible cultural asset-holder] program. Informally, it is known as the *ningen kokuho* [living national treasures] program. It not only honors particular artists and crafts-people for their traditional abilities and skills. It also gives them an annual stipend, so that they can keep practicing their particular arts or crafts, and can pass them on. At the end of the financial year 2001, for example, the Agency for Cultural Affairs recognized 111 such individuals, and 24 groups (Bunkazai hogo-bu, 2000, 14; Agency for Cultural Affairs, 2001, 5).

Under this law diverse aspects of daily Japanese life are also promoted and protected. This includes indigenous peoples like the Ainu, minority populations like that of the Koreans, and diverse agricultural and fishing communities. The folk-cultural practices concerned include prayers for a good harvest, for family safety, and for protection from evil spirits. It also includes customs relating to "food, clothing and housing, to occupations, religious faiths, festivals, etc., [and] to folk-entertainments. . ." (Agency for Cultural Affairs, 2001, 11). Customs deemed most typical or significant are specifically identified as such, and their practitioners are given government subsidies. These subsidies are used to train successors, repair instruments and facilities, produce publicity material, and provide public workshops. No individuals can be nominated, since it is groups who are seen to embody these practices, and groups who are encouraged to carry them on. As of the end of the financial year for 2001, for example, support was being provided to 202 of these intangible properties, out of an estimated 30,000 nationwide (Agency for Cultural Affairs, 2001, 13). Among those given support were rice-paddy ceremonies in Niigata and Hiroshima prefectures, coming of age ceremonies in Aomori and Tochigi prefectures, harvest-related tug-of-war competitions in Aikita and Hyogo prefectures, a tea-drinking ceremony in Gunma prefecture, a seasonal event in Mie prefecture to welcome the spirits of the ancestors, a festival involving a parade of lavish floats in Kyoto prefecture, as well as various local performing arts involving singing, dancing, chanting, story telling, puppeteering, drum playing, praying, and in one case, the spraying of onlookers with hot water (Agency for Cultural Affairs, 2001, 14–17).

Why do the Japanese pay such close official attention to heritage-related practices? Why do they pay such close official attention to the intangible aspect of heritage-related practices?

To answer such questions we have to consider a range of long-standing cultural practices, the first of which entails the preservation of memory in nonphysical forms. The Japanese, Takashina says, have created a number of abstract cultural practices that they are able to pass on, in an intangible way, potentially *ad infinitum* (Takashina, 1996, 3).

The form these practices take is often that of a particular ritual and ceremony. And though the Japanese are hardly unique in preserving their communal memories in ritual and ceremonial fashion, intangible cultural traditions are still very much in evidence in Japan. They continue to pervade the society to a degree uncommon for such an otherwise modernist state.

The rebuilding of *Ise* Shrine is notorious in this regard, the rebuilding process being "not merely a physical process of construction or reconstruction but also a series of sacred rituals" (Takashina, 1996, 4). The rituals are heritage practices, and though they have not remained unchanged, they are ancient, and they are venerated as such. The physical manifestation of these practices (in this case a building) is only their outer form, however. The point of the process is the ongoing repetition of the construction function by ritual and ceremonial means. It is this that constitutes their significance as part of Japan's heritage.

By repeating these rituals and ceremonies it is possible not only to transmit the abstract forms involved, but also to reinforce the sense that time "continually turns back on itself, returning to the point whence it came," thereby perpetuating the sense that time is cyclic, or circular, and can be used to perpetuate memory (Takashina, 1996, 5).

Practices like these put the World Heritage Committee in a quandary. At the meeting of this Committee, held in Australia, in November 2000, a non-governmental advisory body, the International Council on Monuments and Sites (ICOMOS), cast doubt on the list-worthiness of a Nepalese national park because the restoration work on some of the ancient murals in some of the pre-Buddhist monasteries there was being done by local "amateurs" using "acrylics." In its bid to keep the monastery wall paintings "authentic," ICOMOS felt obliged to accuse the local adherents of a living Tibeto-Nepalese religion of not being sufficiently traditional (UNESCO, 2000a, 5). Quandaries like these are most acute where the sacral quality of a site lies entirely in the eye of the beholder. To the indigenous peoples of Australia, for example, a culturally sacred site may be a natural feature of the landscape, like a stream or a rock. The cultural value of a sacred place may have no other referent than the one put there by members of the culture involved. Under these circumstances, site conservation means conserving the culture bearers too. While conservation of the integrity of a particular stream or rock may be extremely important, it can be hard to effect since it is hard to make that object stand on its own, the way a sacred monument can be made to do.

Another nonphysical way in which the Japanese perpetuate their memories is via their sense of their land, the Japanese having long believed that this has spiritual power, and that to benefit from this power they must build it up (Takashina, 1996, 7). Particular places, like those on which shrines are often built, have considerable spiritual significance. In learning to revere such places the Japanese people learn their sense of who they are and what being Japanese means. And though, once again, the Japanese are not unique in this respect, since many peoples profess a profound sense of the land they live on, the degree to which the Japanese do so is of note. The relevant practices do change as modernity proceeds apace, but a non-modernist sense of the spiritual significance of their land is still a marked feature of Japanese cultural life.

There are compelling parallels here with the Chinese attitude toward the past, parallels that may provide a clue as to the historical source of the Japanese attitude. For example, Ryckmans notes a paradox at the heart of Chinese civilization, namely, the way the cultivation of China's ancient moral and spiritual values "appears to have [been] most often combined with a curious neglect or indifference (even at times downright iconoclasm) towards the material heritage of the past . . . ." The same China that is loaded with history and memories is "also oddly deprived of ancient monuments . . . a *material* absence . . . that can be most disconcerting for . . . Western[ers] . . . ," since "[i]n Europe, in spite of countless wars and destruction, every age has left a considerable amount of monumental landmarks: the ruins of classical Greece and Rome, all the great medieval cathedrals, the churches and palaces of the Renaissance period, the monuments of the Baroque era . . . ." By contrast, the Chinese past "seems to inhabit *the people* rather than . . . bricks and stones. The Chinese past is both spiritually active and physically invisible" (Ryckmans, 1986, 1–2).

Ryckmans qualifies this conclusion by pointing out how the Chinese ultimately developed their own antiquarian tradition, though it appeared late in Chinese history, and when it did appear, it remained "closely—if not exclusively—related to the prestige of the *written word*" (Ryckmans, 1986, 4–5). He demonstrates the way the Chinese developed, from a time well before Confucius, the notion that there could be only "one form of immortality: the immortality conferred by history . . . ." Artifacts were deemed useless in this regard, their immobility being considered the opposite of how man "only survives in man . . . through the fluidity of the successive generations" (Ryckmans, 1986, 9). This idea is easy to overstate, but it does help highlight the human dimension to China's cultural staying power, and it does help explain why modernizers in every era have had to confront a Chinese sense of tradition that is "pervasive . . . formless . . . [and seemingly] indestructible . . ." (Ryckmans, 1986, 11, 17).

There are parallels in the modernist West. Along with modernity itself, the practices that make for the rule of law, for example, or for democracy, or for the doctrine of human rights, are compelling examples of intangible forms of heritage. These particular practices are passed on, from one generation to the next, largely by virtue of the sociocultural beliefs they involve. Their material expression—the constitutions, the documents, and the institutions erected in their name—help in this transmission. Without the living message, however, these are dead documents and meaningless patterns of repeated human practice.

The matrix presented in the previous chapter can be applied to demonstrate the significance of intangible heritage in the Japanese case too:

	Tangible (material)	Intangible (nonmaterial)
Products (artifacts)	*Horyuji*	*Noh*; *Kabuki*
Practices (processes)	*Okunchi*; *Ise*	*Giri*

The first quadrant—top left (that of *tangible products*)—is exemplified by Japan's *Horyuji* temple. Mainstream UNESCO modernists have no trouble at all acknowledging this as a heritage item, that is, as a cultural monument that they can detach from the community it represents and put on the World Heritage List.

The second quadrant—bottom left (that of *tangible practices*)—is exemplified by the *Okunchi* festival in Nagasaki, or by *Ise* shrine. This is a more difficult quadrant for UNESCO-style modernists to see as one exemplifying heritage, since it refers to practices not products. At least the practices are tangible, however. At least at *Okunchi* we can see people doing something, while *Ise* shrine is readily reifiable too, being one of the country's most famous Shinto monuments. As noted earlier, *Ise*'s heritage significance lies in the fact that it is entirely rebuilt every 20 years or so, however. This process precludes it from a place on the World Heritage List, since the modernists who compile and police this List consider *Ise* not to be authentic. This clearly highlights UNESCO's bias. The Japanese see *Ise* as completely authentic, and herein lies the (non-modernist) rub (Takashina, 1996, 2).

The third quadrant—top right (that of *intangible products*)—is exemplified by *Noh* stories, or *Kabuki* theater. Though these are nonmaterial, relatively abstract artifacts, they do have a material expression in the form of the *Noh* players who pass these stories on, which makes it possible for UNESCO-style modernists to see *Noh* as "heritage." This is one reason why *Noh* was a successful candidate for UNESCO's Masterpieces list.

The *Noh* stories themselves, however, have to be learned by one generation of players after another. They are nonmaterial artifacts that only exist while the performers are performing. They cease to exist the moment the performance stops. Their expression is "instantaneous, disappearing as soon as it appears . . . ." This means that *Noh* represents little more than a "succession of instants which leave nothing concrete in their wake . . . ." As a consequence "[o]nly persons who happen to be present at that time and place can receive the impression or be moved . . . ," and even then, they must be culturally coached in how to do so (Ueki, 2001, 2).

Because they are intangible, cultural practices like these are always in a state of flux. In the case of *Kabuki*, Kawatake sees the Great Earthquake in Kanto of 1923 as the turning point, not World War II, as was the case for so much else. After 1923, he says, "we . . . no longer find [the] true-blue Edo audience who enjoyed *Kabuki* as a part of their daily life. Instead, the Japanese audience today stand on the same ground as our audiences abroad who . . . appreciate it as classical drama and [as an] object of traditional culture . . ." (Kawatake, 2001, 4–5). Kawatake also cites a ten-year study that compares the interests of Japanese youth. *Karaoke* came first (26.9 percent), and *Kabuki* came last (0.7 percent) (Kawatake, 2001, 5). Those *Kabuki* performances with the greatest appeal, he observes, both overseas and in Japan, are the ones that have a simple, clear plot and a strong dramatic effect. Edo aesthetics are lost on even Japanese audiences today. The *Kabuki* that survives for the next generation or two is likely, therefore, to be a much reduced form of what the art was once. In this form it will speak both to people from other cultural traditions and to the next generation of Japanese themselves. It will be a tradition changed forever, however.

Ueki sees this flux process as characteristic of the folk performing arts as well. Where industrialization and urbanization proceed apace, people cease to practice the relevant cultural forms. These then mutate, or cease to apply, or fall into the hands of hobby groups, and their social meaning then becomes marginal (Ueki, 2001, 3). As Ueki observes: "Folk performing arts were originally passed down through generations by virtue of their being essential to the people themselves. Should the tradition become meant for others, it would then surely lapse into an existence for the sake of administration, for tourism, or to parade tradition before ones guests" (Ueki, 2001, 4). Rather than a spontaneous expression of local communal values and sentiments, folk arts become under these circumstances mere entertainment, and cease as such to draw people together in communities that span generations (Ueki, 2001, 6–7).

The fourth quadrant—bottom right (that of *intangible practices*)—is exemplified by *giri*, that is, the practice of those reciprocal obligations that underpin Japanese society. While there are tangible artifacts that result from the performance of *giri*, like the souvenirs that family and friends expect from those who travel abroad, the souvenir gifts are not themselves *giri* practice, since souvenir products are not identifiable as *giri* gifts unless they are given as such. This makes *giri* hard to objectify and reify.

It is just the kind of cultural artifact modernists are least happy to include on any of their lists of world heritage. It is not heritage as modernists most readily think of it, even though most heritage arguably comes in this intangible form.

A matrix like the one above allows us to see more clearly how heritage encompasses products and practices of *both* a tangible *and* a non-tangible sort. And since it is arguably the case that for most people in this world it is the intangible (nonmaterial) products and practices that most constitute what heritage means to them, being able to see the past in nonmaterial, practice-oriented terms would seem to be a prerequisite to a proper appreciation of how most people think of the past, and of what they want handed on.

This is where the Japanese concept of heritage seems to be of considerable assistance, since it does both at the same time. It construes the concept of heritage *both* in terms of sites *and* in terms of skills. It combines the tangible and the intangible, the artifactual and the procedural, in synergistic ways that demonstrate what is politico-culturally possible in this regard.

The modernist/non-modernist hybrid, as manifest in heritage terms, is still far from straightforward. It involves layers upon layers of meaning, as is immediately evident to those analysts who get close to listen to those involved in heritage activities.

At first glance, for example, the Japanese seem to emphasize the importance of particular cultural practices in a self-conscious way that most other peoples do not. They make an important communalist point about not objectifying heritage, and not having it construed only, or even mainly, in terms of monuments, museums, and national parks.

At another level, however, they seem to do this in a way that objectifies (and even petrifies) the cultural practices concerned. This seemingly negates their use of non-modernist thinking. It seems to reinforce an objectifying, and therefore modernist perspective, rather than a subjectifying, non-modernist one.

By contrast, the French government promotes its preferred cultural practices in a much more interventionist fashion. For example, it defines a *maitre d'art* (a living national treasure) as someone who is able to innovate. It contractually obliges those chosen for this program to stay up-to-date. It finds them apprentices with skills that the masters in this program might be able to learn from themselves. And it views the whole initiative as one able to make "brilliant promises of modernity for the future" (Leclercq and Havel, 2001, 7).

At a deeper level again, the individual Japanese practitioners who receive state subsidies as living national treasures use their mastery to innovate, however, and to seek out new and international contexts in which to do so. To promote and protect their skills they explore new ways in which to realize their art or craft, nationally and internationally. Which highlights once again the dynamic, relatively non-reified character of

Japan's heritage, and its communalist value, despite Japan being highly engaged with the modernist world.

By contrast, Japan's French *confreres* can be found innovating in a relatively superficial fashion. In practice, they promote a notably objectified version of the culture they represent, regardless of the French government's attempts to get them to engage with a less objectified view, and to realize a less reified, more "alive" version of France's national heritage.

A more complex appreciation of what the Japanese actually do, therefore, compared, for example, to what the French actually do, returns us to the conclusion that heritage politics in Japan are both modernist and non-modernist, and in an exemplary way. It leads to a deeper appreciation of why this might be so, and what it is that the Japanese experience has to say to the rest of the world.

Japan, as Watanabe points out, is in the process of constructing a "hybrid culture, different both from its own tradition and from Western culture" (Watanabe, 1998, 175). Most other non-modernist countries are doing the same. The Japanese are doing this in a more deliberate way than most, however, and in a way that demonstrates to the rest of the world what might be possible in this regard.

Part III

Spirituality

Rationalists are not sacralists. They tend to be secularists. This does not mean that the sacral cannot be discussed rationally. Nor does it mean that Rationalism need prevail. Rationalist Christians, for example, depict the modernist project as a neo-pagan heresy (Milbank, 1990, 3), or as the manifestation of the Christian spirit in the human mind.

The point of the modernist project is to eschew all presuppositions so as to give reason as free a rein as possible, and this means eschewing the presupposition that God exists. This means eschewing in turn all sacral ways to know. It is to see sacral conclusions as being either the source of " 'ultimate' cosmological causes," or of "psychological and subjective needs," or of a "sublimity beyond representation" (Milbank, 1990, 1). And it leaves it at that.

This is to posit the sacral as a separate experiential realm (Fox, 2001; *Millennium*, 2000; Dark, 2000). It is to put at a mental distance Rationalism's historical Christian context. It is to dichotomize truth as either reasoned out or revealed. It is to prioritize reason and privatize faith.

The outcome is no end point other than that of the Rationalist's own mental questing. It is to narrow down the concept of reason to a natural faculty only, as free as possible of any and all contextual constraints.

Rationalism did arise within a Christian context, however, and despite all the distancing and the mental exclusion, a historical and analytical understanding of this context remains relevant to any understanding of contemporary world affairs (Jones, 2001). After all, Christianity continues to have effects on the modernist project, and on modernist forms of world affairs, over and above those that specifically Christian individuals and institutions claim to have. As White argues: "[w]e continue today to live . . . very largely in a context of Christian axioms" (White, 1967, 1205). Sovereign states, capitalist markets, individuated individuals, competing classes, and constructivist ideas, are all phenomena that arose within the Rationalist project, which arose within Western European Christianity, and they continue to bear the marks of their sacral origins (McGrath, 2003). Christianity continues to impinge upon every part of the modernist project.

The Christian purpose was first proclaimed by Jesus Christ, in what he is said to have said in his Sermon on the Mount. This sermon suggests that world affairs are best constructed by those who are humble and forgiving, seek peace and not wealth, treat others as they would want to be treated themselves, and affirm life. It is a comforting account of a meta-secular embrace ostensibly available to all who acknowledge the Christian God, and willing to practice mercy and purity, peacemaking and right behavior, giving and forgiving, humility and love (Matthew 5–7).

The Rationalist penchant for untrammeled reason itself owes much to highly rational historical debates about Christian doctrine. In like vein, the sovereign state can be seen as a secularized version of St. Augustine's City of God, world affairs "realism" as articulating Christian concepts of original sin and power "wariness" (Lawrence, 1998, 164), and the modernist concept of the just war as continuing to exemplify the Christian doctrine of the just war. Capitalist marketeering may similarly be seen in terms of Protestant austerity, while the individuated individual can be seen in terms of the sin-bearing self, who must atone for its personal faults if it wants to be "saved." Christian sexism, meanwhile, continues to inform the gendered nature of world affairs, a Christian belief in manifest destiny continues to inform Western ethnocentricity, and Christian ideas about the natural environment continue to inform the world politics of world ecology (McGrath, 2003).

Those Rationalists who look *beyond* Christianity see, not surprisingly, a realm Beyond, about which they say they "cannot speak . . ." (Wittgenstein, 1961 [1921], 74; diagram 0.1). What they see, they say, is the primal ground against which gets configured every other discourse.

The Beyond is accessed using meditation, prayer, religious ritual, and sacral devotion, however. At least, these are the anti-Rationalist research tools that saints and spiritual sages recommend.

Given how subjective these research tools are, Rationalists find it difficult to accept their utility. They find it difficult to meditate or pray themselves, since to do so they have to eschew their modernist assumptions, and ignore the incommensurate character of the sacral ones. They find it difficult to know what a saint or sage is, either, or what spiritual enlightenment might mean (Arberry, 1968). They tend, as a consequence, to see sacral research as dangerously self-delusional (Trungpa, 1973).

The problem here is that those people who do succeed in going Beyond and coming back, may or may not choose to share the experience, while even where they do, they have to use a spiritual language that will be patently anti-Rationalist. (Those spiritual languages that have historically found the most political favor are those we recognize today as the world's main faiths. Though many have spoken in this regard, few have been chosen. And not one such faith has yet received universal acclaim.) Those Rationalists who look beyond Christianity see other sacral languages, therefore, that articulate other ideas about what is real, and why (Morris, 1994).

These ideas can be very different from those used to construct the Christian/Rationalist project, and modernist world affairs. The Buddhist concept of the not-self, for example, is very different from the self-realizing, self-maximizing individual who ostensibly inhabits the contemporary world market. Though the Buddha's first sermon was not written down for hundreds of years after it was delivered, and was subject to diverse interpretations as soon as it was uttered, we can still see in it an ontological principle radically at odds with the one modernist liberals espouse (Huang, 2001).

As the modernist project goes global, there are many struggles with those whom modernists deem nonmodern, the most profound of which pertain to sacral practices and beliefs (Abe, 1985). It was the appeal of Western technology, especially in the commodified form that capitalists created to feed and heal, transport and communicate, entertain and educate, that gave such strength to Europe's imperial push. It is a moot point what originally caused what, however, since "saving souls" has always gone hand in hand with making markets, securing resources, and grabbing land.

There are many attempts at the same time to win sacral "concessions" from the modernist hegemons (Gurnah, 1997, 124). Given the unequal military power of the parties to the exchange, those made marginal do not at first have the same impact as those doing the marginalizing. Modernity does not prevail unaffected by non-modernist concerns, however. Modernists are regularly obliged to come to terms with doctrines different from their own, and this includes both politico-cultural and politico-spiritual ones. It is part of the "cunning of culture" that, even under direct rule, the dominated act back on those who do the dominating (Carroll, 1972). It is part of the "cunning of the sacral" that the acting back process should be a spiritually informed one as well.

A comprehensive account of *world* affairs will include an account of all such codetermination practices, including the politico-spiritual ones. It will account for the "border gnoseologies" that result (Mignolo, 1998, 51). And it will account for the world affairs that are defined by the "*hard irreducibility*" of this kind of hybridity (Dussel, 1998, 22, 30, fn. 81).

Taoist Strategics

The sacral impinges directly upon contemporary strategics. As Carol Cohn notes, in her study of sex and death in the rationalistic world of defense intellectuals: "In a sub-culture of hard-nosed realism and hyper-rationality, in a world that claims as a sign of its superiority its vigilant purging of all nonrational elements . . . the last thing one might expect to find is religious imagery—imagery of the forces that science has been defined in *opposition to* . . . [a]nd yet, religious imagery permeates the nuclear past and present . . . Perhaps most astonishing of all is the fact that the creators of strategic doctrine actually refer to members of their community as 'the nuclear priesthood.' It is hard to decide what is most extraordinary about this: the easy arrogance of their claim . . . or the . . . implicit statement about who, or rather what, has become god" (Cohn, 1987, 702).

While contemporary global strategics can be expected to manifest the marks of their Christian origins, what of other sacral languages? How might anti-Rationalist ideas of a non-Christian kind be seen as impinging upon this particular dimension to world affairs?

What, for example, might Taoists have to say about strategic thinking? What might be learned from the juxtaposition of Taoism, and those doctrines that exemplify the state-making dimension to world affairs, namely, realism, internationalism, and globalism?

The closest contemporary analytical language to the Taoist notion of state-making seems at first glance to be globalism, since globalism is predicated upon the assumption that humanity is essentially good, and Taoists talk, in a similar way, about our fundamental "simplicity and purity" (Ames, 1994, 8, 9). When Taoism was first formulated, however, the dominant strategic issue for most people was how to ensure the survival of their regime in the face of "murderously competing powers." It was one where any idea of system-level protection was simply "unapplicable" (Ames, 1994, 7). Should we be looking to Taoist thinkers for realist responses instead? The Taoist preference is also for small, self-sufficient polities, behaving more cooperatively toward each other than contemporary states tend to do. It is polities like these that Taoists see providing "the small man [*sic*]" (Graham, 1989, 218) with the "circumstances [most] congenial to [his or her] self-realization" (Graham, 1989, 218; Ames, 1994, 8). Which sounds more like internationalism, than realism or globalism.

There is a prior question, however, and that is: what is Taoism? What might it mean to promote and protect the Tao in the context of contemporary world affairs?

This is not easy to say, as the author of the *Tao Te Ching* admits. This germinal text was ostensibly written under the aegis of the sage Lao Tzu. He says explicitly that: "The Way that can be told of is not an Unvarying Way / The names that can be named are not unvarying names / It was from the Nameless that Heaven and Earth sprang" (Lao Tzu, 1997 [480–222 B.C.], 1). We are confronted from the outset, in other words, with the problem of describing a "fluid whole" that defeats any attempt to define and label it (Graham, 1989, 219).

In ancient Chinese *tao* refers, with a small "t" in English, to a road or path. This is not the *Tao*, however. The capital "T" makes the word much more profound and much more ambiguous, conferring such meanings as " 'the way the universe works' " (Waley, 1934, 30), "the eternal order of the cosmos and at the same time its course" (Weber, 1951, 181), the "inherent order that pervades . . . all being" (Loewe, 1990, 91), the "still-undivided stuff" that is "nameless" (Graham, 1989, 221), or "the Great Clod" (Creel, 1970, 33). Waley says Tao also means something like God, but Morris explicitly rejects this, at least where God refers to a spiritual creator. The Tao is totally impersonal, he says, lacking "any reference to a divinity or to a spiritual realm, or to a set of rules to follow, or to rituals to perform" (Morris, 1994, 98).

If we can hold to one side for a moment the injunction against trying to define the Tao at all, we can see from the above that it refers either to a kind of nature mysticism, or to the invariant source of all change. As such it may be little more than a way of talking about the totality of all that is, and the indifference of that totality to the efforts of whoever tries to conceive of it (Creel, 1970, 31).

A closer look, however, shows that the *Tao Te Ching* is offering a definition of a more unconventional, less logical kind. What it tries to tell us is meant to strike us like "successive blows from opposite sides." It is meant to convey a "knack," or an "aptitude," or a "way of living," rather than an explicit account of any ultimate Reality or Truth (Graham, 1989, 199, 220, 218). This is clearly manifest in the way the *Tao Te Ching* asks, for example, who could possibly prefer the "jingle of jade pendants," who once has heard "stone growing inside a cliff . . ." (Bynner, 1972 [1944], 70), an image validated in contemporary times by the discovery of earth tides commensurate with ocean ones.

None of which is very helpful to the student of the world's politico-strategic affairs (though from a Taoist perspective, there is no point expecting such help in the first place). What we can say about the Tao is not what it is, and when we do try to say something about it, we merely demonstrate what we do not know. There would seem little point, as a consequence, in even making the attempt.

This does not deter Taoists, however. They might not be able to offer a logical account of what the Tao means. They do see themselves as being able to offer an analogical account, however, not of what the Taoist reality signifies, but of how this reality feels. This account is not accessed in scientific terms. It is intuited using "stories, verses, maxims" and the like (Graham, 1989, 199–200). To the secular Rationalist, the truth content of such analogical intuitions is fatally compromised by their subjectivity. They are analytically suspect because they do not examine the order and course of the universe in objectified terms. To the Taoist, on the other hand, it is the objectifying character of the Rationalist approach that fatally compromises the truth content of the conclusions it comes to. When Taoists talk of the Tao as an uncarved block, therefore, or as water, with all of water's fluid and life-nourishing power (Lao Tzu, 1997 [480–222 B.C.], 15, 19, 82), they are doing so quite deliberately. They are doing so to provide metaphorical approximations of a principle they do not think can be demonstrated in any other way (Giles, 1961 [1889]).

The same concerns arise when we look at the Tao as a practice, rather than as a principle. Here the focus falls upon the "gradual inward-turning of . . . thought," or what Waley calls "quietism" or meditation (Waley, 1934, 43, 45). Why, the Rationalist asks again, is "mystical illumination" of the kind quietism makes possible going to help state-makers order the interstate system any more effectively than Rationalist calculation can? (Graham, 1989, 234). Do we really want a world where exploitation and global destitution and environmental neglect are met with meditative poise, rather than passionate engagement, and a reasoned commitment to change things for the better? The answer the Taoist gives is to highlight once more how Rationalist state-makers are taught to understand world affairs by objectifying, while Taoists see the conclusions Rationalists come to as being circumscribed by the primary experience (individuation) that makes objectifying possible. They see Taoist meditation as a direct antidote to the limits and distortions of the Rationalist mind-move, and as providing direct access to a way of knowing that allows us to transgress these limits and compensate for these distortions. Consider, for example, human conflict. This can be analyzed objectively in terms of its causes, and the results of these analyses can then be used to manage or resolve it. Conflict can also, however, be analyzed by meditating upon the ways in which we attach ourselves to each other, and to the world. The result of these meditations can then be used to practice a particular kind of watchfulness, a particular kind of non-anticipation, that can then be used to manage or resolve conflict in nonobjectifying ways.

While it would be foolish to try and deal with world conflict by getting state-makers to do Taoist meditation, since few would persist, and the consequences for those that did would be far too uncertain, it might not be foolish to heed the advice provided by Taoists as a result of *their* meditations. Drawing upon the wells of wordless wisdom that underpin our day-to-day awareness, Taoists conclude that "to do is to be," for example, and that the best way to "be" is to try and bring the world "into order" by gaining "greater knowledge and understanding of Nature outside and beyond human society" (Needham, 1956, 33).

As a result of their meditations, Taoists advocate a very active form of pacifism. War does not pay, they say, because war does not get the results that those who prosecute it intend. It also has consequences that are not intended (like it lays waste good land). Where it cannot be avoided, they continue, it should be prosecuted reluctantly, and in non-triumphal terms. Thus: "He who by Tao purposes to help a ruler of men / Will oppose all conquest by force of arms; / For such things are wont to rebound. / Where armies are, thorns and brambles grow." And ". . . he who delights in the slaughter of men will never get what he looks for . . . ." And: "A host that has slain men is received with grief and mourning; he that has conquered in battle is received with rites of mourning." And: "Show me a man of violence that came to a good end, and I will take him for my teacher." And: "The greatest conqueror wins without joining issue . . . This is called the power that comes of not contending." And: "it is the way of Heaven not to strive but none the less to conquer" (Lao Tzu, 1997 [480–222 B.C.], 3132, 45, 72, 77].

In offering such advice, are Taoists contradicting themselves? Creel thinks so, drawing attention to the difference he discerns between the Taoist attempt to have a political impact and the Taoist practice of contemplation (Creel, 1970, 45). Ames repudiates this dichotomy in turn, arguing that "[s]ince Taoist political theory is propounded as a microcosm of their metaphysics in which the operation of the political state is seen as correlative to the functioning of the cosmos, it follows that the ideal ruler can only be 'purposive' if in fact there is some purpose in his cosmic counterpart, the *tao*. The Taoism of the *Lao Tzu* does acknowledge a certain natural 'so-ness' which exists in all things and propels them toward their own realization. But the political theory of the *Lao Tzu* is certainly not purposive in the sense of advocating a specific and artificially contrived political program which enables one to seize and exercise political control . . . . The political theory of the *Lao Tzu* can be accused of being impracticable, but to project selfish desires and base ambitions onto it is a distortion which . . . does violence to the spirit of the text" (Ames, 1994, 218, fn. 23).

In offering such advice, are Taoists simply being impractical? They were certainly critiqued on these grounds from the very beginning. The *Huai Nan Tze* (206 B.C.E.–8 C.E.), for example, castigates Taoists for being naïve and primitivist, and for seeming to provide a "total repudiation of human culture" (Ames, 1994, 219, fn. 34). Many others have said something similar since. Why, they ask, should an active form of pacifism be any more natural than any other policy? Why should a deliberate and conscious attempt to craft the world to human advantage be less in accord with the way the universe works than active nondetachment?

Taoists see all this as missing the (Taoist) point. The active kind of pacifism that the Taoist recommends is a particular form of *wu-wei* ("no unnatural action"). As such, it does not seek to be either practical or impractical (Chan, 1969, 150). It seeks instead not to impose preconceptions. It seeks to use "subtler methods of persuasion." It seeks to let things "take their own course," so that they might bring about the "desired result" (Needham, 1956, 37, 68).

Wu-wei is very easy to misunderstand. When we are standing stiff, for example, and someone tells us to relax, we tend to imagine the opposite of stiff, and go floppy. Not-stiff has another meaning, however, for which there is no precise word in English. Flexible, supple, lithe, (com)pliant, elastic or plastic are all aspects of this other meaning, however, and by *wu-wei* we denote this other meaning, not the floppy one. Likewise, when someone is being too activist in their state making and we advise them to be more pacifist, we tend to think they are being asked not to intervene, and to revert to inactivity. This is the equivalent of thinking of the word "relax" as meaning "floppy," however, which would be disastrous in the state-making case, since a "floppy," "inactive" state-maker would not be likely to hold off domestic or foreign opponents for very long. The advice to be more pacifistic does not necessarily mean making state power inactive, therefore. In practice, it might mean intervention, albeit intervention of a kind that is less single-minded, more adaptable, and more subtle ("not-stiff") than the non-Taoist kind.

Even if we think we do understand *wu-wei*, it still means "no unnatural action," however, which still begs the question, since we still have not said what an unnatural action is, and what the difference might be between an unnatural and a natural one. To the Taoist, the answer to this question comes from meditation not analysis, since natural action is said to mean "rule through *te* ('virtue,' 'power') acquired in trance" (Waley, 1934, 145). Would quietist virtue and power be likely to stop armed marauders or plotting opponents, however? (Creel, 1970, 56). Secular Rationalists tend to see such a suggestion as not only anti-Rational but also ridiculous. Taoists, however, believe there is no "reason" to expect that virtue and power gained this way would not work. Indeed, they see good "reason" to expect that they would and they should.

Natural action is what we are supposed to get when we act in a truly free and spontaneous fashion. It is supposed to allow our relationship with the world to evolve of its own accord.

If asked to be more explicit, Taoists say (as they do in the *Tao Te Ching*) that natural actions are those that are not indifferent but caring, not proud but humble, not profligate but frugal, not assertive but yielding, not learned but wise. They are the kind of action that takes from those "who have too much" and gives to those "who have not enough." They are the kind of action that spares lives rather than takes them, working "like the one who says little" and yet has "laid . . . plans." They are the kind of action that leaves people to themselves and does not interfere, for example, by trying to teach people too much, so that their thinking becomes confused. They are the kind of action that is timely, dealing with big things while they are still small. They are the kind of action that fosters "being content," self-understanding, and self-control, that neither exalts fame, riches, and ritual, nor the overt use of power. They are the kind of action that keeps the state's "sharpest weapons where none can see them," does not portray such weapons as "lovely," and opposes all conquest by force of arms. They are the kind of action that knows "the male, yet cleaves to what is female." They are the kind of action that does not oppress ordinary people but rather seeks to better their welfare, seeing as ordinary people see, and hearing as ordinary people hear; that does not stimulate the desire for products that are hard to get; that does not legislate kindness or morality; and that recognizes the utility of "what is not." They are the kind of action that is helpful, childlike, and down-to-earth, yet values profound thought, gentle friendships, true words, good government, due regulation, and effective deeds (Lao Tzu, 1997 [480–222 B.C.], 81, 77, 75, 49, 37, 32, 31, 29, 11).

Which is a substantial list of considerable specificity, despite all the inbuilt universals. What is meant by wisdom? What constitutes compassion? What is a true word? What is good government? What is an effective deed? Taoists do articulate *wu-wei* practices, however, in a coherent and highly explicit way.

If *wu-wei* should still seem opaque, it can also be seen at work in the practice of martial arts like *tai chi chuan*. Here the power of an opponent is returned or re-directed, making it possible to prevail by yielding and neutralizing, rather than using countervailing force. This has obvious implications for conflict management and resolution, implications that do not escape the Taoist's attention. While it is one thing to re-direct a punch to the face, however, it is quite another to re-direct an invading army heading across a country's border. And yet the techniques of all guerrilla war, whether rural or urban, are basically those of *wu-wei*. Guerrillas will typically avoid a war of position, not wanting to risk direct confrontation for fear of defeat. They will prefer to undermine the enemy. They will prefer to wait for the right moment to apply strategic force, and to prevail that way. The Taoist argues that invasion is best dealt with when the risk is still small anyway, and when strategic intervention is able to preempt the need for conflict altogether.

According to Creel, *wu-wei* can also be seen at work in *judo*, which is a Japanese martial art that uses the same principle as *tai chi chuan*. *Judo* techniques allow weaker people to overcome stronger ones by employing flexible, natural movements that are not retaliatory. Nor do they represent a retreat. Rather, they represent a way of reconciling attack, thereby allowing the defender to prevail despite the attacker's supposed superiority (Creel, 1970, 67).

The same logic is found in *aikido* as well, which is another Japanese martial art of the Taoist kind. And though *aikido* has largely ceased to be a spiritual *do* or "way" by now, having mostly mutated into other arts, or having reverted to the performance of physical technique (*aiki-jutsu*), it is still possible to find in one or two of its schools ongoing research of the *wu-wei* kind.

Aikido is a non-violent form of self-defence whose founder, Morihei Uyeshiba, sought to create a martial art of harmony and love, not discord and hate. Its purpose is not to fight. It is not to try and win. It is rather "to reconcile the world and make human beings one family," thereby allowing the "completion of everyone's mission." In unmistakably Taoist language, Uyeshiba also says that "[t]he secret of Aikido is to harmonize ourselves with the movement of the universe and bring ourselves into accord with the universe itself." Winning under these circumstances means "winning over the mind of discord in yourself." Nor is this simply theory, since Uyeshiba says it has to be practiced before it becomes possible to accept the "great power of oneness with Nature" that it ultimately represents (Uyeshiba, 1963, 177, 180, 178; Pettman, 1993).

Aikido is not just a martial art, since its principles can be applied in daily life, up to and including state making. For example, *aikido* has been called a "highly germane metaphor" for describing and explaining the international relations of Japan, since it describes and explains the country's preference for foreign policy initiatives that are not assertive, as well as its dependence on covert economic rather than overt military power to gain regional and global influence. Both have been explicitly characterized as an international demonstration of *aikido* at work (Hook et al., 2001, 376).

The idea that a major state, like Japan, should be conducting its foreign policy along such lines is an intriguing one, not only making possible a more Japanese interpretation of Japanese state-making (albeit one offered by Westerners), but also providing a demonstrably effective—if somewhat unfamiliar—alternative to any state-maker faced with the question of what he or she should actually be doing. It does not accept the premises of the modernist construction of world affairs. It prefers to reach beyond the limits these premises set for antimodernist premises that posit antimodernist politico-strategic practices instead.

The collaborative nature of the aikidoist/Taoist approach stands in marked contrast to the dog-eat-dog competitiveness that characterizes contemporary politico-strategic realism, and the tit-for-tat cooperativeness that characterizes politico-strategic internationalism. At the same time it is not globalist, despite the parallels suggested at the start. Indeed, it has nothing to do at all with the modernist strategic spectrum that puts competition at one end and cooperation at the other (Pettman, 1998, 176). It posits collaboration instead, not of the negative kind inferred by the idea of "going along," but of the positive kind inferred by the concept of "self-realization." It posits an affirmative, non-conflictual approach, not in terms of the "self," but in terms of the "Self" (Pettman, 1998, 177).

What, then, do Taoist strategics entail? What does this particular sacral discourse have to say to the white, Western, realist, state-making males who dominate contemporary global state making (should they ever be able to shut up long enough to listen)?

As noted at the beginning, strategics are conventionally read in military and diplomatic terms. They are read in terms of the changing balance of power, and of serial challenges to state and interstate security.

Less conventionally, they are read in politico-economic, politico-social, politico-cultural, and politico-sacral terms as well. Which is why issue-areas once considered marginal receive more mainstream consideration now, issue-areas like those of labor migration, terrorism, drug smuggling, people smuggling, piracy, gender, and the environment. This is consistent with a general move toward expanding the compass of strategic concerns from realist readings of national security to include, first, ideas of collective and common security, and second, ideas of cooperative, comprehensive, and even human security (Dupont, 1995).

To the more conventional strategist, Taoists offer *wu-wei* (or "no unnatural action"). Taoist teachings recommend security practices that maximize the ability to act freely and respond spontaneously, that spare lives whenever possible by using overt force reluctantly, that keep the use of force to a minimum when use is unavoidable, and that involve keeping one's own counsel while planning ahead for whatever strategic challenges changes in the regional balance might present. They mean keeping the state's "sharpest weapons" out of sight, and generally eschewing armed conquest. And they mean strategic intervention earlier rather than later.

To the less conventional strategist, Taoists offer the same general advice. In this regard, "no unnatural action" means not stimulating the desire for products that are hard to get, and not attempting to legislate kindness or morality. It is also deemed to mean taking from those "who have too much" and giving to those "who have not enough," keeping an eye on problems so that they can be dealt with in a timely fashion, acknowledging "the male" while cleaving to "what is female," and generally promoting policies that are helpful, down-to-earth, effective, good, and true.

Of the various current concerns, both conventional and unconventional, that face the analyst and practitioner of world affairs, one strategic issue involves Taoist practice in a more immediate way than most. This is the putative threat presented to the global and regional security balance by the growing power of China.

Does China constitute a potential threat to the international order? Its *realpolitik* record certainly suggests that this might be so. Historically it has long played a central role in regional affairs, and as it recovers from the inroads made by nineteenth-century European imperialists, and subsequent attempts to reconstruct the country along marxist/maoist lines, there seems no reason not to think that it will play such a role again.

Despite the rapid economic growth made possible by the liberalist rethink of more recent times, analysts like Harding continue to conclude that "China's domestic situation is so complex and uncertain that it would be unwise to draw premature conclusions about its emergence as a major international power" (Harding, 1996, 109). Others, however, talk of China as posing a "daunting challenge for Asia Pacific order" and of a "rise" that will "continue to strain the existing structure of relations within the region" (Senior Policy Seminar, 2001, vii–viii). Chinese leaders themselves, meanwhile, talk of being open and peaceful, while noting continued American hegemony (the "U.S. question"), the Taiwan issue, and a range of claims to islands in China's seas to the south. They also acknowledge that economic development has strategic implications of its own, like the need to protect the shipping lanes along which vital raw materials come in (like oil), and Chinese goods go out.

Much turns upon assessments of China's strategic intentions. No matter how powerful China becomes, if its leaders have no intention of using that power to threaten others in the region or the world, then force levels and the like have little strategic significance. Harding, for example, observes that "[a]t present, the international intentions of Chinese leaders appear largely benign" (Harding, 1996, 109–10). Is this observation accurate? And if it is, why are China's leaders not more outgoing?

One answer would be a materialist one. In this view a benign China would reflect no more than a desire for rapid economic development, and the need to ensure a security environment that maximizes the country's productive potential. The willingness on the part of China's leaders to do security deals with neighbors, like India and Russia, and to resolve regional conflicts, like the one with Vietnam over Cambodia, would be no more than an expression of the kind of commercial ambitions clearly evident, for example, in the way the Chinese deal with global organizations like the World Bank, the International Monetary Fund, and the World Trade Organization, and regional organizations like the Asian Development Bank and the Asia Pacific Economic Cooperation (APEC) one.

Another answer would be more mentalist. In this view, China has been catapulted without choice into the modernist world. It has nonetheless retained elements of its own strategic culture, a culture notably different from that of the modernist world in which the Chinese have come to live. Over time, as the influence of Euro-American modernity has grown, this difference has decreased. The Chinese still have their own ideas about world affairs, however, and about how international order should be maintained. Nor are these ideas necessarily congruent with those that have emerged in the Euro-American part of the world. Analytic attention is regularly drawn, therefore, to the problem of "parachuting" European perceptions and European expectations into the Asia-Pacific region. It also gets drawn to the way Chinese leaders may use the "Western vocabulary of international relations," but remain well aware of their own "civilization," and the need to protect China's "core culture" from "external contamination," a need still said to be "as important a component of national security as territorial security" (Baker and Sebastian, 1996, 25).

From this perspective it is significant, perhaps, that China's strategic culture is one that still has within it the sense that conflict is "aberrant" or at least "avoidable," and that force should be used "defensively, minimally, only under unavoidable conditions, and then only in the name of the righteous restoration of a moral-political order" (Johnston, 1995, 24). Johnston calls this sense Confucian-Mencian, and says that it is not the dominant one. It is more accurate to call it Taoist, however, and even if it is not dominant, it might still help explain why Chinese "realists" tend to think in defensive rather than expansionist terms, and why Deng Xiaoping, in his bid in the late 1970s and early 1980s to replace Mao's "war and revolution" line with a "peace and development" one, talked of China keeping a "low profile," and never taking the lead (Finkelstein, 2002, 24).

It is difficult to establish the influence of a heritage like the Taoist one in a direct and unambiguous way. However, when Wang Jisi, Director of the Institute of American Studies at the Chinese Academy of Social Sciences, says in an assessment of China's international environment that "[i]f China thinks of danger in times of peace and does a good job at home, some external troubles can never become internal disturbances" (Wang, 2002, 7) are we not hearing—albeit in a muted and mediated form—the Taoist preference for timely intervention and contingency planning ("thinking of danger in times of peace"), and for seeking to better the welfare of ordinary people ("doing a good job at home")? And when Lin Limin, Deputy Director at the Division for World Politics Studies in the China Institute of Contemporary International Relations, says that China should be "prudent" instead of "arrogant," even if it becomes "very strong," that it should practice "strategic self-restraint" because "[o]nly such a big power can fate always smile upon," and that it should hide its capacities "biding its time" (Lin, 2002, 40), are we not hearing the Taoist injunction to be humble, and to follow not lead ("when [the] flower blooms, it naturally sends forth a fragrant odor")? (Lin, 2002, 40).

So: there is evidence of Taoist practices at work still, and there is reason to think that these practices continue to temper what Chinese state-makers think and how they behave. Therefore, China might reasonably be expected to be a relatively benign member of the international community.

Wu-wei makes for a particular kind of strategic thinking, one where the international use of force is not necessarily seen in *realpolitik* terms. Any assessment of China as a rising threat needs to take the susceptibility of its leaders to such thinking into account, since it might well be that Chinese leaders are at least a part-exception to the *realpolitik* rule. If this is the case, then treating them otherwise might only induce the very response that non-Chinese leaders fear the most. This is one possible example of Taoism at work in world affairs. It also suggests how Taoism, and the politico-strategic dimension to world affairs, might be profitably juxtaposed. In the process it helps show the limits modernity places on our understanding of world affairs, the distortions that modernity causes, and how these constraints and misconstruals might be countered by sacralist means.

Chapter 6

Buddhist Economics

To adopt some fastidiously imitated form of Buddhism would both be quite artificial and also would indicate immaturity with respect to our own social and religious roots. Yet it is very worthwhile for westerners to sift and to search the Buddhist tradition of Asia. It bears insights which ought to contribute to the emerging global culture of modern times . . .

—Pye, 1979, 140

Economics is part of the market-making dimension to world affairs. It is that particular part of political economy that describes and explains market behavior. In terms of the dominant accounts of the discipline, it is puzzle solving for liberals, as opposed to puzzle solving for mercantilists and socialists, for example, or marxists and neo-marxists, or feminists and environmentalists. As such, it carries the cause of modernist Rationalism into the heart of the marketeering dimension to world affairs, where it gives voice to a wide range of analytic dialects, ranging from Keynesianism to anarcho-capitalism.

Each analytical language articulates a different assumption about human nature or human nurturing practices, as conceptualized not in the romantic or phenomenological terms used to document the lived world, but in the Rationalist terms used to describe and explain world affairs. Liberalism is one such language. Liberalists assume that individuals, rather than behaving as utterly unpredictable individuals, do so in a calculating way. Mercantilists, by contrast, assume that we behave essentially badly, while socialists assume that we are capable of behaving well. Marxists, who eschew such views of an essential human nature, see us as behaving in the way the material nature of the nurturing environment determines; neo-marxists assume that we behave in the way our material *and* our mental environment determines; while constructivists assume that we behave the way the mental environment alone determines. Radical feminists assume that we behave essentially the way our biology decrees, or the world's patriarchs decide. And so on.

Taken together these doctrines provide detailed accounts of economic nationalism and protectionism, world trade and investment, and world production and consumption. Because they are posited in terms of their particular assumptions, however, they constrain all talk about marketeering to the articulation each assumption allows, distorting our understanding of world affairs accordingly.

Given the above, what might a Buddhist economics be? What kind of account of the production and consumption dimension to human experience does the particular spiritual discourse that the Buddha articulated provide? What premises did the Buddha posit (as far as we can tell), and what does the attempt to describe, explain, and prescribe for the world in terms of these premises tell us about liberal marketeering, for example?

In Rationalist parlance, Buddhist economics is a contradiction in terms. As a politico-spiritual language, Buddhism is anti-Rationalist. Economics, on the other hand, is a secular, modernist discipline, and as such Rationalist, anti-sacral, and anti-Buddhist. From the Rationalist point of view these languages represent two very different projects, the one having essentially no bearing on the other.

In sacralist parlance, however, it is entirely possible to locate liberal marketeering in the context of Buddhist knowing. The Buddha was not a liberal, but what he seemed to say impinges directly upon liberalism, and provides a radical alternative to liberalist thought and practice.

If we are to explore this particular politico-spiritual alternative, we have first to ask: what is Buddhism, however? More particularly, what can we say that the Buddha had to say?

Contemporary Buddhism presents a diverse array of Buddhist dialects. There is no definitive version, that is, of the Buddhist account of the world. There are different versions that articulate different interpretations that promote and protect different Buddhist ideas. There is no one interpretation that commands the assent of all who call themselves Buddhists.

There was, however, a historic individual who first articulated this particular sacral doctrine, and all Buddhists do ostensibly subscribe to what this individual said, even though the " 'original' doctrine of the Buddha . . . cannot be isolated and described as it was by itself" (Conze, 1962, 32). Thus while many Buddhist discourses "look back" to the teachings of the historical Buddha, "none can be specified with certainty as being his own words" (de Bary et al., 1988, 100).

The uncertainty arises because the Buddha spoke what he thought and believed. He did not write it down. Or if he did, we have no record of these writings. Others had to remember what they thought he said and pass their memories on, creating oral traditions that were used to preserve his teachings until various initial attempts were made, most of which are now lost, to create a written record of them (de Bary et al., 1988, 100). Knowing what the Buddha himself taught is not possible, in other words. We have no unmediated account of what his teachings were (Pye, 1979). We have only secondary accounts, all of which are subject to interpretative bias.

This said, the accuracy of the oral tradition that preserved the Buddha's teachings was arguably quite high, while the one comprehensive written account that we do still have (the Pali Canon, or *Tripitaka*), from all the early attempts to compile a written form of the Buddha's teachings, does include an account of his first sermon. He is said to have given this sermon in a park outside Varanasi to a group of five monks (Buddha, 1959

[100 B.C.E.]). It begins "Thus I have heard . . . ," thereby highlighting its second-hand character, but if we stay as close as we can to this sermon, we have a reasonable chance of understanding the gist of what the Buddha himself tried to said. By applying the ideas expressed in this sermon directly to contemporary economics, we might then be able to get a sense of how the Buddha's thinking might apply to contemporary liberal marketeering.

The Buddha's first sermon, "Setting in Motion the Wheel of Truth," was reportedly on the topic of two of his most basic insights. One of these was the Middle Way. The other was the Four Noble Truths, the last of which leads onto the Noble Eightfold Path.

The Middle Way was the Buddha's injunction to avoid the extremes of "sensuality and self-torture" (Parrinder, 1977, 29). It was about the "two ends" he is said to have said were "not to be served by a wanderer," namely, the "pursuit of desires and of the pleasure which springs from desire," as opposed to the "pursuit of pain and hardship" (de Bary, 1988, 101–2).

The first of the Four Noble Truths was that of the fact of Sorrow (or suffering or pain), as manifest by our "birth . . . age . . . disease . . . [and] death," as well as by " . . . contact with the unpleasant . . . separation from the pleasant . . . [and] every wish unfulfilled." It pertained, "in short," to "all the components of individuality (forms, sensations, perceptions, psychic dispositions, and consciousness)."

The second Noble Truth was the fact of Sorrow's fundamental cause, that is, "craving, which leads to rebirth, which brings delight and passion, and seeks pleasure now here, now there . . . ." It is the "craving for sensual pleasure . . . for continued life . . . for power."

The third Noble Truth was the certainty of Sorrow's cessation, which only comes about by eliminating craving, so that "no passion remains . . . ." This means facing craving and "leaving it, being emancipated from it, being released from it, giving no place to it."

The fourth Noble Truth was the way to stop Sorrow. This was the Noble Eightfold Path, namely, Right Views, Resolve, Speech, Conduct, Livelihood, Effort, Mindfulness, and Concentration (de Bary et al., 1988, 102).

The Buddha's ultimate promise was one of clear inner vision. From clear inner vision came wisdom, he said. This in turn resulted in insight, peace, enlightenment, and finally, Enlightenment or *nirvana* (de Bary et al., 1988, 102).

From what can be ascertained elsewhere in the *Tripitaka*, the Buddha also sought to construct integrated communities, centered on monasteries, where monks and nuns tried to become Enlightened, while serving the spiritual needs of the community as a whole. In such societies lay believers could engage in worldly pursuits, while making spiritual progress by providing monks and nuns with the necessities of life.

Buddhists do live in such communities, though few practice assiduously and consistently what the Buddha taught (few Christians practice assiduously and consistently the principles Christ preached, either). A Buddhist world community is as conceivable as a Christian one, and arguably as likely, given the competing conceptions of sacral practice preferred worldwide.

The next step in this chapter is to explore liberal marketeering. Marketeers say that our primary purpose is to buy and consume the goods and services that markets provide. The more liberal minded among them assume that we are individuated, self-maximizing producers and consumers, and entrepreneurs and workers, assumptions commensurate with those that inform the modernist mind-gaze as a whole. Economics is characterized, therefore, by the pursuit of private interests, that taken together are deemed to serve the collective good. These are interests that have seemingly little to do with spiritual ideals. They serve secular, rationalist, material gain (Smith, 1892 [1776]).

The Buddha, on the other hand, wanted Right Mindfulness. He enjoined monks to be not only "fully conscious," but also aware of the individual self as "not . . . enduring" that is, as a "composite and transitory collection of material and psychic factors" (de Bary et al., 1988, 102, fn. 5). The Buddha saw the self as an illusion. He did not think the ordinary self does not exist, but rather, that the "essence of existence" is impermanence (Morris, 1994, 59). Which is why he considered it inappropriate to say " 'I have no self' . . . [or] 'I have self' . . . ." Both, he said, are "fetters." The Buddha also thought it inappropriate to hold "opinions or views." We should try, he said, to see things "objectively as they are without mental projections." When we do so, what we call "I," or "being", begins to look like a concatenation of physical and mental aggregates, working together but manifesting endless change. Nothing, the Buddha concluded, is "permanent, everlasting, unchanging and eternal in the whole of existence" (Rahula, 1959, 51, 66).

How does this apply to economics? If we are not-selves, that is, if the self is an emergent outcome of no particular significance, then our needs must have little significance either. And if our needs are not significant, then our production and investment systems, and our places of exchange, must be more like monuments to suffering and desire, rather than the liberal miracles of production and supply that economists so admire. "What follows 'I' immediately is 'my' or 'mine'—the possessive self. With the false apprehension of an egoistic self, man craves blindly to possess things. Buddhism rejects the existence of self and thus, the possessive self collapses . . . Thus, Buddhist economics has, as its basis, not the search for supply, but a questioning of . . . human demands" (Satha-Anand and Wongwaisayawan, 1979, 40–1). In the Buddha's terms, that is, our demands are fleeting, and any system of market supply that caters to them will be radically ill conceived as well. It will be sustained more by false consciousness than by any collective sense of what we truly need.

Is the self only possessive and needy, then? Non-liberal accounts of the market, like socialism, suggest that we can be caring, cooperative, and compassionate as well. They suggest that we can be altruistic and self-denying, not just wanting and selfish.

In the Buddha's eyes, however, these traits are illusory too. Which is why "true" compassion is not the compassion that contradicts competition. It is a trait that lies outside the competition/kindness dichotomy altogether. True compassion is not the "active brotherliness" of self-denial. It is the "cool stoic equanimity" of one who truly knows (Weber, 1958, 211–3).

How might true compassion be brought to bear upon market practices? Some Buddhists think that by positing an idealized kind of socialism, where rich and poor work together for the benefit of all, and society's wealth is used to alleviate every instance of human suffering, we can apply such a sentiment (Buddhadasa, 1989, 194–7, 206; Payutto, 1994, 53, 62). Others envisage true compassion perfecting liberalism, by making possible a level of trust that allows markets to become completely efficient (Bubna-Litic, 1998, 209).

The Buddha himself seems to have seen true compassion as the expression of a not-self that is a non-dual self, and as a state of mind portending material practices much more radical than those that result in centralized market planning. The non-dual sense of self is one where no distinction arises between "agent, act, and object . . . ," where every action is performed as if it were "dynamic, unbroken, and unrepeatable," and where every life situation is part of an "interdependent, seamless whole . . ." (Batchelor, 1990, 179). It is a non-objectifying, non-individuating self, coterminous with everything that is. It is not part of any dichotomy or continuum that competitiveness and kindness create, since the individual who competes, or who practices kindness, still does so as a separate individual. It posits a completely different alternative, one where any sense of separation ceases to exist, and true compassion prevails. It is also "empty" (Batchelor, 1990, 180), in that it does not appeal to either "God, nature, energy, [or even] emptiness [itself]" to give it substance or content (Batchelor, 1990, 180). Positing "emptiness" as our essential being, however, means positing plenitude as well (Batchelor, 1990, 180). It means replacing a picture of individuated individuals, in a reified natural setting, with one where individuals are unique, and "nature" consists of discrete rivers, rocks, and trees. At this point, the form of the self that informs liberal economics has clearly been transformed, and with this transformation, market provision in terms of individuated consumption has ceased to apply. This does not mean self-denial, or social affirmation. It means something else altogether.

The Buddha's approval may look like it lies between the desire for material satisfaction and the desire for spiritual satisfaction. It may look like it lies between sensual excess and ascetic self-denial, between free market behavior and the pursuit of subsistence (Payutto, 1994, 69–70; Schumacher, 1973, 238).

It really lies somewhere else, however. It does not chart a path between those attached to secular satisfaction, like economists, and those who eschew all such attachment, like spiritual ascetics. It posits the "complete elimination of any form of inner-worldly motivation," and the possibility of another kind of awareness (Weber, 1958, 222).

What stops us achieving the emptiness/plenitude posited here? Most radically, it is the objectifying mind-gaze and Rationalist abstraction. In the Buddha's first sermon he infers that Rationalism, being a psychic disposition, and one of the five components of individuality (de Bary et al., 1988, 102), is one aspect of our fundamental Sorrow. As such, it can only obscure our understanding of our "present situation." Thus while Rationalists may recall objectified views of the past, for example, and anticipate objectified views of the future, their attempt to create a modernist mind-point requires them literally to overlook the moving moment, and with it the concrete experience of being alive. The result being, in Buddha's parlance, that they live the "mere idea of life." They do not live life itself (Batchelor, 1990, 181).

Realizing emptiness/plenitude means confronting the objectifying mind-gaze with its Buddhist alternative, and radically reversing the practices that modernist knowing involves (Batchelor, 1990, 181). It is much more radical than the romantic attempt to recover what we feel about things, as opposed to what we think about them. It requires a sustained attempt to see the "world as it is," a world without its veil of analytical languages and ideological perspectives (Batchelor, 1990, 182). It means sustaining a mind-gaze of undivided sacral attention, focused on the present moment. It means Buddhist meditation, in other words, since it is only through mental training of this (anti-Rationalist) kind that, we are able to bear witness to that "stream of causes" that begins as "mental conditions," but ends as economics. It is only by meditating that we find alternatives to our compulsions and longings and fears. It is only by meditating that we realize our "true well-being" (Payutto, 1994, 82–3).

Does Buddhist economics mean calling upon all economists to meditate, then, the way Taoist strategics seems to call upon state-makers to do? Is this the only way for us to know what economics truly entails?

Systematic meditation does provide for a calm, focused, and poised frame of mind, relatively free from confusing attachments (Buddhadasa, 1989, 65). Modernist economists may aspire to such a mental state, but they turn their reason out upon the world, and upon their minds in that world. They do not habitually turn their reason in, to understand their awareness as this presents to the mind itself. Some do meditate as a stress management exercise. Most are too imbued with secular Rationalism to do any more than this, however. The results are also too limited and uncertain to let us think of a global market being made this way.

Short of meditating economists, we still have the advice of the Buddha himself, though, advice that articulates a profound state of sacral understanding. This includes concrete prescriptions of direct relevance to material life in general, and to liberal marketeering ("economics") in particular. And though it was first formulated in an agricultural era, in a very different social and political context from that which predominates today, it is perennial advice, seemingly appropriate for any place and age.

As noted above, for example, the Buddha saw the middle way (beyond self-indulgence and self-mortification) as requiring eight particular modes of behavior. In following this compound path, he said, we free ourselves from all suffering and pain ("Sorrow"). We are able to become dispassionate, detached, and truly free. "[S]uch was the vision, the knowledge, the wisdom, the science, the light," he said in his inaugural address, "that arose in me with regard to things not heard before" (Buddha, 1959 [100 B.C.E.], 94).

Two of these eight aspects he described as Right Action ("Conduct"), and Right Livelihood. By Right Action, he seems to have meant "moral, honourable and peaceful" conduct, that is, not stealing and not being dishonest. By Right Livelihood, he seems to have meant not making one's living from a profession that brings "harm to others, such as trading in arms and lethal weapons, intoxicating drinks, poisons, killing animals, cheating, etc.". Or in the words of a later commentator, living off professions that are "honourable, blameless and innocent . . ." (Rahula, 1959, 47).

Though the injunctions not to steal and not to be dishonest are straightforward enough, the injunction not to work at what brings harm to others is less so. While involvement in the global armaments industry would seem to be clearly contraindicated (Hanh, 1994, 246), what about those who practice law? Even when acting honorably, lawyers can do great harm, as well as great good. And what about sales people, who are obliged to highlight what is right with a product rather than what is wrong with it, and who may regularly blur the line between "dealing with indecision in human nature" and "subtle trickery?" (Bubna-Litic, 2000, 202, 203). What about the whole capitalist mode of production, which obliges those without means to sell their labor for wages, and to suffer work that is often of little or no personal worth, to make a living? From the Buddha's point of view, the whole capitalist economy could be said to be built upon the wrong kind of livelihood.

Concepts like Right Action and Right Livelihood are problematic for those accustomed to the language of economics. They sound quaint and preachy until we ask: does modern industrial capitalism really satisfy human desire? The fundamental equation that underpins the dominant economic system of our day is that more wealth equals less suffering. This equation is even enshrined in economic legislation, company directors having a legal duty, for example, to maximize their shareholders' income (Bubna-Litic, 2000, 205). And while the liberal market certainly does make for happiness, particularly if we define happiness in terms of the ability to buy a better class of misery, does the liberal market deliver deep, abiding joy? Is it a system that prevents more suffering than it creates? Do the global corporations that scour the globe for markets, resources, and cheap labor, for example, do more good than harm? Does the capitalist work ethic, that holds up material wealth as the ultimate measure of status and worth, create more satisfaction than despair?

If material consumption really did satisfy our basic needs, then we could readily accept the conclusion that maximum consumption equals maximum satisfaction, as liberal economists maintain it does. We could embrace liberal economics as the one true economics, forever.

Maximum consumption does not lead to maximum satisfaction, however. There is much to suggest, for example, that whatever else they may make possible, liberal markets result in disparities in wealth, while contributing at the same time to spiritual impoverishment. Which suggests, in turn, that the question of consumption may have to be looked at more closely, and with it, the question of production as well.

In terms of what the Buddha seemed to say, we suffer until we understand that the key to suffering is desire. Liberal economists see desire prompting consumption, prompting production (and vice versa), with the exchange process regulating both. Liberal economists prioritize entrepreneurial freedom, therefore. They are not averse to workers being unemployed as part of the exchange process, so long as they do not upset the system as a whole. The Buddha, on the other hand, would seem to have placed a priority upon all people being employed, and creatively so. More generally, he could be said to have prioritized non-attachment, and a world where one who "conquers" him or herself is more respected than one who "conquers" millions of others by "economic warfare" (Rahula, 1994, 26).

The injunction to transcend desire does sound like an insult to the world's poor, particularly if it amounts to telling them to contemplate their mental navels, rather than strive for a fair share of the world's material wealth. Nor is such an injunction likely to raise the awareness of the world's rich.

There is such a thing as right rather than wrong livelihood, however, and global well-being might well come to depend upon an ability to tell the difference, not just in global terms, but in all the local ways in which people live day-to-day. In other words, the Buddha's advice may be sounder than it sounds (Goodman, 1994, 46).

So, what do Buddhist economics entail? What does Buddhism have to offer the market-making males, particularly the white, Western, liberalized males, who dominate the world political economy?

First, it offers insights into the way liberal economics works, and its fundamental reliance on a sense of self that may not be as absolute or as desirable as it is believed to be (Harris, 1999). No elite can ignore the power and influence of the contemporary economy, particularly where it comes in capitalist form. This is reflected in the way most politico-economic elites actively collude in spreading its power and influence. Capitalism's fecundity is undeniable. So is the appeal of the many commodities capitalists make and sell. The resources they buy, meanwhile, including the labor resources they buy, means wealth for those prepared to act as its agents, compradors and wage slaves. Capitalism is not practiced everywhere in the same way, however. In Buddhist countries it acquires a Buddhist cast, which may be more or less superficial, but is part of the story nonetheless, and is part of a larger story, too, of how modernity spreads. Understanding Buddhist versions of this story is part of understanding contemporary liberal economics and contemporary world affairs.

Second, Buddhism offers Buddhist advice. In the process, it offers the chance to have an economics that is arguably more humane, more fulfilling, and less crass.

In general human beings prefer to live by more than bread alone. Bread is necessary, but it is usually not sufficient. While those born into a Christian context learn to eschew it for Rationalist reasons, where do they then turn for advice on insufficiency? Should they turn back to Christianity? They may. They may also, however, turn to other politico-spiritual languages for advice on what sufficiency might mean.

The Buddha prioritized a sense of our selves as ephemeral and impermanent. He extolled a way of absolute compassion, that involved specific practices to do with Right Action and Right Livelihood (Rawlinson, 1997; Morris, 1994, 53, 58). All these ideas bear directly upon political economy.

He seemed to suggest the avoidance of extremes, and a muddling through approach familiar to most economists from their attempts to reconcile market supply and demand. He seemed to counsel a measured and instrumental response, as opposed to revolutionary politico-economic change.

The Buddha's "middle-way" practices are potentially much more profound than this, however. In the first instance, the Buddha counseled honesty. He also counseled making a living in ways that do least harm, thereby requiring us to think about the practical implications of what we do, and whether our work creates more suffering than it alleviates. Most basic of all, however, he extolled the not-self, the realization of which has profound economic implications. This is not just the opposite of the self that inhabits liberal economies. It is completely beyond this analytic ken. For example, the Buddha's notion that nothing else ever happens other than an "arising and passing of bodily and mental phenomena," or the notion that there is "no separate ego-identity within or without this process" (Morris, 1994, 64), is a far cry indeed from the liberal subject, with its private, concrete, and highly personalized wants and needs.

By highlighting how "I" suffer because of "my" attachments and "my" desires, and by showing how Self-realization and detachment can bring an end to suffering, through the simple expedient of repudiating this "I," the Buddha seemed to advocate a kind of spiritual suicide. This only seems so if we fail to understand what the Buddha considered essential, however. What is killed here is not, in his terms, real. Once "it" comes to an end, it is unreality that ends, not existence. At which point enlightenment ensues, that is, a state of awareness neither individuated nor non-individuated, a state of awareness that is spiritually emancipated in a completely different way (Arnold, 1998).

What kind of economics would enlightened not-beings practice? No economics at all, one suspects. The truly wise would be too aware to need an economy. If they did find themselves confronted by marketeering imperatives, they would likely use them not only as an opportunity to provide tangible proof of life's spiritual purpose, but also to show marketeers, in practical terms, how to mitigate their greed and their selfishness, and the sense of "me" and "mine" that makes marketeers so materially acquisitive. They would demonstrate what it means in market terms to promote true compassion (Green, 1990, 223).

For those still aspiring to such a state of awareness, a truly Buddhist economist would not say that marketeering is bad in itself. Rather, he or she would say that it is how marketeering is done that matters most. It is how marketeers think and feel about what they do in the market that denotes the sacral worth of their intent, and the spiritual significance of their material aspirations.

Economic scarcity is clearly undesirable, since it causes people to suffer. Economic surfeit is also undesirable, however, since it causes people to suffer too, allowing them to meet their material needs but not their nonmaterial ones. Which brings us back to economic sufficiency, and the material benefits the Buddha believed would come from taking the Middle Way. The most fundamental problem for Rationalists with the Middle Way is that it is not Rationalist enough, and herein lies the rub. Economists are Rationalists, and in their terms at any rate, Buddhists are not. This does not necessarily make Buddhists wrong. But are they right?

Basically, in the terms the Buddha espoused, wealth is only ever a means to an end. It might be an indispensable means, in that the material conditions favorable to spiritual success might have to be met if the "higher and nobler end" is to be achieved (Rahula, 1959, 81). Wealth is only ever the figure, however, to a much more fundamental and comprehensive ground.

In Buddhist terms, then, economics is not a separate body of systematic knowledge at all. It is part of a vast web of social agreements, all of which are at work "within the individual, within society and within the environment" (Payutto, 1994, 35). There is no "economics." There is only more or less awareness of the Middle Way.

CHAPTER 7

ISLAMIC CIVICS

Talk of *civics* in a work on world affairs means talk of the modernist citizen, and of the identities that being such a citizen entails. With talk of this kind we enter the politico-social dimension to world affairs, and we articulate the three key analytic languages it represents, namely, nationalism, individualism, and collectivism. Each language is based upon an assumption about human nature. More specifically, nationalism articulates the sense that we are (or in this case, "they" are) essentially bad. Individualism articulates the sense that we (that is, we who prioritize reason as an end in itself) are essentially calculating. While collectivism articulates the sense that "we" are essentially good. Taken together, these languages highlight nation making, human rights advocacy, the international attempt to install democracy, the esteem afforded constitutions and contracts, the proliferation of social movements, and the growth of a global civil society.

All three of these principles are Rationalist. They are predicated, therefore, upon individuated individuals. These individuals are alienated individuals, whose skills in objectifying result in them making mental distance from those similarly en-selved. While exhilarating for some, this social distancing can also estrange. Attempts to compensate for the resultant alienation can include, on the one hand, atavistic efforts to reawaken the solidarist feelings that ostensibly predate the whole project, and on the other hand, efforts to cast forward to create the associative feelings that come from sharing a common cause or interest. The former leads to nationalism, and if extreme enough, to fascism. The latter leads to collectivism, and the divers social movements that constitute the global civil society.

Though it is somewhat arbitrary to choose from the world faiths that currently confront us, the following analysis will look at the way Muslims deal with modernist en-selving. More specifically, it will look at how Muslims accommodate a doctrine like that of nationalism, which makes for a different identity than that of the global Islamic *umma*. How do Muslims accommodate a doctrine like that of human rights, which clearly valorizes the individuated status of the modernist self, endowing that self with moral entitlements rather than communal responsibilities? And how do Muslims accommodate a doctrine like that of collectivism, which is Rationalist and associative rather than sacralist and solidaristic?

The ultimate reference point for any Muslim response must be the *Qur'an*. For Muslims, this is the literal Word of God (*Allah*), as voiced by the archangel Gabriel (God in this case being that indefinable, infinite, eternal, and incomparable Being that is the "Uncaused Cause of All That Exists") (Asad, 1984, 985 [112/2]). As the Word of God, the *Qur'an* prescribes all Muslim forms of behavior and belief. It is "divine thought and divine law incarnated in words: it is mysterious sound which has everlasting life and existence . . . [it is] God's eternal speech" (Smart, 1989, 281). And though God thinks and speaks in the *Qur'an* in the idiom of ancient Arabia, one would hardly expect Him to do otherwise. It would have made no sense to His Arabic-speaking agent, Muhammad, if He had spoken in contemporary Chinese, despite the fact that it was clearly within His competence to do so. (It would have made even less sense for Him to speak in His own language, whatever this could be said to be.)

The *Qur'an* consists of 114 chapters (*surah*), which taken as a whole, provide a fundamental template for all human behavior. The *surah* are believed to give all the guidance that humanity requires. Once the individual submits to *Allah* and therefore to His template (the *da'wa*), the soul can be enlightened, right and wrong can be determined, the bad can be denounced, the good can be exalted, alms can be paid, justice can be done, and a transnational spiritual community can be constructed.

The first *surah* was revealed, in the seventh century of the Christian era, to a middle-aged male Arab trader of the *Quraysh* tribe. When he was 40 years old, Muhammad began receiving the word of God. This continued for 23 more years, until just before he died. He was subsequently acclaimed a Prophet by those inspired by what he was reporting. He was also deemed, by those persuaded of the veracity of what was revealed to him, to be the "last and the greatest of God's message-bearers" (Asad, 1984, 998).

As noted already, the purpose of Islam is to live as the *Qur'an* prescribes. Many Muslims, however, accept the *sunna* as a second source of instruction, that is, those teachings of the Prophet apart from those God apparently told him, like the *hadith*. For most Muslims a third set of instructions is to be found in the *shari'a* (literally, the "path"), namely, the laws made by consensus by religious scholars, in their ongoing attempts to interpret the Prophet's teachings properly.

In living as a Muslim, truth is paramount. As the God of the *Qur'an* says: "We have not created the heavens and the earth and all that is between them in mere idle play . . . We hurl the truth against falsehood, and it crushes the latter . . . " (Asad, 1984, 489 [21/16, 18]).

In living as a Muslim, justice is also paramount. The *Qur'an* says that by being just we come "closest to being God-conscious" (Asad, 1984, 143 [5/8]).

The kind of justice the Islamic God requires is uncompromising and highly explicit. In the case of theft, for example, the Islamic God says that the hand of the man or woman who steals should be cut off " . . . as a deterrent" (Asad, 1984, 149 [5/38]). In the case of adultery, the Islamic God says that the "adulteress and the adulterer" (this includes intercourse between the unmarried) should be given a "hundred stripes" before a "group of . . . believers." (Those who bear false witness in this regard should be given eighty stripes.) Nor, He says, should we "let . . . compassion with them [the adulterers]" keep us from carrying out "this law . . . " (Asad, 1984, 532 [24/2]).

Generally we get our just desserts when we die. It is then that we will be judged as sacral beings. It is then, the Islamic God says, that we will "come to understand!," for it is "on that Day" that we will be "most surely. . . called to account for [what we have done with] the boon of life!"

The Islamic God's expectations are not necessarily particularly high, however. As He points out, with characteristic forcefulness: "[y]ou are obsessed by greed for more and more . . . until you go down to your graves . . . " (Asad, 1984, 1973 [102/1, 2, 4, 8]).

Nor does the instruction the *Qur'an* provides apply to individuals only, since it provides social rules as well. The sense tends to be strong among Muslims, therefore, that "individual righteousness cannot become really effective . . . unless there is agreement within the community as to the social rights and obligations of its members . . . [as defined by] the practical *laws* which should govern the behaviour of the individual within the society . . . " (Asad, 1984, 37, fn. 47).

This reflects the high priority placed upon having a sense of community itself, and the feeling that each Muslim individual is an integral part of a religious whole. This is the *umma*, that is said to invite "all that is good"; the *umma* that in practice enjoins all that is right, and forbids all that is wrong.

As a member of the spiritual community of Islam, the Muslim individual does not have the sovereign status the modernist doctrine of individualism strives so hard to confer. The Muslim individual is not supposed to feel the need to seek solace in nationalism or collectivism. After all, Muslims are already cupped by what is said to be " . . . the best community" (in the words of the *Qur'an*) "that has ever been brought forth for [the good of] mankind . . . " (Asad, 1984, 83 [3/104, 110]).

Although a member of the *umma*, the Muslim individual is found in many different social contexts. While in principle the contemporary Islamic community is a singular spiritual nation, in practice it is a wide range of different communities. There is "no monolithic Islam." There is a diverse Muslim world instead, that spans the globe (Lawrence, 1998, 4). Thus while the *umma* of today totals more than a fifth of the world's population, there are more Muslims in Africa than in Arabia, and more Muslims in Asia than in Africa, and "no single body, political or religious . . . " able to speak for Islam as a whole. We have a range of bodies, that is, "some political, some juridical, some academic . . . which interpret law and tradition as they see fit and which appeal to all Muslims to follow them" (Halliday, 1995, 155).

All Islamic societies have had to face the same modernist revolutions as everyone else. They have had to come to terms with the same "taken-for-granted hegemony" that the Christian/modernist project represents (Lawrence, 1998, 8, 9).

They have had to come to terms with sovereign state making, for example, since the Islamic community is now found spread across 50 or more supposedly independent, supposedly equal, territorially configured, and centrally governed sovereign nation-states. The *umma* of today, for example, is found in Saudia Arabia, Iran, Indonesia, Malaysia, Algeria, and Pakistan. Islamic instruction is provided in state-centered contexts, and politico-strategic agendas often prevail, like the need to balance international power, forge international alliances, and promote national interests (Ayubi, 1991, ch. 1).

The Muslim societies that constitute the contemporary *umma* have also had to come to terms with global marketering. The world capitalist system, for example, creates growing numbers of Muslim wageworkers and Muslim entrepreneurs. The *umma* of today is spread across such diverse firms and unions as the Saudi Basic Industries Corporation ("Our Power to Provide is both God-given and man-made"), the Emirates Tele-communications Corporation, the Riyad Bank, and the Pakistan Workers' Confederation. Islamic instruction is given in market-centered contexts, and market-oriented agendas often prevail, like the importance of promoting corporate viability, or protecting workers' rights (Ayubi, 1991, chs. 7, 8).

The Muslim societies that constitute the spiritual nation of Islam have also had to come to terms with the making of modernist civic identities. Growing numbers of people, for example, identify with the notion of the nation now. Modernist nationalism has made it possible for secular state-makers to displace Islam as a motivating force, though sometimes nationalists will use the symbolic force of the Faith to augment that of the doctrine of nationalism itself. Nationalism is typically employed today to consolidate support within a specific border for the state this border defines. It has come to do what religion did in the premodern era, that is, "direct the hopes of the majority toward its norms, while . . . engaging their energies in its public life" (Lawrence, 1998, 15). In practice, then, because the *umma* is found in various ethnic guises, like that of the Arabs, Berbers, Persians, Turks, Kurds, Pashtuns, Tajiks, Bengalis, Javanese, and Malays, Islamic instruction is given in nation-making contexts like these. Nationalistic agendas often prevail as a consequence, like the protection of ethnic integrity, the promotion of ethnic autonomy, and the construction of identities commensurate with the membership of a modernist sovereign state.

The Islamic response to the spread of modernist nationalism has usually been either reformist or conservationist. As Muslim leaders have struggled to maintain the Islamic "difference," that is, as they have struggled to maintain the experience of Islam as the prime context in which politico-social ideologies like the modernist/nationalist one are practiced, they have sought either to accommodate recent developments (despite the divided loyalties this can create), or to hold the Muslim line.

Islamic reformists accept the need to make a distinction between the sacral and the rational. They deal with modernism by accepting its fundamental premise.

Islamic conservationists draw no such distinction. As either revivalists or fundamentalists, they see no difference at all between the religious and the secular, the material and the spiritual, the public and the private, the divine and the mundane, the outer life and the inner one. They speak of religious and political practice "in a single, equal accent," calling for direct engagement in this world, but only as a necessary consequence of believing in the next. They also exalt the institution of the mosque, as the primary place of worship, education, regulation, and rule (Lawrence, 1998, 33, 14).

Which is not to say that radical conservationists *reject* Rationalism, since the *Qur'an* itself stresses *"reason* as a valid way to faith." By insisting on the "inseparability of the spiritual and the physical . . . ," however, and the inseparable character of daily behavior and spiritual life, the *Qur'an* does make it difficult for non-Muslims to accept its claim to be "predominantly rational" in its approach to "all religious questions." Most Rationalists, for example, more used to conceiving of spiritual experience in terms of the "thrill of numinous awe before things hidden and beyond all intellectual comprehension," find it difficult to accept the *Qur'an's* claim to provide guidance with regard to what is worth attaining here and now, and not just "hereafter." They find it difficult to accept the idea that all the concerns of the "flesh and . . . mind . . . sex and economics . . . individual righteousness and social equity" are best met in terms of the specifically Muslim idea of the kind of life that ostensibly follows death (Asad, 1984, ii–iii).

Sacral rationalism is not rationalism in the modernist sense, since it does not denote the attempt to detach the use of reason from trammeling factors like faith. Quite the contrary, it denotes reason as a faculty embedded in a spiritual context. It denotes reason as rationalization. And though this is no impediment to thinking in systematic and critical ways, it does preclude the eschewal of the initial sacral premise.

The most incensed of the Islamic conservationists are prepared to resort to violence to defend and promote their beliefs, even though this means having to explain away the *Qur'anic* injunction against imposing Islam by force rather than example. There are similar extremists in most of the other global faiths. The use by Muslim conservationists of terrorist tactics, particularly against the United States, has made the issue of the Islamic response to modernity more prominent than most, however.

The less incensed of the conservationists prefer to see Islam prevail because of the compelling character of its truth-content alone. They seek to demonstrate what the *umma* of Islam offers as an alternative to the analytic language of modernist nationalism. They consequently refuse to draw the distinctions that modernists consider mandatory, and in not resorting to violence, they see themselves positing an "Islamic difference" they consider sufficiently comprehensive and sufficiently benign to render ethnic diversity redundant. They see Islam as being capable of providing a context in which all international, interethnic animosities can be resolved. In positing the construction of a spiritual nation out of those who believe in the Islamic God, and by subsuming all ethnic and national differences under this primary loyalty, it is possible, they argue, to imagine these differences ceasing to matter, or at least, becoming ways to learn about each other, rather than to despise each other.

The Muslim record from nigh on eight centuries of rule in Spain is heartening in this regard, though historic and contemporary counter-cases of the *umma* conspicuously failing to realize its reconciliatory potential are noteworthy as well. A world entirely Muslim would still be one of diverse societies. Specific Muslim governments, like the Turkish one, for example, would still be likely to repress minority Muslim peoples, like the Kurds. And though a world entirely Muslim might indeed see an end to interethnic strife, this would ultimately depend on the degree of subservience to Islamic ideas and ideals. Hence the ongoing significance of the other global faiths, all of which claim to transcend nationalism-as-tribalism, and each one of which offers its own politico-spiritual language as a description and explanation of life's ultimate meaning, a language that the adherents of other faiths steadfastly refuse to learn.

Until there is a universal sacral language able to subsume ethnic and national disparities, therefore, the differences between the main religious beliefs will continue to exacerbate such disparities, as well as mitigate them. Islam has no way to contextualize and contain such contention, except to invite conversion to Islam. Muslims have so far failed, however, to persuade the other four-fifths of the world's population to take up the Islamic invitation to submit to *Allah's* will, since the proponents of the other global faiths hold to similar beliefs they consider equally self-evident, beliefs they articulate in their own terms and not those of Islam.

It is a feature of the modernist project that it offers its own universal politico-social language for reconciling international strife. This is the secular, rationalist language of politico-social individualism.

A notable feature of this language is its articulation of the concept of human rights. Being Rationalist, this concept is secular. It does not preclude sacral sanction, but it does not require it, since it is figured apart from any spiritual ground. Indeed, Rationalists see human rights defining a secular measure that can be applied to all faiths, and a standard to which any sacral tradition can be asked to measure up if it wants to be considered civilized.

The principles the proponents of human rights articulate are predicated upon personal autonomy, individuation being both their premise and their prize. Rights are seen as both the privilege of the en-selved individual, and the most basic way of protecting the individual against social incursions deemed universally undesirable. Yet, individuated individuals also form associations. Most notably, they form neo-communalist associations like modernist nation-states, and forward-looking collectivist ones, like social movements. Hence, the advent of the idea of collective or group rights, which were originally mooted by ethnic minorities and indigenous peoples to advance (premodernist) claims for self-determination, but were subsequently articulated by (modernist) collectivists as well, in their bid to promote their shared interests and causes (Freeman, 1995, 40).

Being modernist, the human rights doctrine is a contemporary one, but the Islamic response to it is contemporary too. Liberal Muslims argue that the doctrine is compatible with their faith, while the more radical of the liberals are even prepared to see it as the preferred moral expression of modern-day Islam (Tibi, 1998). Equally contemporary is the response by conservationist Muslims, however, some of whom seek to relocate the rights doctrine in the context of their own beliefs, having "long viewed" Islam as "more equitable, less racial, and more humane than Western political thought" (Moussalli, 2001, 4). The more radical of the conservationists repudiate the rights doctrine altogether, prioritizing Islam's own ideas about moral entitlement. Prominent contemporary examples of the latter include the *shari'a*-inspired penal code that Jaafar Nimeiri introduced in the Sudan in 1983, the regulations the Ayatollah Khomeini introduced in Iran in 1987, and the regulations the Taliban introduced in Afghanistan in and after 1996.

A number of attempts have been made to date to reconcile the teachings of Islam with the principles of human rights, and to devise formal declarations of a distinctively Islamic version of them (Farraq, 1990; *Universal Islamic Declaration of Human Rights*, 1981; *Cairo Declaration on Human Rights*, 1990). These declarations jar with Rationalist/individualist/liberals, however, not because of what they say, so much as what they do not. They do not say, for example, anything about the Islamic God's injunction against Muslim women marrying Christians or Jews, even though this injunction contravenes modernist human rights, and remains a widespread Muslim prohibition.

From the radical Rationalist point of view, it is not possible to reconcile the politico-spiritual purpose of Islam (where God is seen as the ultimate reality, and truth is revealed) with the politico-cultural purpose of modernity (where human reason is the ultimate reality, and truth is always contingent and empirically tested) (Heinemeijer, 1990, 146). The two are simply incommensurable. On the one side, there is the devout modernist/Rationalist, who sees reason as an end in itself. To such an individual—and it is an individual—nothing is sacred, and any truths that might result from revelation (including Islamic truths) require critical rational scrutiny if they are to be considered reliably so. While on the other side there is the devout Muslim/sacralist, who sees truth as God-given, and literally sacrosanct; who sees the human capacity for reason as God-given, and the search to know the meaning and purpose of life as the search to know the mind of God. In these terms reason is a means to an end. It is never an end in itself. The modernist/Rationalist who suggests otherwise is a heretic, and human rights, as a modernist concept, is heretical too.

There are less radical arguments on both sides. The proponents of these arguments would rather avoid a straight fight since there is little to be said in a language that repudiates religious belief, to those who put faith at the center of their worldview (Ahmed, 1992, 264). The less radical promote a sense of the difference between reason and revelation that is less absolute (Arberry, 1957). Thus secular Rationalists try and conceive ways of knowing that Islam might access that they cannot. While Muslim sacralists try and come to terms with modernist knowledge, so that they can offer (reasoned? revealed?) conclusions about the costs and limits of modernity, and about how best to put the modernist project in the context of Islam.

The less radical dialogue is difficult to sustain, however. In Fukuyama's judgment, for example, "Islam . . . is the only cultural system that seems regularly to produce people . . . who reject modernity lock, stock and barrel" (Fukuyama, 2001, 21). Halliday, meanwhile, thinks that it is "ahistorical and artificial" to take "odd quotes" from the *Qur'an* and the *hadith* and to try and justify their human rights standing (Halliday, 1995, 161). Devout Muslim sacralists also see no contest. More relevant to them are the words of the thirteenth-century Persian poet Jalal al-Din Rumi (1207–73 C.E.), to the effect that "no man of reason will ever know the heart's rapture of the reason-lost" (Arberry, 1968, 57). For them faith subsumes everything, including any and every other kind of cognition. It simply comes first.

What room for maneuver does this leave Muslim modernists? The language of Muslim texts is largely a language of duty and obligation, service and obedience. It is a language of surrender, not self-assertion (Vincent, 1986, 42). And yet, as Mayer argues: "I have not run across a single instance where a Muslim conversant with the international human rights norms voluntarily acquiesced in the violation of the right on the grounds that Muslims were not entitled to claim the same rights as other human beings or that rights protections were alien to Islamic culture" (Mayer, 1991, 218, n. 16).

At which point we might want to reconsider what Islam provides as an alternative to attempts to compensate for individualist alienation by nationalist or collectivist means. It is an undeniable feature of world affairs that contemporary Islam has created a range of spiritually grounded communities, most of which are not traditionalist, and most of which have been highly durable, have protected local mores, and have maintained a creative tension between justice and law. Muslim communities are not only able to be pluralistic, that is, they can also empower, and they can work in ways that Rationalist attempts to compensate for individualism can fail to do. If we compare these Muslim communities with non-Muslim attempts at communitarianism, for example, and particularly with those non-Muslim attempts that refuse to repudiate the doctrine of individualism, thereby ending up as yet another form of it, the difference can be instructive. If we also compare these communities with the neo-tribalist fraud that nationalism so often represents, or the desperate attempts that individuated individuals may make to find collective solace by forming social movements, then it is not necessary to be a Muslim to appreciate the significance of Muslim alternatives in this regard.

Islam has another card up its sleeve, however, and that is Sufism. Every religion has its mystic heart, and Sufism is the mystic heart of Islam. The term is certainly "highly contested" (Ernst, 1997, xvi). Sufis, however, can be said to seek "direct knowledge or personal religious experience of God's presence." This presence they see as always immanent in daily life, although it is one that is ordinarily "hidden from view . . ." (Esposito, 1998, 107, 108).

Sufism is both different from and more than the usual state of Islamic submission, with its religious rituals, and its legal routines. It is an attempt to recreate the state of mind in which Muhammad received his initial inspiration, by going "beyond the letter of the law" to realize its "spirit" instead (Esposito, 1998, 103). In the process it promotes the purity and simplicity that seems commensurate with such a state of mind. It also promotes the practices that result in such purity and simplicity, eschewing material attachment, and exalting meditation. Often using music or dance, Sufis seek to discipline the body, quieten the mind, and liberate the soul (Esposito, 1998, 102). Some of them are relatively temperate, while some are euphoric in the extreme. All seek a way of knowing and living in the world that is loving and ecstatic, rather than righteous and routine.

Sufism has developed over time its own diverse regimens, as befits the highly personalized ways in which its teachings and practices have been transmitted. These are typically centered on charismatic teachers (*shaykhs*), whom orthodox Muslims tend to castigate for encouraging their followers to get to God by eliminating the ego. This they see as a denial of the essential difference between the individual and God, and therefore as blasphemous. The Sufi movement as a whole they tend to see as being corrupt and subversive and a distortion of the faith (Cooper et al., eds., 2000, 71). Non-Muslims, on the other hand, often see in Sufic ways seductive traps for the suggestible. They note how the "high ground of sound and sober mysticism" is all too often inundated by those prepared to exploit human ignorance and human superstition (Esposito, 1998, 109). And they note that Sufism is often susceptible to this charge.

Despite the very real dangers (which are present in all systems of belief) of spiritual corruption (Trungpa, 1973), honest forms of Sufism do continue to provide a communal context in which individuals can experience world affairs in cosmic terms, and the sense of true love that goes with that experience. This is sacral inspiration in its "widest and most universal sense" (Affifi, 1958, 178).

To quote Bawa Muhaiyaddeen, a Tamil peasant from Sri Lanka, and a twentieth-century Sufi sage: "[P]lease look at your hearts. You should search [there] for the qualities and inherent characteristics of God. That is . . . the perfect treasure . . . No matter how long we may live, the world we live in does not belong to us; neither does the place we dwell in belong to us. This is merely a school where we have come to study about birth and death, good and evil, heaven and hell, man and God, human beings . . . and beasts . . . beauty and ugliness . . . happiness and sorrow . . . We have to learn what we came here to learn . . . and leave as people with pure faith . . . We must dispel the part that is us, and that which is Him must pray to Him" (Muhaiyaddeen, 1997, 213, 225, 227, 228).

Or to quote Rumi once more, who began as a Muslim theologian and preacher, and subsequently became a Sufi ecstatic: "Since it has become certain to my heart that you [God] are the soul of the soul of the soul, open the door . . . for you are the stay of a thousand worlds" (Arberry, 1979, 121).

Honest Sufis are a perennial thorn in the side of proponents of modernist politico-social identities like the nationalist, individualist, and collectivist ones, since nationalism and collectivism in particular pale into insignificance beside the kind of non-individualistic identity that a personal sense of divine presence provides. Particularly when that presence is known to be, and can be shown to be, synonymous with loving everyone.

How could it be possible to prefer any of the dialects of the doctrine of individualism, when there is such a luminous form of awareness in the offing? What can human rights do, for example, that a sense of cosmic consciousness cannot do and more, particularly when pursued and practiced with sufficient ardor? Why would any sane person want to seek any other sense of self than the sense of Self that honest Sufis hold out? Why would those who construct these world affairs want to promote any other purpose? The fact that they do, preferring in the main to pursue much more earth-bound objectives, does not mean they are right to do so. The fact that most people make do and get by, seemingly satisfied with material well-being, does not mean that they fail to feel the need for, or deserve as individual human beings to feel the need for, something more exalted (Bending, 2002).

Any modernist/Rationalist who looks to honest forms of Sufism to augment their choices in conducting world affairs (rather than automatically repudiating Sufism as being too subjective) finds extraordinary options offered there. Radical Rationalists repudiate such offers outright. The more agnostic remain more curious, however, and accepting of the possibility that there might be something worth listening to and learning from.

What are the options that honest Sufis offer? What does the imagination, couched in the idiom of this particular sacral discourse, provide as an alternative to what secular analysis provides? What might be a specifically Sufic account of contemporary world affairs?

One option would be to whirl with dervishes. In the right political context this could work the way the Czech revolution did. Rationalists would likely ask what the point might be of doing so in front of advancing tanks, however, or how this might feed those dying of malnutrition, or how it might get people out of prison who have been incarcerated and tortured for their political beliefs.

Another option would be to sit with a true *shaykh* and listen. The point here would be to learn how to prevent tanks being sent in the first place, or to prevent malnutrition before it began, or to prevent regimes from crushing people before they have the power to do so.

To modernist ears, both options sound ludicrous. And yet, those about to despatch tanks, or impoverish a populace, or incarcerate opponents as a matter of political convenience, could arguably derive considerable benefit from the conscious and heartfelt attempt to remember the name of God in the more rather than less loving way that Sufis recommend (*dhikr*). More indirectly, ordinary people who attempt such a remembering can have an impact on world affairs too. "Remember God often" is a recurrent Qu'ranic injunction. Many Sufis interpret it to mean constantly recalling a sense of oneness with what they define as God (Arberry, 1950, 22). Though few non-Sufis aspire to such a mystical state, that does not make the aspiration of those who do illegitimate, or their efforts insignificant.

Honest Sufism is one politico-spiritual dialect among many of what is only one politico-spiritual language among many. It is a well attested way, nonetheless, of putting modernist/Rationalist world affairs in a sacral context, so that any individual, including any individual leader, can see more clearly the particularity of contemporary world affairs, how he or she might move in affirmative ways beyond the limits these affairs set, and might compensate for the distortions they create. Modernist/Rationalists tend not to acknowledge such particularity, and where they do, they tend not to recognize other and better ways of knowing and living. Thus we have a modernist philosopher like Passmore saying that "the attempt to substitute for ordinary human relationships and . . . achievements a supposedly 'higher' relationship and . . . achievement" is in practice a "lower form of life, inferior to what human beings daily accomplish in their ambitious, proud, anxiety-ridden way . . . ." Passmore specifically decries the idea of "union with an undifferentiated unity," proclaiming it inferior to "loving a woman [*sic*] . . . writing a poem, or cultivating a farm" (Passmore, 1970, 287). Is it inferior to invading an enemy, however, or colluding in unfair trade and investment practices, or torturing political prisoners? Passmore does not say.

What would a more affirmative world look like in Sufic terms? Honest Sufis are on home ground here. It is firm ground, too, far from the modernist/Rationalist parody of the mystic as someone engaged in nothing more than a careless form of play (Passmore, 1970, 302). The true mystic knows that the holiest war is not against others, but against one's own lack of wisdom and understanding, which is why, for the honest Sufi, Islam does not denote militant resentment. It denotes peace within and, therefore, peace without (Muhaiyaddeen, 1987).

So, what do Islamic civics entail? What does Islam have to offer the white, Western, nationalistic, individualistic males, who dominate the global political society?

First, in putting modernist nationalism, individualism and collectivism in the context of Islam, it puts these doctrines in the context of a form of loyalty that shows how particular and limited they can be, and at what cost they come. It subsumes the identities that these principles create under ones more spiritual and more profound. This does not necessarily mean less divisive, and more cohesive, as the religious factor in world affairs amply demonstrates. It holds out its own hopes for global community and world peace, however, hopes more high since they harbor such depths of human meaning.

Second, it provides a politico-spiritual language, Sufism, that honestly practiced, provides world affairs with a sense of higher purpose. If world affairs did not have an ultimate meaning, we would probably not have the ability to ask whether they did or not. Sufis are certain that we do have this ability, however, and that there is a meaning to what we do beyond that which we can rationally ascertain. Theirs is not the only discourse to do this, but it does do this, and it does so in a humane way that holds out hope for much more than a just world peace. It prompts world-makers to think creatively when faced with the dilemmas of day-to-day international relations. And it sees in sacral remembering a mitigating factor that would help make these politics less harmful and more humane. There is no formula for getting modernist leaders, or their soldiers and citizens, to practice the appropriate thought-forms. Generations of good *shaykhs* provide luminous examples of what it might mean to do so, however, and how being a Muslim in ways like these can promote the practice of civic virtue.

CHAPTER 8

CONFUCIAN MARXISM

Having looked at sacral alternatives to the kind of modernist languages that articulate assumptions about our essential human nature, the focus now moves to sacral alternatives to the kind of modernist languages that articulate assumptions about our nurturing practices. In the parlance of modernist world affairs these assumptions are either materialist (mainly marxist) or mentalist (constructivist), or a mixture of the two (neo-marxist).

The concept of Confucian marxism confronts us with something of a paradox. Like Taoist strategics or Buddhist economics, it would seem to be a contradiction in terms. Nonetheless, successfully implementing marxism would arguably seem to require, if not Confucian principles, then ones much like them. The dictatorship of the proletariat, if it is not to end in oppression of its own, requires the dictators to subscribe to an extremely high sense of civic duty. Where is this sense to come from, however, if not some sacral context of the Confucian kind?

There is another paradox, too, in that Confucianism is seemingly more philosophical than spiritual. It is neither theistic nor mystical, deeming a life of self-discipline and self-mastery more important than devotion to a deity or any attempt to achieve a state of divine awareness. If Confucianism is to be defined as a world faith, therefore, it must be defined as one where the "sacred elements are elusive . . . ," and even, perhaps, secular (Rule, 1986, xiii, 31).

This particular paradox may mostly be an artifact of modernist thinking, though, since neither Confucius himself, nor the culture in which he lived, dichotomized the sacral and the secular to the extent that modernists do. Both were steeped in sacral sentiment. *Kongzi* (Master Kong) himself—or Confucius, as the sixteenth-century Jesuit latinization has it (Jensen, 1997, 7)—believed in heaven, ancestor worship, magical powers, and the sacral significance of traditional rites. For him, as for the Chinese society he lived in, "[f]amily life, [and] government" were "in many respects 'sacred' activities . . . " (Rule, 1986, 196). The rituals they involved were not just social conventions, therefore. They were practices that had profound spiritual meaning, and served profound spiritual purposes.

Confucius was first and foremost an advocate of order. He believed that order was best based, in turn, upon "ethically correct" behavior on the part of both the rulers and the ruled (Tamney and Chiang, 2002, 3).

What kind of ethic makes for orderly behavior? Before we answer this question directly, it is worth noting that Confucius found the answer to it, not in anything innate, but in what we are taught. Confucius argued that the good is learned. This is why, at the heart of the Confucian doctrine, there is a close relationship between education, morality, and political power (Tamney and Chiang, 2002, 3; Leys, 1997, xxviii–xxix). Taken together these three elements provide the "true," Confucian vision of a "grand and powerful . . . culture rooted in a unified polity, the whole deriving its inspiration from a unified literature, language and ceremonial forms . . ." (Fingarette, 1972, 61). They provide the "guidance of wisdom," harmony and peace. And since the guidance comes from mastering a number of classic Chinese texts (Yao, 2000, 26, 25), Confucius saw the relevant education as the acquisition of an intimate knowledge of these texts.

Rule should be by moral example, he said. Order is derived from virtue of the kind manifest in contemporary times by a leader like Nelson Mandela (Ames, 1994, 28–9).

Confucius also exalted effective government, defining effectiveness in terms of the communal ability to endure. If the "common people . . . have confidence in their leaders," he said, then this will prove more important than weaponry, or even food (Ames and Rosemont, 1998, 155 [12.7]).

The Confucian doctrine predates Confucius. The man was born into a civilized milieu that was already a millennium old. And though he is the figure with whom Confucianism is most closely associated, and in whose name it was carried well beyond its country of origin, Confucius was not the doctrine's originator, nor did he claim to be (Rozman, 1991; Tu, 1996).

The ideas that were later to be identified most closely with Confucianism were first systematized by a duke of the Zhou dynasty that Confucius revered, and had lived under himself. These ideas were originally designed to develop a pool of learned officials, able to act as competent administrators and wise counselors. Over time they acquired a much wider doctrinal range, however, as many different minds, including that of Confucius himself, strived to make them compatible with contemporary politico-cultural projects (Yao, 2000, 4–9).

Confucius did not, that is, invent the forms of self-cultivation and self-transformation that he espoused. Nor could he be called a "Confucian" in terms of the revered doctrine that generations of followers made in his name (he died more than three centuries before Confucianism became the official ideology of the Chinese state). The Confucian way is nonetheless his way, the *ren* way (honorable, authoritative, benevolent); the way of shamans originally, and then of masters of ritual, and ultimately of scholar–bureaucrats like himself (Yao, 2000, 16–21). And though temples to the memory of "the Sage" did eventually appear, the cult that they represented is a somewhat artificial one (Smart, 1989, 103).

It was not certain for some time that the Confucian doctrine would ever be very successful, either, since some of its rivals were highly influential. These included the Legalists, who were more authoritarian, and the Mohists, who were more technocratic (Brooks and Brooks, 1997, 6). There were competing politico-spiritual projects as well, like that of the Taoists, who were more mystical, and later the Buddhists, who were more accessible.

Confucianism did ultimately play a key part in Chinese culture, however, and for 70 generations, mainly because of its political utility, it served the emperors well. As formulated by the duke of Zhou, and in turn, by Confucius, it was able to survive even in the face of fierce opposition from dynasties like the *Qin* (221–206 B.C.E). The last civil service examination to be based on the core Confucian texts was held only a hundred years ago, in 1905 (Ames and Rosemont, 1998, 10). For more than two thousand years, in other words, it was arguably the country's main cultural resource, so much so that many of its tenets are simply taken for granted now as what it means to be Chinese (Ames and Rosemont, 1998, 18).

Who was this man? By most accounts he lived from 551 to 479 B.C.E., as a scholar, a teacher, and a minor aristocrat of humble means. He was born at a time of considerable politico-strategic confusion. The Zhou dynasty was collapsing. Several independent states were competing militarily for hegemonic power, and for the chance to head what was to become the first empire of China (Ames and Rosemont, 1998, 2). The relatively anarchic nature of this context prompted Confucius and his followers to turn to the thinking of an earlier era to articulate the way that "peace and harmony" might be achieved and maintained (Yao, 2000, 7). Confucius himself seemed to have defined this way in terms of how the mystical sage-kings of old were supposed to have behaved. He also seems to have considered the early Zhou years as a golden time, and espoused the practices of that period as exemplary ones.

Like other great teachers, in what was still an oral rather than a written tradition, Confucius spoke rather than wrote (Tu, 1993, 41). The best-known account of his teachings is the one contained in the *Analects (Lun yu)*, the "selected sayings," though these were compiled in the two centuries that followed his death and as Pound remarks, were arguably little more than the "oddments which Kung's circle found indispensable" (Pound, 1933, 7). None of them may be the sayings of Confucius himself (Waley, 1989 [1938], 25). Thus Brooks and Brooks argue that of the 20 books or chapters that constitute the contemporary arrangement of the text, it is only the fourth that preserves "something like" the "actual voice" of Confucius himself (Brooks and Brooks, 1997, 11). The other 19 books are by others; they say his immediate disciples, and later theirs, and then theirs. Each generation sought to work out the implications of their chosen doctrine, as they strove to promote its practice, and to defend it against other forms of thought.

Though the *Analects* may be a compound work, they are also a coherent one. They convey throughout a "vivid sense" of the importance of holding to "right principles . . . [and of] working toward the . . . humane, public outcome" (Brooks and Brooks, 1997, viii). And while they may well be the voice of many, and not just one, the message the *Analects* conveys is vibrant and clear.

They also convey a sense of Confucius as having been a strong and complex character—charismatic, self-confident, sympathetic, well-balanced, thoughtful, humorous, and kind. This sense, as Leys says, is the backbone of the whole work (Leys, 1997, xxi; Creel, 1949, 30–3, 60–1). It reflects the world Confucius lived in, where the administration of the day was falling into the hands of "artisans and other palace-connected individuals." These people espoused a "profit rather than a service ethic." A long-established feudal order was collapsing, and the warrior elite was being displaced by lower orders. Confucius opposed this displacement, and the parallel rise of a culture of self-interest and personal profit that it seemed to involve (though some see him as having welcomed this displacement, which he then defined in a new way) (Brooks and Brooks, 1997, 3, 13; Leys, 1997, 107).

The emphasis Confucius came to place upon the consistent practice of right principle, or *orthopraxy* (proper behavior), does not tell us what "right and proper" mean, however (Tamney and Chiang, 2002, 4). If old-world, virtuous behavior was required of an authoritative elite, what here was "virtue" meant to entail?

Turning to the Confucius of book four for an answer, we find him extolling, in the Brooks and Brooks translation, the cardinal value of *ren*, or the code of the warrior and of the feudal aristocracy this warrior was supposed to defend. Not for nothing do Brooks and Brooks counterpose their translation of this part of the *Analects* with a photo of a bronze sword.

As far as they are concerned (having removed those sections of the chapter that do not support their case) "right and proper" means a code of martial honor. It means an "austere code . . . adjusted but not bent to the different needs of the new-society courtier" (Brooks and Brooks, 1997, 11; Allen, 1999, 4). It espouses qualities like "strength, courage, steadfastness in crisis, consideration for others, [and] capacity for self-sacrifice" (Brooks and Brooks, 1997, 15). Or in the quaint translation that Ames and Rosemont make, it is "manhood-at-its-best" (Ames and Rosemont, 1998, 49).

If we turn to the "book four" Confucius that other translators provide, however, we find a notably less Athurian picture, and a considerably more civil one. For Ames and Rosemont, for example, the virtuous person is the authoritative person. He is not just the decorous feudal warrior (Ames and Rosemont, 1998, 48). For Waley, he is the Good Man, that is, the sublimely unselfish man, the man who is primarily, even mystically, concerned for the feelings of others (Waley, 1989 [1938], 102, 28). For Legge he is the "superior" man—worthy, unselfish, righteous, cautious, earnest, and nonassertive (Legge, 1970 [1861], 165–72). For Lau, he is the benevolent gentleman, who loves his fellows (though not necessarily the commoners among them), and who is wise and courageous, honest and trustworthy, reverent and dutiful (Lau, 1979, 14–17, 22–6). For Leys, he is the academic gentleman. He is not necessarily one born to that role. He has, however, qualified as such. He is demonstrably educated and decent. He is not merely rich or well connected. And he is recognizable for what he is, rather than what he has. For Pound, he is simply "he," a plain-speaking, laconic character, speaking about real life in pithy, vernacular, no-nonsense terms (Pound, 1933, 24–7).

"Right and proper" behavior is learned, not innate, and it is learned via a Confucian education. Such an education attempts to replicate the exemplary individual. It attempts to cultivate character rather than administrative skills (Ames and Rosemont, 1998, 7). It attempts to inculcate a particular sense of obligation to the family and the community, a particular sense of humility and altruism, a particular sense of indifference to material possessions, and a particular love of social equity. It attempts to teach a premodernist kind of humanism, and one that fosters communal unity as well (Moore, 1968, 96).

Early translators, like the Jesuits, whose sixteenth-century invention of Confucius aroused the curiosity of Enlightenment European philosophers, saw in the construction of the virtuous leader and bureaucrat a crucial cultural reference point (Rule, 1986, ix). Through these translators, Confucius came to figure in the politico-cultural awareness of Europeans as a symbol for rational respect for morally exemplary authority, and for government by ethical example rather than judicial regulation. Statements like: "Lead the people with administrative injunctions . . . keep them orderly with penal law . . . and they will avoid punishments but will be without a sense of shame. Lead them with excellence [however] . . . keep them orderly through observing ritual propriety . . . and they will . . . order themselves" (Ames and Rosemont, 1998, 26 [2.3]), seemed to signify a distinctive Chinese approach to maintaining political order.

Analysts like Jensen argue that it was the Jesuit form of Confucius that the Chinese later reappropriated for themselves. It was the European interpretation, he says, that Chinese leaders themselves ultimately took back and offered as a Chinese approach to the "new 'age . . . for the Pacific Rim'" (Jensen, 1997, 4, 11, 15).

Arguments like these do underestimate the indigenous significance of Confucian thought, though. It was, after all, the modernist values most compatible with Confucian concerns that were those that won the readiest acceptance in China. Mao argued early, for example, for a Confucian form of marxism, built upon the Chinese people's own sense of what was morally ideal (Metzger, 1977, 194–5, 156, 220, 222). Making marxism Chinese helped him mobilize and unite a geographically disparate peasantry against the invading Japanese. It also helped him create a revolutionary communist party able to take control of the whole country. As he said: "We should sum up our history from Confucius to Sun Yat-sen and take over this valuable legacy." And: "Being Marxists, Communists are internationalists, but we can put Marxism into practice only when it is integrated with the specific characteristics of our country and acquires a definite national form" (Tse-Tung, 1965 [1938], 209; Nivison, 1972, 209, 211; Schram, 1989, 70–2).

The power of indigenous thought forms was also evident in Mao's idea of what a political elite was, and how it could only rule in the light of a "correct" ideology. Despite his talk of a people's democracy, Mao was, after all, a traditional, strong-state autocrat, struck straight from a local mould that is four millennia old (Hsiung, 1970, 300; Schram, 1989, 93).

Reappropriating Confucius played its own role in confronting nineteenth-century European imperialism. The European intrusion prompted radical change right across the Asian region. It helped define it as such, prompting a radical reassessment of the intellectual resources required to keep the Europeans at bay, and active attempts to match their productive and military power.

This part of the story starts for the Chinese with the Opium Wars of 1839–42. This was the episode that first alerted Chinese intellectuals to their country's extraordinary vulnerability. Though Confucianism was seen as having contributed to this vulnerability, the initial response was to try and graft the superior scientific and technological knowledge of the Europeans onto the local root stock, in a bid to compensate for what Confucianism was not (Tu, 1996, 140; Yao, 2000, 248, 267). It is claimed that the European presence, and the impact of European knowledge, even provided an "escape" for Confucianism, since it caused radical change without requiring the Chinese to find the capacity for change within their own thought-world (Metzger, 1977, 215, 217–18, 231).

It was not until the end of the *Qing* dynasty, in 1911–12, that Confucianism was repudiated, root and branch. By this time Confucian thought was seen as too closely associated with the kind of China that European imperialism had humiliated to deserve continued support, and the choice was finally made not to keep reinventing it as a way of thinking through the Chinese experience (Yao, 2000, 274).

Decisive in this regard was the May Fourth Movement of 1919. This was a call both to end foreign domination and to embrace European ways. It was a call, for example, to repudiate the idea of education being based on an intimate knowledge of classic Chinese texts, in favor of a more Rationalist curriculum.

The generation who initiated this movement sought European-style Enlightenment. They sought an end to a whole system they had come to consider nonprogressive, ethnocentric, and sexist, as well as politically corrupt, economically conservative, and socially inegalitarian (Jensen, 1997, 24; Tu, 1993, 177; Yao, 2000, 271). Counterclaims that Confucianism still had a potentially constructive part to play in making China modernist, and that Confucianism might even be preferable in terms of its capacity to provide life-affirming values beyond that of reason as an end in itself, were rejected as being no longer appropriate, and no longer supportable.

With the Communist Revolution of 1949, the elite embrace of anti-Confucian ideals seemed complete. Despite Mao's earlier endorsement of Confucian values, the Chinese Communist Party that came to power seemed to associate Confucian thinking with a feudal past it sought specifically to overthrow (Louie, 1980). A socialist China needed a socialist citizenry, it was argued, and that meant a Chinese marxism imbued with modernist socialist values, not traditional Confucian ones (Dirlik, 1994b).

Mao's subsequent decision to wage a Cultural Revolution to counter threats to his power from within his own party, as well as threats to the outcome of his attempts to reform Chinese society, only strengthened this embrace. Which is why a later campaign, against the "ultra-rightist," Lin Biao, was cast in terms of an attack on Confucius as a historical reactionary, who had purportedly hindered the change in the Chinese mode of production from slavery to feudalism (Meisner, 1986, 213; Louie, 1980, 108–17).

At the same time Mao's admiration for *haojie* (men of outstanding character and ability) seemed fully congruent with traditional Confucian ideals (Metzger, 1977, 40–1). The stress he placed on the "irresistible moral power of pedagogy" bore more than a passing resemblance to Confucian-style thinking. In making the study of "Mao Zedong Thought" the "ultimate weapon against all 'counterrevolutionary' evils," and in using the model of the *Analects* for his own little Red Book, Mao was preserving and perpetuating a recognizable form of Confucian practice, despite repudiating Confucianism as a political practice (Leys, 1997, xxix, 132).

Mao was, after all, a member of the last generation to be steeped in Confucian learning. He had memorized the classic Confucian adages in school, plus the principles they represented, and the assumptions they helped articulate. These informed his worldview for the rest of his life. Tellingly perhaps, the books he had with him on first entering Beijing as head of the communist regime, were not books by Marx, but books by Ssu-ma Kuang, whose eleventh-century manual on imperial Chinese statecraft, *The Comprehensive Mirror for Aid in Government (Zizhi tongjian)*, provides an account (in the author's own words) of the merits and demerits of former ages, and of the reasons for the rise and fall of the great Chinese dynasties (Beasley and Pulleybank, 1961, 152, 153–4). As Mao had taken selectively from Marx in his attempt to make marxism relevant to China, he was not averse to taking from the Chinese classics, either, to make marxism work (Schram, 1989, 135, 141).

Mao believed in the Confucian idea of society as a huge school for moral education, and of the social order as dependent not only on the law (as a Rationalist might construe it) but on the "preservation of 'correct' human relationships" too (Hsiung, 1970, 250). As a consequence, Mao repeatedly asked the Chinese people to ask not how "marxist *theory* [might] be translated into *fact* . . . ," but rather "(h)ow can I, a Marxist in *name*, become . . . a Marxist in *fact?*" The former was a social scientific question. The latter required an answer in individual ethical terms (Nivison, 1972, 210). It recalled in turn the Confucian idea that the good and virtuous action is the right and moral one (Short, 1999).

The choices made in China after Mao died to reinvent Confucianism, as an adjunct to modernist marxism-plus-capitalism, have resulted in a steady stream of politico-cultural innovations (Yao, 2000, 276). These innovations are not traditional but contemporary, not old but new (Dirlik, 1995, 235). Their proponents are well aware of the difficulty of trying to re-traditionalize what people think, using Confucian ideas. The lack of success the ruling regime in Singapore had when it tried to legislate filial piety and make Confucian values part of the school curriculum, is a case in point (Dirlik, 1995, 239). Attempts have been made, nonetheless, to reanimate the rituals of a scriptural Confucianism long thought defunct. Confucian-style values, for example, have been invoked as a nationalistic counter to (bourgeois) individualism, and as the ethical rationale for a theory of economic development at odds with the hegemonic contemporary liberal one (Tamney and Chiang, 2002, 192, 202; Nivison, 1972, 216; Dirlik, 1995, 251, 243, 264–73; Liu, 1998, 172–3, 177). Indeed, Chinese neo-Confucianism would seem to provide evidence that globalization, at least in this instance, is not a "reworking" of the "local" in the way that the world's owners and managers might prefer, but rather an attempt to arrive at a viable identity that is more homegrown (Nivison, 1972, 215; Dirlik, 1995, 271).

Weber saw Confucian values as being incompatible with the private ownership of the means of production, and as the reason the Chinese did not initiate historically a modernist project of their own (Weber, 1951, 152, 227). Criticism of contemporary neo-Confucianism may be a rerun of the same argument, though this time in a bid to denigrate the achievements of Chinese-style socialism.

The outlook for those who would reinvent Confucianism is not good, since there has been little systematic Confucian education for a hundred years (Munro, 1996, 107; de Bary, 1981, x). Reteaching Confucianism, whether it be to foster Chinese nationalism, or to reinforce a more robust sense of China's developmental identity, would be a major enterprise. It would have to be done in the face of what China has now become.

What about the possibility of a non-Chinese reinvention of Confucianism? "Confucius" as a contemporary phenomenon is said to be a Jesuit invention. The current "East Asian Confucian revival" may be a similar attempt to turn a "native culture into a capitalist narrative" (Dirlik, 1994a, 350). Then again it might be something more radical, such as a Euro-American attempt to re-invent Confucianism in a bid to find out something "momentous" that Euro-Americans need to know, but modernist assumptions prevent them from knowing (Hall and Ames, 1987, 328–30).

Confucian marxism might best be seen as one response to the growing disparities in wealth that seem to accompany the spread of world capitalism. Marxism talks about world affairs in terms of the globalization of contemporary capitalism, and about growing conflict between those who own and manage the factories, firms, and farms, and those who sell their labor for wages. Neo-marxists are acutely aware of the way this growing conflict has not resulted in a global working-class revolution. They analyze the ways in which the owners and managers normalize and naturalize the exploitation process, so that they are not overthrown. *Confucian* marxism combines the marxist and neo-marxist ways of talking about world affairs, with a Confucian concern for having decent leaders, recruited on merit, capable of winning widespread support, and dedicated to constructing a neo-communal form of humanist utopia. Perhaps only a hybrid doctrine like this could countenance a marxist revolution, by recasting the result in Confucian terms to obviate the seemingly inevitable advent of corrupt, communist party rule.

While this essentializes marxism and Confucianism, characterizing both in terms of a "few general traits, deprived of all history and complexity" (Dirlik, 1995, 273), it does highlight the integral character of global poverty (marxism), and the need for altruistic, exemplary leaders (Confucianism) as a way of winning the trust and support of the poor. Lenin talked of a vanguard seizing power to effect revolutionary change. He said nothing, however, about that vanguard being Arthurian and virtuous, dutiful, and meritocratic. He said nothing about it realizing the will of the people under a mandate from heaven. Perhaps if he had, the Soviet experiment might have taken a different road.

Consider a relatively small, relatively poor country, where the depredations of transnational companies, aided and abetted by comprador elements of the local elite, continue to make for a growing gap between rich and poor. What are those who live in such a country to do, and particularly, what are the poor to do, given the disempowering nature of their poverty, and the way the modernist state system gives those who can successfully claim to be the state-makers a monopoly over the domestic means of order and repression? Classical marxists would say that the poor should embrace market capitalism, and the class struggle it creates, with a view to overthrowing the entire system. Neo-marxists would highlight the need to counter the ideological efforts the rich make to confound and confuse those who would expose their exploitative practices. Confucian marxists would not only endorse both prescriptions. They would also empower those of their number, deemed sufficiently learned and moral, to lead the charge against the capitalist profiteers and their ideological aides. Leaders like these would draw in turn from the relevant cultural traditions, not only to enhance production, but also to promote alternative concepts of governance, welfare, social security, and education.

The modernist liberal democrat might ask what the disadvantaged should do if those so empowered betray the trust placed in them. They might point to the corrupt character of historical Confucian bureaucracies, and of the communist parties that have historically ruled in Marx's name, to make their point. How, in the event of betrayal, might Confucian marxist rulers be reformed or fired? What is to stop them becoming corrupted ("power tends to corrupt; absolute power corrupts absolutely") and ignoring all attempts to hold them accountable? The ultimate constraint upon Confucian bureaucrats was the right to replace them forthwith. Given that there were no generally agreed rules of the game to expedite the non-violent rotation of elites, this rarely happened. The only constraint upon bad marxist parties is the same one. It is what self-discipline provides, and when self-discipline breaks down, there is no mechanism for regime replacement.

Modernist liberal democracy is arguably less democratic in practice than it is in principle, however. When it becomes a smokescreen for bourgeois rule, for example, democratic elections are only able to replace tweedledum with tweedledee. Marxists note the failure by liberal capitalists to implement large-scale, long-term changes in the distribution of power, status, and wealth, turning the democratic case on its analytic head in the process.

Enter Confucian marxists, who look to moral leadership under any conditions, democratic or otherwise, to make a difference to those most in need. As marxists, Confucian marxists highlight class-based disparities in power, status, and wealth in the world, and the need for more equitable global outcomes. As Confucians, however, they see no point to changing these disparities without a Confucian-style commitment, on the part of those who come to power, to right and proper rule, that is, to a leadership code of courage, steadfastness, self-sacrifice, integrity, and true consideration for those they rule.

CHAPTER 9

HINDU CONSTRUCTIVISM

While Confucianism may seem somewhat less of a sacral discourse than other politico-spiritual doctrines, Hinduism may seem more so. Hinduism covers the whole gamut, from the most materialist of thought-worlds to the most spiritually abstruse. It is an entire sacral universe, sufficient unto itself.

Here the focus is placed upon those Hindu ways of thinking that "definitively empty human existence of any meaning other than that of a perfect integration into a transcendent whole" (Biardeau, 1989, 161). In short, it highlights *Advaita Vedanta* since it is arguably this aspect of Hinduism that mounts the most radical challenge to modernist Rationalism, and to that way of articulating modernist world affairs called global "constructivism."

Hindu ways of thinking are referred to by Hindus themselves as *dharma*. The connotations of this word are not captured by English equivalents like that of religion or faith, since *dharma* refers to the universal and eternal law that defines the structure of the entire cosmos, including human society itself. It is the sociomoral law and order of the whole universe. In a fundamental sense it *is* that society, including the caste system that permeates and regulates nearly every devout Hindu's life "from before birth to after death" (Klostermaier, 1998, 2; Organ, 1975, 19).

How meaningful, therefore, is the use of the word Hinduism to denote a world faith? Quite apart from its social significance, Frykenberg argues that there has "never been any such . . . thing as a single 'Hinduism'" since there has never been a single Hindu community that covers all, or even part of the subcontinent (Frykenberg, 1991, 29). Stietencron argues likewise, saying that Hinduism is a politico-cultural civilization "formed and enriched by a group of [related but distinct, separate but interacting] Hindu religions . . . ," and that any attempt to use the word in the singular should be abandoned forthwith (Stietencron, 1991, 16, 21).

Perhaps we should start with the word Hindu, then, which comes originally from the Persian form of the Sanskrit word *sindhu*, and was first used by non-Indians, two and a half thousand years ago, to categorize the peoples of and beyond the Indus river region. After Muslim incursions from the eighth century on, the Persians apparently used the term to nominate the non-Muslim part of this population. The early European imperialists of the seventeenth century simply spoke of *gentoos*, that is, heathens.

The concept of the Hindu is an ancient one, therefore, though the concept of Hinduism is not, having first come into common English parlance as a derivative of Hindu, and as a nineteenth-century covering concept for "anything 'Native' or 'Indian'." At this time it was still possible to talk of "Hindoo" Christians or "Hindoo" Muslims, for example (Frykenberg, 1991, 31). The word was also used, however, as it was much earlier, to talk of the components of Indian culture and religion exclusive of Christians and Muslims and the like, as well as to talk of those components of Indian culture and religion of "Aryan, Brahmanical or Vedic" origin (Stietencron, 1991, 13).

In the minds of most nineteenth- and twentieth-century Indian nationalists, and indeed, in the minds of most nineteenth- and twentieth-century Western orientalists, the core of the concept of Hinduism is the sacred wisdom enshrined in four collections of ancient oral teachings called the *Vedas*. These anthologies are said to be unauthored, in that their origins are long lost. In Sanskrit, the language in which they are couched, they are said to be *sruti*, "that which is heard," or that which is articulated "without beginning" and without discernible cause (Nikhilananda, 1964, 13). As such they were read—or more often heard—as the germinal account of the whole culture, and the source of a "natural" faith, since they were not revealed to any particular prophet, at any particular place or time (Mohanty, 2000, 125).

Such a derivation was subsequently used to promote the idea of a continuous Hindu heritage, and this despite the fact that the religious beliefs of ordinary Indians draw much more directly upon epic stories like the *Mahabharata* (which includes the *Bhagavad Gita*), or the *Ramayana*, or the non-Vedic "old books," or the *Puranas* (which many Hindus consider to be just as divinely inspired as the *Vedas*). The idea of a Vedic taproot makes Hinduism seemingly more compatible with Christian notions of a singular truth expressed in scriptural form, which is one reason why European scholars tend to talk of an underlying unity to Hindu beliefs (thus playing down India's sacral diversity). In making comparisons between world faiths, for example, Euro-American analysts often talk of Hinduism as if it were one belief-system. When they talk of different Hinduisms they talk of them as different sects, thereby managing to elide differences "at least as . . . fundamental as those between Judaism, Christianity and Islam . . . " (Stietencron, 1991, 16).

Even the most fervent of those who talk of many Hinduisms, however, agree with Indian nationalists and Western orientalists that the various expressions of Hindu faith do incorporate "largely the same traditions" (Stietencron, 1991, 20). Whether its practitioners are aware of it or not— and not many Hindus today would be able to say what the ancient texts contain—Hinduism has a fundamental reference point in the *Vedic* teachings, and in the ritual recitation of these teachings by Brahmins, who are the "closest Hinduism gets to a legitimizing authority," and who have labored for many generations to give Hinduism some kind of sacral order (Flood, 1996, 12). Like the Indian notion of the divine itself, Hinduism is infinitely diverse *and* fundamentally unified. It is both many and one

(Knott, 1998, 108), the many being the different doctrines it encompasses, the one consisting of that "complex, stable system of values, beliefs and practices" that underpins the different doctrines, and makes them comprehensible (Biardeau, 1989, 3, 15).

The most ancient of the traditional texts, the *Rig Veda*, is said to be more than three millennia old. It is an anthology of a thousand or so short, often quite worldly hymns, that reach out into "every aspect of life" (O'Flaherty, 1981, 229).

The *Rig Vedic* hymns token a keen attempt to understand the First Cause. They also indicate a clear awareness of the limitations our cognitive capacities place upon our understanding in this regard, and of the paradoxes that confront those who seek to experience something other than what these limitations allow.

"What was the base," the *Rig Veda* asks, "what sort of raw matter was there, and precisely how was it done, when the All-Maker . . . created the earth and revealed the sky in its glory? . . . What was the wood and what was the tree from which they carved the sky and the earth? You deep thinkers, ask yourselves in your own hearts, what . . . did he stand on when he set up the worlds?" Having failed to discern the All-Maker in any form, being "glutted with the pleasures of life . . . [or] wander[ing] about wrapped up in mist and stammering nonsense . . . ," we are then asked: who do we turn to for help? Who is able to tell us how to think and feel and act so that our mind might become more discriminating? (O'Flaherty, 1981, 36 [10.81–2]).

At this point the text turns to the great sages, who out of the "fullness of their illumined experience" are prepared to lend us a hand (Radhakrishnan and Moore, 1957, 37). The *Upanishads* are literally the things that are learned "sitting down near" those who know. In textual terms, the *Upanishads* are the fourth and last part of each of the *Vedas*. They are the teachings of the wise of old as to what brings spiritual wisdom, what is ultimately real, what the absolute might be (*Brahman*), and how to find it in the Self (*Atman*). As such, they are said to be the source of the "spiritual monism" that "in one form or another characterizes much of Indian philosophy," as well as the source of the sense that "intuition rather than reason" is the "true guide to ultimate truth" (Radhakrishnan and Moore, 1957, xvi).

There is no reason why the answers to the questions the *Rig Veda* asks cannot be couched in scientific terms. As the *Isa Upanishad* argues, however, an analytical approach can be worse than no approach at all:

> Into blind darkness enter they
> That worship ignorance;
> Into darkness greater than that, as it were, they
> That delight in knowledge.
>   (Radhakrishnan and Moore, 1957, 40)

Summarized and systematized over centuries, the insights of the Hindu sages were turned into several different schools, each with its own set of fundamental aphorisms or verses (*sutra* or "threads/strands"). These are the so-called orthodox schools (Eck, 1981, 7). They include *Yoga*, which focuses upon the practice of highly disciplined forms of meditation, and the deconstruction of the every-day sense of self so as to take the meditator beyond what he or she currently knows. They also include idea- and belief-systems crudely equivalent to what have been called schools of logic (*Nyaya*), atomism (*Vaisesika*), dualistic discrimination (*Samkhya*), ritualism (*Purva Mimamsa*), and scholasticism (*Uttara Mimamsa* or *Vedanta*). There are other, less orthodox schools as well, like that of the *Carvaka/Lokayata* materialists (Mittal, 1974), who marxists in particular consider to be more important than bourgeois Indologists care to admit (Anikeev, 1969). Nor is it to downplay the significance of the *Jainas* and the Buddhists, or those who would analyze language itself (*Vyakarana*), or those who believe in loving devotion alone (*bhakti*). Nor is it to downplay the differences within these schools as well as between them. All of which is the merest hint of the breadth and depth of Hindu attempts to articulate what they think of as the sciences of salvation.

Advaita Vedanta comes out of the last of the orthodox schools, and with it comes the best known and arguably most influential defense of the sense that *Brahman*, the absolute, is *Atman*, the inner Self. The *Advaita Vedanta* version of this key proposition is not the only one. Because of its appeal to nineteenth-century Euro-American intellectuals, like the British Hegelians, however, it is the one best known in the West.

The fundamental principle of *Advaita Vedanta*, that reality is not dual (*Advaita*), and *Brahman* alone is real, is found in the *Vedas* at large, as well as in the *Bhagavad Gita*. It is also found in the *Brahma Sutra*, which was an early summary of the *Upanishads*, designed specifically to refute the argument that awareness and the material world are separate, and that the Self might be conceived in non-*Brahman* terms.

The most eminent of the advocates of this principle (non-duality) was the eighth-century philosopher and theologian Shankaracharya [Sankara], who argued that any sense that the inner Self (*Atman*) and the absolute (*Brahman*) are not one is merely a symptom of the way the world appears to be not what it is (*maya*). This argument led him to conclude that on the one hand there is the truth, as it appears to those not enlightened (for whom the One is Many, and God is separate from the Self), and on the other hand, there is the Truth as the enlightened know it (which is awareness of the absolute as "all-pervading, imperishable, auspicious, uninterrupted, undivided and devoid of action") (Mayeda, 1979, 120 [I, 8.3]).

To know this "firmly," Sankara said, is to be blessed. To know it without interruption, he said, "is helpful to people, as a boat [is helpful] to one wishing to get across a river," though the other bank here represents an end to, and our release from, that which binds us to the wheel of spiritual transmigration, and causes us not only to live after we die, but also to live in ignorance, in the moment-by-moment illusion of the difference between ourselves and the absolute (Mayeda, 1979, 211 [II, 1.3]).

Sankara's thoughts are all meant to confirm the fact of "not two-ness," and the sacral emancipation this confirmation ostensibly provides, though his thoughts are said to have proceeded—somewhat ironically given their basic purpose—along three different paths. The first path, a theological or cosmological one, confirms the absolute as the inner Self (*Brahman* as *Atman*). The second path, a psychological or epistemological one, confirms the inner Self as the absolute (*Atman* as *Brahman*). The third path is an appeal to the sacral authority of the ancient oral teachings in support of both conclusions (Mayeda, 1979, 18–58, 160 [I, 17.8]).

This can be somewhat confusing, but Sankara says that however we choose to know it, whether by sense–perception, inference, or verbal authority, the identity of *Atman/Brahman* is the ground upon which all the rest of our figuring out is done. As a consequence, he concludes that "[o]ne should always grasp *Atman* alone . . . and abandon the object of knowledge . . . " (Mayeda, 1979, 117 [I, 6.4, 6.6]). He also concludes that " . . . when there is discriminating knowledge, nothing but the highest [*Atman*] exists, not even [the intellect] itself" (Mayeda, 1979, 118 [I, 7.6]).

Is this no more than the objectifying mind-move, that the Western Rationalist makes, carried to its logical extreme? Does the objectifyer cease at this point to be a discrete thinker, and move Beyond? Is this the point at which the rationalistic, individuated objectifyer either goes mad, or becomes divine (the obvious intention here)?

In Sankara's terms, any attempt to posit this point in modernist terms is to reinstate a dichotomy that does not exist, however. It is to fail to apprehend the identity that was always there, that makes the one a One, as neither "agent nor object nor result" (Mayeda, 1979, 137 [I, 14.18]). The secular Rationalist who looks Beyond anticipates finding everything available there to the objectifying mind-gaze. Sankara sees this as an illusion, since it still assumes a separate perspective. This, he argues, is the source of our ignorance and all our "great fears" (Mayeda, 1979, 120 [I, 8.6]).

For Sankara, the preferred mind-move is not one away from the world toward the Beyond, and absolute objectivity. Rather, it is one where mental movement ceases completely, thus allowing recognition of what was all pervasive in the first place. The freedom that then follows, he says, the freedom from delusion, desire, cause-and-effect thinking, and sorrow, is like the freedom of the "unborn." It is like something "altogether stainless" and pain-free, he says, "as in the sleeping state," where awareness of the body disappears. It is "ever-shining," like the sky (Mayeda, 1979, 120, 123 [I, 8.6; I, 10.3, 10.1; I, 12.5]). It is to have an understanding of understanding itself (Mayeda, 1979, 123 [I, 10.4]).

Moreover, Sankara offers these conclusions as the result not of some analytical or experimental procedure, or some mystical experience, but as the result of reading the *Vedas*. He does talk about meditating (Flood, 1996, 242), but he seems to believe more in the liberating effect of a particular kind of knowledge, and what he calls "adequate reasoning," that is, reasoning not as an end in itself, but reasoning based upon the "salutary counsel of the wise . . . ," and the "meaning of the Vedanta" (Shankaracharya, 1974, 5, 16).

Sankara's disciples differ as to how illusion works, and how the absolute might be realized. Not all agree that the proper study of the *Vedas* is enough. There are those, for example, who prefer the practice of *Yoga*, and similar forms of sacral research. There are others who believe in sacrifices, or in ritual, or who seek to exhaust the mind's capacity for logical thought by meditating on the way language represents reality in Great Sayings like "thou art that" (*tat tvam asi*), or "I am Brahman" (*aham brahmasmi*), sayings which are known to allow meditators to dispense with all distinctions, and to apprehend for themselves the common ground that Sankara says is always there.

Sankara's critics, on the other hand, like Ramanuja, an eleventh-century devotee of the Hindu god *Visnu*, tend to reject the abstract nature of his concept of the absolute, and his ideas about illusion, preferring to see the latter as evidence of the gods at play, or as the source of human creativity. Some believe sacral liberation not to be possible by those still possessed of a physical or material or some more subtle body. Sankara himself sees illusion as a matter of "superimposition" (*adhyasa*), by which he means false attribution. This is like the way we superimpose the qualities of one thing upon another, to false effect. In their ignorance (*avidya*), people attribute ordinary qualities to what is sacral, for example, and vice versa. They attribute to the inner, sacral Self (*Atman*) qualities that are not *Atman*, in the way that they can mistake a snake for a rope in the half-light of dusk (Mayeda, 1979, 77–8 [II, 2.51]). In terms of this metaphor, the absolute (*Brahman*) would be the "locus of the world," in the same way that a real rope would be the "locus of a snake illusion" (Phillips, 1995, 29).

The *Upanishads*, upon which Sankara builds his account of sacral understanding, invert the modernist model of representation. They put sense perception and rationalist thinking at the bottom of the pile of states of consciousness, where things exist, time passes, and change takes place. They put dreaming and dreamless sleep next. And they see *turiya* or "pure consciousness," as the highest, innermost, and only real state of mind. Thus while scientific knowing has its place, Sankara saw this as being notably inferior to sacral knowing. Ultimately, he saw no "place" for modernist representation, since sacral knowing in his view meant eschewing the thisness and thatness of the material world (*neti, neti*), in favor of understanding nothing ("no-thing") (Klostermaier, 1998, 89, 90). Or to quote Gauda Pada, who was the guru of Sankara's guru: "If the world were really to exist, it would undoubtedly disappear" (Pereira, 1976, 190).

Though observations like these can seem highly abstruse, they have profound consequences for the world affairs constructivist. Contemporary constructivism is the attempt to prioritize the mental rather than the material possibilities that human practices make possible. It highlights the way, within the context of the modernist project, we use our beliefs, ideas, and values to construct the world affairs we currently do. Compare this, then, with the conclusions Sankara comes to, and the findings of *Advaita Vedanta* Hinduism. If the only way to understand the true construction of the world is to realize the absolute (*Brahman*), what are we to make of world affairs, and what are we to make of the modernist project of which it is a part?

If any version of the world that is non-absolute is "merely" phenomenal, and if ultimate wisdom comes from eschewing phenomena, including the phenomena we mentally construct, we must eschew constructivism to know the absolute. We must reject its modernist, Rationalist premises, and with these premises, constructivism too.

If ultimate wisdom comes from knowing that only one idea matters, that is, and only one construction of the world is really real, namely, the sacral one, then other forms of reality must be less real. And while we are hardly likely to stop playing with lesser forms of (phenomenal) reality any time soon, or constructing world affairs in any way we care to think of it, Sankara would see us as playing with illusions. He would see us as playing with forms of reality that, while certainly substantive enough to cripple and even kill, are the delusory result of a radical lack of sacral understanding.

As Rationalists, constructivists reject the reliability of the knowledge claims upon which Sankara's conclusions are based. They ask, for example, how it is that we can know whether the knowledge the *Vedas* enshrine can be trusted, despite our respect for the teachings they contain, and despite the willingness of their exponents to share their knowledge of what these teachings say.

Why should sacral reality be superior to the empirical one? Might sacral being not be the lower truth, and Rationalist understanding the higher one? Why should we not prefer the constructivist kind of account, where knowledge is sought by objectifying Rationalism, rather than meditation on transcendental texts? Might constructivists not be justified in seeing a dichotomy between faith and science, and in cleaving to the latter as the more dependable way to know?

The *Vedantist* response is to say that the Rationalist dichotomy between matter and its "minding" is precisely what obscures the significance of that form of consciousness which is neither. If mind is matter organized in a particular way, as modernist Rationalists tend to claim, then what are we to make of mind when the matter from which it emerges is an emergent property of energy states we cannot directly see? Moreover, what precisely is it that these energy states manifest?

Is it so unreasonable, as a consequence, to posit an underlying principle that animates and permeates all? Might there not be a universal Absolute that manifests in material terms as conscious mind, but is not that mind? And might this Absolute not reach out into the world in mind-making terms, much as the mind itself reaches out into the world, with its various senses, projecting themselves upon that world, rather than sitting in the head awaiting stimulation? The eye, for example, is a direct extension of the brain, and is used to put onto what it sees as much as it takes in. It grasps for the objects it visualizes with the perceptual categories that "vision" entails (Eck, 1981, 10). Might the principle that animates the entire mind, or the entire cosmos even, not work in this kind of way?

Direct human experience of such a principle could only be subjective. It would be impossible to verify it by the intersubjective means that modernist Rationalists favor. This does not make such experience untrue, though to show why this is so is to articulate a radical alternative to the modernist way of knowing and being. It is to propose a post–Euro-American epistemology of a profoundly non-modernist kind.

Consider how the modernist Rationalist is taught to pull away mentally from the world toward a subjective self-point of absolute objectivity, and compare this with the *Advaita Vedantist*, who learns instead that our true nature is the objective self's Absolute subjectivity (*Atman*). Compare the Self of the *Advaita Vedantist* with the self of the modernist Rationalist. The Rationalist aspires to be the eye of God, conceptualized in terms that are absolutely Other. The *Advaita Vedantist* aspires to be "ontologically identical with the absolute . . . ," in a state of Absolute sameness (Flood, 1996, 241). The two are not the same, however. The latter is fundamentally different, not only from day-to-day reality, but also from what lies Beyond it (and of how that Beyond might be manifest in the here-and-now). The Hindu conclusion is profoundly at odds with the modernist Rationalist one. It represents a "sophisticated theoretical structure of self-universalization and self-isolation" that renders all else otherwise. It is a sacral insight "so comprehensive" that it is "not conducive to any serious involvement with what is different and apart . . . " (Halbfass, 1988, 187; Sinari, 1970, 10, 107). And that includes world affairs.

On the basis of ideas like these, the nationalists of the Hindu Renaissance—the neo-Hindus as opposed to the traditionalist Hindus—argued for greater intercivilizational dialogue. "Do you know what my idea is?" said Swami Vivekananda, a leading, Western-educated, nineteenth-century Hindu reformer (Halbfass, 1988, 221). "By preaching the profound secrets of the Vedanta religion in the Western world, we shall attract the sympathy and regard of these mighty nations, maintaining for ever the position of their teacher in spiritual matters, and they will remain our teachers in all material concerns" (Vivekananda, 1964, 174).

By promoting the Vedantic perspective, however, the neo-Hindus were asking Euro-Americans to accept a very different version of reality, and the idea of a kind of emancipation much more comprehensive than the one Euro-Americans had in mind. Sri Aurobindo, Sarvepalli Radhakrishnan, and Rabindranath Tagore, all articulated a similar message. As Tagore said to an audience in Oxford in 1930, for example: "Our teachers in ancient India realized . . . [that a]ny limited view of man would . . . be an incomplete view. He could not reach finality as a mere Citizen or Patriot, for neither City nor Country, nor the bubble called the World, could contain his eternal soul . . . " (Tagore, 1967 [1930], 184).

With notable exceptions, such as Schopenhauer or Voltaire, Fichte or Heidegger (Taber, 1983), Euro-Americans have largely ignored the invitation to enter into a dialogue with neo-Hindus. They favor monologue instead. They favor the kind of discourse designed to secure the planetary dominance of European thought, and to explore the anti-sacralist implications of their own approach (Halbfass, 1988, 84–99, 169).

Despite the undeniable success of the modernist project, however, the disdain with which it treats others and the environment has come to pose a growing threat to species survival. As a consequence simpleminded neo-Orientalist dichotomies are coming back to haunt the West, for example, in the form of questions as to what modernists might learn from Hindu sacralists that might help modernity endure. Given that the "meaning of progress, the significance of science and technology have become thoroughly questionable . . . The search for alternatives now appears as a matter of life and death" (Halbfass, 1988, 440). Which is why ancient Indian thinking, however incommensurable with modernist Western thinking, may not be as "obsolete" as it might (to the modernist) appear (Halbfass, 1988, 442).

The alternative offered by Hinduism of this kind is the capacity to think the unthought. This not only involves freeing thinking from the constraints of modernist discourse but also engaging with what Rationalism leaves "unthought," that is, with the "other few, really great beginnings in human history" in epistemological terms. It means making a new start in how to think, and gathering the requisite resources (Mehta, 1985, 233). It means recognition that the "complete unfoldment of life" might depend on completely different thinking, and it means casting our mental nets accordingly (Taber, 1983, 137).

In modernist world affairs the only analytic language likely to encompass intercivilizational discourse is the constructivist one since only constructivism is sufficiently uncommitted to essentialist assumptions about human nature, or materialist conceptions of human nurture, to think the unthought. Constructivism valorizes an account of world making in idealist terms. As such it has no commitment to any particular set of ideas. Its only commitment is to the idea of the importance of ideas themselves, and to Rationalism, of course, upon which all modernist accounts of world affairs are predicated, including constructivism. There is nothing, for example, to stop constructivists from expanding on ideas about what counts as valid ideas. The only inhibiting factor is the constructivist commitment to Rationalism itself. And constructivists have already been known to look beyond the modernist realm to expand upon ideas otherwise seen to be "irrational . . . magical . . . mythic . . . symbolic . . . poetic and fanciful . . . ." There is nothing to stop them questioning their Rationalist foundations, either, and not just in postmodernist (Rationalist) terms, but in anti-Rationalist terms as well, terms that ask for a sacral reassessment of what thinking is, and what the "experience of thought" might be (Mehta, 1985, 241, 254).

What is more, help for radical constructivists is at hand from those Hindus aware of the hazards of modernist thinking and aware of the all-pervasiveness of what is spiritually real. The result is Hindu constructivism, that is, the deconstruction of the Rationalist form of constructivism, and its reconstruction in anti-Rationalist terms. Hindu constructivists take the Rationalist account of world affairs in terms of the play of shared ideas, and remake this account in terms of the play of one sacral Idea. They make constructivism into Constructivism, which is anti-Rational idealism of the most radical kind (in)conceivable.

If life is about the identity of the inner Self and the Absolute, that is, *Brahman/Atman*, then modernist reason employed as an end in itself seems rather paltry by comparison, and these world affairs rather pale into insignificance. To the Hindu constructivist, global capitalism, sovereign statism, liberal individualism, anti-ecological masculinism, and all the other Rationalist attempts to describe, explain, and prescribe for world affairs, look like so many toy-like attempts to make illusion seem more real than ultimate Reality.

What might this mean for something as mundane as the global balance of power, then? Imagine a world of realist state-makers advised by wise *Advaita Vedantans*, rather than by senior bureaucrats, senior military personnel, or professors of international relations. Imagine these wise men and women confronting the dilemmas of world affairs, and instead of responding in kind, as state-makers do, reminding these leaders of the cosmic context in which their policy decisions are couched instead. This would certainly put state making in perspective. Imagine what kind of a world these state-makers might then construct. Imagine the same for the executives who head transnational corporations, and those who lead global social movements.

The objections to this line of argument are obvious, and that is the point, and in a way, the problem. Those who make them continue to engage the analyst in Rationalist discourse, when Hindu constructivists have already eschewed such a discourse completely. And not as a mere debating ploy, but as a source of political humility of a potentially world-saving sort.

Chapter 10

Pagan Feminism

—Tao Te Ching *(chapter 6)*,
trans. Ursula Le Guin

The modernist project is an objectifying project. Its proponents believe that by putting mental distance between the world and themselves they acquire a unique perspective on it.

From this perspective they see themselves as being in an "environment." They see the world as "stuff," and this stuff as malleable and exploitable. They mould and exploit it, to their own ends, and now to the point where they are doing so much damage that they are beginning to degrade the quality of their own lives. They then look for ways to control the consequences of their penchant for control, and become "environmentalists," espousing a doctrine which is not particular to any one of the analytic languages outlined in the introduction, and as a consequence, can be articulated in all of them.

As modernists stand back from the world, and themselves in the world, they take with them (amongst other things) a range of cultural assumptions about gendering practices. For example, modernists tend to prioritize the public power of males, while peripheralizing that of females. They tend to accept this as normal and natural and "rational." Instead of a gender-indifferent world of individuated individuals, which is what Rationalism portends in principle, we get in practice a gender-riven world of males and females, and a gender hierarchy dominated by men. Those who want gender parity become feminists, which is to argue, from another one of modernity's margins, in all of the languages modernists use to describe, explain, and prescribe for world affairs.

The next two chapters look at these two marginalized discourses, the feminist and the environmentalist ones, in the light of two more sacral languages, Paganism and Animism respectively. These are not mainstream discourses, and these are not mainstream religions, either. This does not mean they are insignificant, however, as the next two chapters hope to show.

As to Pagan feminism, first. One of the most notable features of modernity, and of modernist world affairs, is the extent of male dominance there. The mental and material revolution that the modernist project represents was mostly made by men, for men, with the result that these world affairs are almost exclusively still in male hands.

Not coincidentally, we have a Lord's Prayer, so that it is "Our Father, who art in Heaven," even though the Christian God is not supposed to have a sex, and Jesus Christ could just as well have been born a woman (Gibson, 1992, 66, 67–9; McFague, 1989). Not coincidentally the Christian God is also one with an all-seeing gaze, which is said to extend into the most "private recesses" of our lives. Compounded by patriarchy, this can deepen the "alienation, objectification, and self-doubt" that modernist females often say they feel (Hunter, 1992, 24).

What came before modernity's Euro-Christian origins, however? What was the ground in which Christianity itself took root? What politico-spiritual languages did Europeans speak before the advent of Christianity, and what politico-cultural values did these languages articulate? More particularly, how might an understanding of pre-Christian beliefs and practices contribute to an understanding of the male dominance that characterizes these world affairs?

While it was the Euro-Christian denial of female spiritual agency that is mostly at issue here, and more particularly, the way this helped create the gender inequities that currently characterize the global distribution of power and resources, there were Old European antecedents of quite a different kind, that can be explored in their own right. In studying those who came before Euro-Christianity, we encounter politico-spiritual practices long forgotten or repressed, while remembering and recovering them provides for a much wider palette of contemporary possibilities.

It seems to be the case, for example, that the female sex was sacred for many thousands of years in old Europe, that women as a gender were more highly respected then than they are (on the whole) now, and that this has important implications for discussions of intergroup violence. It is the basis for an argument, for example, that a return to "feminine sacredness," and to greater gender-parity, might make for a more peaceful world affairs (Ann and Imel, 1993, xix).

In Christian terms, all those who lived before God revealed Himself (*sic*) in the guise of his Son, are Pagans—literally, country dwellers (Adler, 1986, 9–10, 25). The more extreme Christians think of Pagans as Satanists, that is, as evil incarnate, though even the more moderate of them may use the word in a derogatory way, to refer to those who do not worship in the Christian fashion as heathens or idolators.

Usage like this is archaic, however. Pagan is employed today to refer mostly to nature-worshippers, and to small groups of usually indigenous peoples who generally lack the global means to fight the conceptual slur it has largely become.

When the messianic fervor of the Euro-Christians was at its height, it may have made sense to have a blanket term with which to refer to those considered Unsaved or otherwise Benighted, but as modernist world affairs become more global, they become the world affairs of Judaism,

Islam, Buddhism, and Hinduism as well. It ceases to be appropriate for Euro-Christians to divide the world into a Christian "us" and a non-Christian "them." And they generally refrain now from doing so. Jews, Muslims, Buddhists, and Hindus all actively participate in contemporary world affairs. They do not respond well to being referred to as mere non-Christians, so a designation like the Pagan one will seem demeaning. To those who see Christians as the benighted ones, this will seem even more so.

At the same time, Pagan as a term has gone on to acquire more neutral connotations. For those who see in pre-Christian ideas a continuing source of inspiration, it even has positive connotations now. It is no longer derogatory, for example, to use Pagan to refer to archaic practices which may have been more gender-equal and less patriarchal (Frymer-Kensky, 1992, 1).

In pre-Christian terms, Pagan is mostly used to refer to the Old Europeans, that is, to those who lived in the Neolithic and the Chalcolithic eras, in the southern and eastern parts of Europe and the Aegean. These people seemed to have believed in the Goddess, an entity otherwise described as Mother Nature (Heliotrope, 1999, 48), the "living unity" (Baring and Cashford, 1991, xi), the "living earth" (Simos, 1988, xvi), "the binding force that holds together the universe" (Simos, 1989, 180), the animating force of the Tree of Life (Gross, 1996, 223), the "holder of the Blood Mysteries" (Batten, 1995, 16), or the "absolute and parthenogenetic . . . foundation of all being . . . [and] of the Great Mystery of life . . ." (Leeming and Page, 1994, 7, 10, 16).

The Goddess had a myriad masks. She was, for example, both Good and Bad. She had symbolic minions who represented her fertility, and her role as the Killer-Regeneratrix. She was the Mother of the Dead as well as of the Living (Gimbutas, 1989, 316, 319). She was also a warrior, and was manifest in the form of those goddesses who sanctioned the sovereignty of kings (Benard and Moon, 2000).

Archaeologists infer this fact from the earliest archaeological objects they have found from Old Europe. These objects represent the Divine as being gendered, and female. And while we will never know the mental and spiritual context in which these objects were originally made, for at least 25,000 years they appear to have been symbolic of all human "origin" in this region, as well as of the human "goal" there. They appear to have represented both the "giver of life and [the] dwelling place of the dead." They appear to have stood for she who is the "transformer of the life," who brings this life out of herself, and then takes it back again in a cycle of time "as perpetual and enduring as that of the moon" (Baring and Cashford, 1991, 42). Archaeological objects that represent the Divine as male are only found at site levels that correspond to the last 5,000 years.

The art and artifacts of ancient peoples provide lasting evidence of what they believed and what they worshipped (Gimbutas, 1974, 236). How are we to read this evidence, though? Can we be sure what these artifacts mean?

The inferences outlined above are speculative, since interpretations of the evidence do differ. For example, the complex designs that the Old Europeans drew have been said to be significantly more than decorative geometric motifs. They have been seen as symbols, for example, of the primary characteristics of the Goddess. So consistent are these symbols that one analyst believes them to be an "alphabet of the metaphysical" (Gimbutas, 1989, 3, 1). Other analysts, confronted with the same art and artifacts, do not concur, however, and find such an interpretation far too fanciful (Tringham, 1993). It is hard to know as a consequence what these politico-spiritual artifacts tell us about the societies that made them, and about what these societies believed the status of women to be. Were they really meant to represent a sense of the earth as somehow the same as the (female) human body? Those who think that they were, see them as ways in which these societies talked about the "roles and nature of women . . . ," and of "women writ large . . ." (Frymer-Kensky, 1992, 14). Those who think they were not, disagree.

Despite these differences, the art and artifacts of the ancient Europeans are evidence of something, and some of these artifacts are images of gestation that may well be of sacral significance, since they do seem to refer to a female form of Divinity notably different from that provided later by more "phallic fiat" (Ruether, 1989, 101). Whether Old European societies were more egalitarian because they had female Divinities, though, or whether they had female Divinities because they were more egalitarian—that is not clear. Contemporary anthropological studies lend weight to the conclusion that God's gender goes together with ideas about nature and secular power, since men are dominant where the sacral realm is male, for example, and vice versa (Sanday, 1981, 6). Where the spiritual pantheon is more mixed and egalitarian, so seemingly is the society. Power seems to be accorded "whichever sex is thought to embody or to be in touch with the forces upon which people depend for their perceived needs" (Sanday, 1981, 11) (although particular circumstances can have more particular consequences. Societies under "adverse circumstances," like those forced to migrate, can be "heavily dependent" on the "aggressive acts of men," while descent and residence rules that follow maternal lines tend to be more evident in settled, agricultural societies-like the Old European one (Gimbutas, 1999, xix; Young, ed., 1993, xxiv)).

Neo-Pagans are among those persuaded by such evidence, who use the archaeological record to contest the authority of patriarchal faiths like Christianity, and highlight the arbitrary character of the male bias that patriarchal faiths help impose upon contemporary world affairs (Simos, 1979, 1989). As long as "goddess feminists" are only able to make their case by reversing "exclusivism," they remain tied to Christian thought forms (Ruether, 1989, 101). Which is why establishing the historical priority of female-centered belief systems, and their superior inclusiveness, is so important to them. It allows neo-Pagans to highlight the way in which later faiths like Christianity were implicated in the subjugation of women, first in Europe, and then elsewhere through European expansion. It allows them to posit a human capacity for egalitarian ways of living, ways that seem to have existed in pre-Christian times, and that given the appropriate sacral and material context, could conceivably exist again. Hence, the contemporary feminist interest in Old European Paganism, and in the "highly developed, artistic civilization" that it served. Hence, too, the emphasis on the fact that these societies seemed to have a "comfortable standard of living . . . [and lived in] harmony with nature and each other for several thousand years" (Christ, 1996b, 53).

Christian feminists are not persuaded. They prefer to advocate female emancipation in post-Pagan terms, and to categorize Pagan feminism as an uncritical heir to nineteenth-century romanticism (Coakley, 2002, 97). They reject outright what they see as a distorted reading of the archaeological and anthropological record (Ruether, 1983, 40–1).

Rationalists are not persuaded either. Having learned to put faith at a mental distance, having struggled historically to dichotomize church and state, having managed to get reason prioritized as an end in itself *en masse*, and having managed to marginalize those who use reason to articulate their assumptions about God, modernists are not about to accept pre-Christian beliefs as relevant to a description and explanation of contemporary world affairs. Those who have seen the light of the mind that modernity makes possible, that is, are not about to have it occluded by the votive candles of the neo-Pagans (Stone, 1976). Hence the fervor of those Rationalist archaeologists who decry any concept of a pre-Bronze Age pan-European "symbolic unity," built on a belief in the Goddess. Hence the assiduous way in which many of these analysts hunt for gaps in the argument that Gimbutas, the main advocate of the idea of such a unity, has tried to provide (Gimbutas, 1989, 1991), and their aversion to what she has to say about particular buildings, particular engravings, and particular figurines (Tringham, 1993, 197). Hence the critical counterargument that this case is not one that can be closed by "selecting pieces" from "scattered sources," or by attributing "every nuance of style and decoration . . . to religious or mythological motives, ignoring social or decorative influences" (Barnett, 1992, 170–1).

As Rationalists, modernist feminists are not persuaded either. The more liberal among them, for example, who would emancipate women by promoting the concept of human rights (Sharman and Young, eds., 1999, 2), reject the neo-Pagan case as a religious mode of emancipation, and as anti-Rationalistic. Marxist feminists are similarly dismissive, since they see women's liberation being achieved by revolutionary means, that is, by heightened proletariat consciousness and the overthrow of the (modernist) bourgeoisie. Sacral modes of emancipation, like those neo-Pagans offer, they see as one of the ways this bourgeoisie uses to keep the masses toiling (including the female masses) and unaware of class oppression.

And even though postmodernist feminists do critique modernity (Lovibond, 1989), they find sacral arguments problematic, too. They see these arguments helping, not hindering, the modernist promulgation of "colonizing idioms and hierarchical paradigms" that oppress women (Lelwica, 1998, 117, fn. 19).

Pagan feminists respond by highlighting how Christianity is sexist, how the Christian-inspired form of modernity is sexist and nihilist, how both beget brutality (Lelwica, 1998, 123), and how the pre- and post-Christian valorizing of a female God provides an alternative. They highlight modernist research (like that of Gimbutas) that demonstrates that Old European societies may well have allowed women better access to power and resources than they enjoy today, and to the antiwar effect that that access may have had. They use a combination of reconfigured faith and research findings to challenge the idea—sacral and historical—that patriarchy is inevitable, and should be preferred.

More fundamentally, Pagan feminists point out how modernists have failed successfully to confront the highly particular and radically skewed nature of modernity itself, and the consequent need, as they see it, to counteract the prejudices that modernist Rationalism promotes. These prejudices derive from the assumptions about the self that make such an objectifying mind-gaze possible. Counteracting these prejudices is best achieved, they argue, by locating modernity in its sacral context, and more particularly, in its pre-Christian/Pagan context.

For example, Pagan feminists point out how, by prioritizing a mind-gaze that allows reason to be used as an end in itself *en masse*, modernists put themselves in the place of the all-knowing Christian god who preceded them, and that this God is male. In adopting this god's objectifying perspective, modernists are not obliged to be male, and indeed, the individuated individual who gives reason free rein is not in principle a biologically sexed or a culturally gendered one. Liberalism, the doctrine that articulates this abstract self in terms of world affairs, is not in principle sexed or gendered either, hence the liberal feminist support for the "human" rights doctrine. In practice, however, it was men, in the main, who assumed the synoptic gaze of the male Christian god. It was men, in the main, who used their untrammeled reason to construct the kind of world that relatively untrammeled reason made possible. And it was men, in the main, who did so in male-centric ways. What had the potential to emancipate women, therefore, came to hide a systematic failure to do so behind a purported capacity that continues to remain unrealized.

As Pagan feminists see it, the progressive path that modernists take is also extinguishing the "very conditions for life on earth." As the results of human alienation from the "vital roots" of "earthly life" become clearer to them, they see the Goddess reemerging from modernity's margins to bring hope for the future in the form of a return to our pre-Christian sacral origins. They see the historical cycle that began in Old Europe, when patriarchal warriors ended an extended age of peaceful intergroup living, and laid the basis for Christianity and the spread of the "philosophical rejection of this world," as finally turning back to the Goddess, and to everything she stood for (Gimbutas, 1989, 321).

So: what are we to make of all this argument and counterargument? What of these pre-Christian female Divinities, the relatively exalted status they are supposed to have enjoyed, and the egalitarian, non-warring societies that ostensibly gave them that status (and the warring societies that ostensibly succeeded them?).

In restating the Pagan feminist case, the first issue to be addressed is the purported way, "[i]n Neolithic Europe and Asia Minor (ancient Anatolia [modern Turkey])—in the era between 7000 B.C. and 3000 B.C. . . . it was the feminine force that pervaded existence" (Gimbutas, 1999, 3). Central to this observation are one hundred thousand or so ceramic figurines of animals, humans, and abstract objects, excavated by archaeologists working across the entire region. Since we have no other records from this time, the meaning of both the figurines, and their symbolic markings, must remain unknown (Mellaart, 1975, 274; Gimbutas, 1989, xv). The ritual contexts in which these figurines are usually found supports the idea that they were spiritually significant, however, while the idea that God may then have been a woman is corroborated by contemporary folk practices that perpetuate a belief in a female divinity that gives and takes life, before giving it again. Large numbers of Neolithic artifacts distort the female form in ways highly suggestive of "sacred sexuality." Whether this distorting force was understood as one that gave all and took all; whether it was understood as a female Creator, "from whom all life . . . arose, and to whom everything returned" (Gimbutas, 1999, 5); this is less certain. What is certain, however, is that no image of a Father God is to be found in the entire prehistoric record. Those representations of male gods that appear later are only, arguably, adjuncts to the female Goddess—perhaps her consort, or her son (Gimbutas, 1982, 24).

The second issue to be addressed is that of social equality. The implication that women played an equal role in the life of Old Europe is supported mainly by studies of the grave goods of the time. These goods tend to be similar, in quantity and quality, despite the sex of the body in the grave. Indeed, women's graves often contain more goods than men's graves, which does not preclude entirely the possibility that these were male-centered societies that passed on their wealth via women, but is at least suggestive of societies of a more egalitarian kind (Keller, 1996, 83; Spretnak, 1996, 95).

The third issue to be addressed is the outcome of the incursion into Old Europe, from the fifth to the third millennium B.C., of seminomadic, horseriding Indo-European pastoralists from the Pontic (Volga) steppe. These incursions have been verified by genetic mapping (Cavalli-Sforza et al., 1993, 642; Cavalli-Sforza, 1997). Driven by drought (Keller, 1996, 84), these invaders moved west in three main waves, overrunning the agricultural societies they encountered, and imposing their own presence and their own beliefs in their stead. These were very different beliefs. Thus while the sacred myths of Old Europe were redolent of "the moon, water, and the female . . . ," those of the interlopers invoked "the sun . . . planets . . . thunder and lightning." Thus while Old Europe was "matrifocal, sedentary, peaceful, art-loving, earth- and sea-bound," the Kurgan invaders (named as such for their burial mounds) were "patrifocal, mobile, warlike, ideologically sky oriented, and indifferent to art" (Gimbutas, 1982, 23). Their deities bore weapons and rode chariots, wore "starry cloaks adorned with glittering gold," carried "shining daggers . . . and shields," and venerated the "magical swiftness of [the] arrow and [the] javelin and the sharpness of the blade . . ." (Gimbutas, 1982, 31).

The Old European civilization survived intact longest on island margins in the Aegean, like Crete (Gimbutas, 1999, 129). With the end of the Minoan and Mycenaean societies, the "Neolithic vision" was lost, however, and a "unique insight . . . into how human consciousness might have continued to evolve . . ." simply disappeared. It is "no wonder," Pagan feminists say, "that, many centuries later, Classical Greece looked back to Crete as to a lost Golden Age . . ." (Baring and Cashford, 1991, 144).

What was lost included gender parity. While the Kurgans were masculinist, nomadic, rude, and war-loving, the Old European societies were female-centered, settled, civilized, and peaceful.

The historic result of their encounter also raises important questions about the relationship between the "preeminence . . . [of] male gods; the necessity of war; [and] the inevitability of male dominance . . ." (Christ, 1996a, 34; Sanday, 1981). To realize world peace, for example, should we attempt to reinstate a pre-industrial, agricultural mode of production (which would be the materialist argument), or one where the people also worship female deities (which would be the sacralist argument), or both?

Short of an end to the industrial revolution, reinstating agriculture as the planetary mode of production would seem highly unlikely. Reinstating the Goddess would seem highly unlikely too, particularly in the light of the limited response neo-Pagan ideas have so far evoked. The Gimbutas account of Old Europe remains debatable then, as a valid and viable vision for contemporary world affairs. Even if Old Europe did represent a more egalitarian and peaceful way of living, and one that warlike, hierarchic males forced us to digress from, do we really, in these more self-reflexive times, have a chance to return to it, or reinvent it? (Keller, 1996, 86).

It is a more than an awkward fact that modernity, and the progress it makes possible, is male-centric, however. The power that Rationalism gives us over nature and each other remains masculinist power, of a kind that may well erode the basis for its own capacity to survive.

Which is why it might be timely to remember, as the Pagan feminists bid us do, that there may have been more gender-equal societies in the past that manifest little evidence of organized warfare for extended periods of time, and that lived in greater harmony with the environment. Historical memories like these can inspire confidence in the idea that sustained peace is possible. The fact that Old European towns were not heavily fortified, especially when compared with other early places (like eighth millennium Neolithic B Jericho in Palestine, with its huge defensive wall and ditch (Mellaart, 1965, 33)) , the fact that Old European towns were not usually sited in locations designed for defence, the fact that there is not much evidence of extensive violence between these towns, and that there is little (in what remains of their arts and technologies) to suggest that organized fighting was common (the plentiful evidence of head wounds at a site like Catal Huyuk in Turkey being considered evidence of a "lot of quarrelling," commensurate with a "vigorous people living in . . . a closely cooped up society," rather than war) (Mellaart, 1978, 16)—all bodes well in this regard. None of the buried dead in Old European towns died from the wounds of war (Mellaart, 1967, 225). Indeed, for close to a thousand years the particular Old European town most carefully studied was "never conquered . . . a stretch of peace and prosperity . . . hard to parallel in later periods in history" (Mellaart, 1978, 17). As a result it would seem that an "ecologically embedded, egalitarian, nonmilitarisic society is not a pipe dream. It is part, at least, of our human heritage" (Spretnak, 1996, 96).

Which bears directly upon those modernist assumptions that our essential human nature is the cause of large-scale violence. When put together with anthropological evidence that women "as a group" do "not willingly face death in violent conflict" (Sanday, 1981, 211), Old Europe seems to show that it is possible to live in greater harmony with nature, and with each other, than we do today. Perhaps our ancestors had achieved something we have not yet been able to. Perhaps they had something that we lack, and have something to teach us after all (Baring and Cashford, 1991, 25). Perhaps wisdom can be old as well as new.

The story of the Kurgan incursions is central to any conclusion here, since it was they who seemingly brought large-scale war to the Old European world, and it was they who seem to have systematically denied female agency and power. It is arguably because of them and their descendants that these world affairs, the world affairs beyond 2000 in the Christian calendar, should be so male-dominated and war-prone (Frymer-Kensky, 1992, 80; Lacey and Danziger, 1999, 195).

Which is why Pagan feminists highlight the radical Kurgan separation of earth and sky, and their preference for a panoptic form of cosmic consciousness. Much has come from this kind of consciousness, including the ability to sight the world and each other with the ". . . naughty thumb / of science . . ." (whose only alternative is Spring) (Baring and Cashford, 1991, 154, 486, 659). No wonder Pagan feminists would reconceptualize God as a verb, not a noun (Daly, 1979, 213), and as the kind of verb, moreover, that promotes an awareness of what obtains without male intervention (Ruether, 1983, 266). It was the Kurgan incursions, after all, they say, that instilled a belief in gods who provide order from above. It was the Kurgan victories that made the individuation of the individual possible, they say, first in the form of heroes (with their exemplary capacity to master and change the world) and then in the form of all men (who do likewise albeit in less exalted ways) (Baring and Cashford, 1991, 154–5). Note master, and note men. And note how "[i]n our Western culture there is now formally no goddess myth and so no feminine dimension in the collective image of the divine. This means that contemporary experience of the archetypal feminine as a sacred entity is no longer available as an immediate reality . . ." (Baring and Cashford, 1991, 660–1, 667). Which is extraordinary, they say, and comes at no small global cost.

And which is why Pagan feminists would renegotiate the terms of the original Kurgan victories in a bid, if not to reinstate the sense of a female Divinity and a more gender-equal world, then at least to provide such ideas as alternatives of historically proven worth. To do this, they say, it is necessary to understand the nature of that faith that once exalted the female. Only then, they say, will we understand that patriarchal societies are cultural constructs, and relatively recent ones, and that they only seem natural and normal. They can be changed (Spretnak, 1982, 396; Daly, 1986, 13).

Would renegotiations like these allow us to engage with the virility as well as the fertility of the world? Would they make it possible (to quote D.H. Lawrence) to draw life into ourselves out of its "huge vitalities," as he saw the Etruscans (one of the Kurgan margins) as having done? (Baring and Cashford, 1991, 664). Would renewed respect for the status and achievements of the women of Neolithic Europe allow us to move beyond the male/female dichotomy, as a more Rationalist and liberalist account of the world's future would want us to do? (King, 1987, 216). And would any attempt to answer questions like these only distract us from more mundane and pressing issues, like how to feed the starving, how to stop war, and how to repair the planet?

It is hard to say. In seeking renegotiations like these, however, Pagan feminists are saying that a world at peace is conceivable, and they are suggesting that the Old Europeans achieved this for thousands of years. Whether we can achieve it again is highly uncertain, but it has been achieved before, for a sustained period of time, and over a wide geographic area. This makes it a distinct possibility that it could be achieved again.

For Pagan feminists, the keys are female Divinity and gender equity, and they unlock a potential for less war and for more civilized ways of living. And while Pagan feminists cannot supply these keys themselves, nor can they promise they would fit even if they could, they do provide astute suggestions as to where these keys might be cut.

CHAPTER 11

ANIMIST ENVIRONMENTALISM

One notable consequence of the Rationalist mind-gaze, and therefore of modernist world affairs, are changes in the condition of the planet's environment. There is global warming, for example, industrial pollution, deforestation, and species extinction. There is depletion of vital resources as the size of the human population continues to grow. And there are the uncertainties that attend our attempts to manipulate that "marvellous living alphabet" inside the cell from which all life is constructed (Eiseley, 1988, 141). These all have consequences for world affairs. Indeed, without a viable planetary environment, there are no world affairs, modernist or otherwise.

Despite these changes, the world as an ecological system remains relatively peripheral to world affairs. Planetary ecology is still of marginal concern to foreign affairs practitioners and analysts, and attempts to negotiate international protocols to reduce the level of dangerous atmospheric pollutants, for example, or to protect endangered species, have had limited success to date.

Though degradation of the contemporary kind is only possible because of advances in the scientific technologies that provide modern hygiene, medicines, food, and industrial commodities, it is the Rationalistic mind-gaze of the scientists themselves that has allowed these advances to be made on such a vast scale, without the creation at the same time of an equally profound concern for the viability of the planetary environment. In particular, it is the objectifying, reifying character of this mind-gaze that allows us to put the planet at a mental distance, and in the main, to think that we are in charge, and that what we do is under our control.

This mind-gaze was first given widespread credence in the context of European Christianity, an ethos not noted for its reverence for the earth or for other species. "By destroying pagan animism," White argues, "Christianity made it possible to exploit nature in a mood of indifference to the feelings of natural objects . . . [M]odern Western science was cast in a matrix of Christian theology," and has carried on accordingly (White, 1967, 1205, 1206; Wilson, 1984).

We have not always had such an impact. We have not always loomed so environmentally large. This is partly because in previous times and places there were fewer of us (during the Pleistocene, perhaps only one hundred thousand) (Agar, 2001, 40). In these earlier times human lives were lived in much greater proximity to the natural world, which made a difference, since it made it much more difficult to put the natural environment at a mental distance, and much easier to think of the world as something to be lived in, as a place of spirits, rather than as something to be lived with, as a resource, or a sink, or a physical platform.

It was Edward Tylor, in the last part of the nineteenth century, who first called the belief in nature as a place of spirits "animism," and who arranged the mind-move from a belief in spirits in nature to a belief in organized complexity into a progressive sequence. He saw the belief in spirits as being most characteristic of tribes and races "very low" on the ladder of humanity. We ascend from here, he said, into "high modern culture," by which he meant Christendom and science.

Tylor thought that animist beliefs originated in the puzzle presented to even the most "primitive" of thinkers by the difference between a living body and a dead one. He imagined these "primitive" thinkers wondering: what causes waking? What causes sleep or trance? What causes disease or death? (Tylor, 1903 [1871], v.1, 428).

Another puzzle was presented, he thought, by the "human shapes" we see in "dreams and visions . . ." (Tylor, 1903 [1871], v.1, 428). Tylor imagined ancient peoples wondering what these phenomena might be, too.

Tylor saw ancient intellectuals solving these puzzles by first inferring that everyone has two components, a life and a "phantom," and then by combining these two ideas, in the concept of the spirit or soul. This had the benefit of explaining the way the body and mind worked, including the dreaming mind. It also had the benefit of explaining the clairvoyance of shamans and seers, and what happens after death (Tylor, 1903 [1871], v.1, 436, 438, 457–67).

In many cultures phantom souls were seen to be an attribute not only of people, but also of birds, animals, and plants. Even inanimate objects, like rivers, stones, weapons, boats, food, ornaments, and clothes, could have such spirits. As a result even inanimate objects could be "talked to, propitiated, [and] punished for the harm they do . . ." (Tylor, 1903 [1871], v.1, 477).

The concept of the phantom spirit or soul makes for a radically different awareness of the world. So much so that Tylor saw the difference between the great world faiths as trivial by comparison. The "deepest of all religious schisms," he argued, is that between animist spiritualism and scientific materialism (Tylor, 1903 [1871], v.1, 500–2).

To understand this "childlike" stage in mental development we need only, Tylor said, evoke memories of our own "childish days" (Tylor, 1903 [1871], v.1, 477–8). The psychologist, Jean Piaget, subsequently went one step further. He identified a general human tendency, from the age of two to that of six or seven, to regard inanimate things as sufficiently willful to perform natural tasks. He attributed this tendency to the failure to discriminate between the self and the world, and to differentiate between psychical and physical ideas. This was not a matter he said, of projecting the personal will onto what is inert (Sugarman, 1987, 14), since at this age things appear to be "necessarily animate." At this age, nature is seen as constituting a "*continuum* of life, such that every object possesses activity and awareness in some degree . . . ." He called this the *diffuse* animist stage, to distinguish it from the more particular forms of animism he saw exemplified by such statements as: "the sun and moon follow me." And while Piaget specifically avoided portraying "primitive" peoples as children, his whole approach assumes that the individuated individual, who prioritizes reason as an end in itself, is the mental norm (Piaget, 1929, 169–70, 231, 233, 236, 250). He was, after all, a modernist/Rationalist, and as such he looked not only for evidence that children individuate as they grow up, but for evidence that might confirm his politico-cultural assumptions about the social centrality of this process. In looking for evidence that showed how (European) children learn this most important of mental lessons, it never occurred to him that logical, moral, and effective behavior might be manifest by adults who do not prioritize the objectifying mind-gaze, and who do not separate the self from its context in the preferred, Rationalist way. It never occurred to Tylor either.

Tylor saw animism as extraordinarily persistent. As such, he argued, it was "the groundwork of the Philosophy of Religion, from that of savages up to that of civilized men" (Tylor, 1903 [1871], v.1, 426). "[M]en still act," he said, "as though in some half-meant way they believed in souls or ghosts of objects," even when their knowledge of physics and biology and psychology was well beyond so "crude" a philosophic faith (Tylor, 1903 [1871], v.1, 500–1). For example, he observed how "the conception of the human soul is . . . continuous from the philosophy of the savage thinker to that of the modern professor of theology," and how as an "animating, separable, surviving entity . . . [it remains] one principal part of a system of religious philosophy which unites, in an unbroken line of mental connexion, the savage fetish-worshipper and the civilized Christian" (Tylor, 1903 [1871], v.1, 501–2).

Tylor did see animism undergoing change, however. Consistent with his Rationalist/progressivist outlook, he saw the animism of his day as being a more "developed product" than that of earlier times. He saw it as an animism "more appropriate to advanced knowledge . . . ," "more conformed to positive science . . . ," and "less complete and consistent" (Tylor, 1903 [1871], v.1, 500).

As a sacral doctrine, however, it was a hardy perennial that always performed the same basic ontological function. It was the natural faith. It was the faith human beings come to by reason rather than revelation (Tylor, 1903 [1871], v.1, 500). As thinking beings, we invent animist beliefs, Tylor said, even if we do not already have them, since they are the most rational way to understand our environment. They are the most basic intellectual response we can make to the mysteries of the world in which we live. They do not require a sense of cosmic awe or rapture. They do not require spiritual devotion or fear, or the need for sacral recognition, heavenly succor, or divine justice (Tylor, 1903 [1871], v.2, 356). They arise because of overinterpretation. And though this may be a mistake, where it is hard to tell what is alive and what is not, as Guthrie argues, erring in favor of the decision that something is alive favors survival, and is likely to be selected for as a psychological trait. We would expect to find it, therefore, and we would expect to find animism, "throughout the sentient world . . . ," not as an anomaly but as an inevitable and reasonable result of "normal perceptual uncertainty and . . . good perceptual strategy" (Guthrie, 1993, 41, 54, 204; Boyer, 1994, 2001).

Tylor anticipated attack from those who prefer to highlight sacral feelings rather than sacral reflections. He knew that he had written "soullessly of the soul" and "unspiritually of spiritual things." He recognized that he had eschewed any mystic sense of transcendent emotion. And he offered no apology for having done so, since he saw himself as a scientific progressive (Tylor, 1903 [1871], v.2, 359). As the student of anatomy maps the physical body, he said, without being distracted by the emotional implications of such work, or the student of war analyzes armed conflict, without feeling compelled to put it in the context of Christian sentiments about loving thy neighbor, he saw himself doing no more than his good, modernist, nineteenth-century, analytic duty. Writing at the same time, Herbert Spencer saw the same "primitive" philosophers as being driven by their religious instincts (Spencer, 1904, 11, 276). Robert Marett also rose to Tylor's challenge. He noted Tylor's admission that he preferred the intellect to the emotions, and accused him of being too narrow (Marett, 1914, xxxi). He saw him as being mistaken in seeing such an emotive aspect of human experience in such an exclusively philosophical way, and posited a pre-animist stage to the same evolutionary sequence. The pre-animist stage he defined in terms of our emotional and physical animation, with Animism being built upon prior experiences that were raw and rudimentary and in "awe of the mysterious." Animism was not so much "thought out," he said, as "danced out" (Marett, 1914, 1, xxxi).

Suspect in principle for being psychologically unsophisticated, historically unconfirmed, and culturally mechanistic, Tylor's evolutionary logic is more than a little redolent of the arrogance of empire as well. Tylor was after all, a representative of a Christian/modernist society infamous for its imperial behavior. The fundamental flaw in his logic is epistemological, however. The dichotomy Tylor saw between modernity and savagery, occluded both the extraordinary variety of premodernist traditions, and the extraordinary variety of modernist ones. His social scientific reification of concepts like "primitive" or "spirit" was reductionist. It caused him to see similarity (and difference) where there was none, and to find simplicity where there was complexity. His evolutionism ultimately failed, therefore, as did the empire of which it was part, and which it helped to promote (Bolle, 1987, 302).

While Tylor's evolutionary logic may be deemed defunct, animist conclusions continue to be drawn about what is life and what constitutes its vitality. Tylor expected animism to remain an abiding intellectual inference. He thought it would be one ongoing response to the puzzles life sets, and in this respect, he was correct. For example, Pagan feminists talk of a Life Force and a Mother Nature, without whose (female) power "nothing is born or glad" (Budapest, 1989, xxv, 3). The biologist Rupert Sheldrake talks of formative causation, morphogenetic fields, and a morphic resonance which acts across space and time to create physico-chemical systems at every level of complexity (Sheldrake, 1981, 1990, 87–90). Sheldrake's active principle is Tylor's animistic spirit or soul, restated in contemporary scientific language. He specifically denies this (Sheldrake, 1990, 135), but his appeal for experimental validation cannot disguise the vitalist character of his core concerns. The physicist David Bohm talks in similar terms of field variables, a superwave function, unbroken wholeness, holomovement, and an implicate order "enfolded in everything," as each thing is enfolded in it. He sees this order in world affairs, and ultimately, in the way the universe makes a "mirror" with which to "observe itself." These are animist concerns also (Bohm and Hiley, 1993, 8, 352, 382, 386, 389). Field variables are not spirits one can talk to, pray to, bargain with, or implore. They have no consciousness or will. One implication of Bohms's work, however, is a concept of consciousness and will as emergent properties of complex systems, and therefore, as being much more common than we think. Perhaps, Bohm infers, the ancient intuition of an animated environment is more accurate than our more mechanistic contemporaries like to think. Tylor's expectations are also met by advocates of "deep ecology," who see all life as having intrinsic worth, and picture humanity as part of a much larger whole, with which human beings can and should identify (Tobias, 1985; Naess, 1989; Sessions, 1995; Barnhill and Gottlieb, 2001). Deep ecologists see humanity as having an "obligation" to articulate a "total view," of the kind that the various "ecosophies" (like the sacral and secular philosophies committed to realizing a larger Self) try to provide (Bodian, 1995, 28; Naess, 1995, 28).

Animism remains, then, a seemingly rational response to the puzzles life sets. It continues to be restated in contemporary scientific terms, and recast as a less singular account of the world.

Anthropologically, this is associated with uncertainty, that is, with a felt lack of the ability to predict and control the environment, which is why animist beliefs are highly characteristic of hunter-gatherer societies, where survival is never simple (Levinson, 1996, 8). Modernist science and technology have largely eliminated hunting and gathering as a mode of production, but they have not eliminated uncertainty. For example, recent scientific evidence suggests that mass extinction events are "necessary" to the maintenance of life on Earth (Boulter, 2002, 67). There have been at least five notable extinction events in the planet's history (450, 350, 250, 200, and 65 million years ago), and for the last 10,000 years (the timescale precludes certainty), it is suggested that our planetary system has entered "free fall" toward another (Boulter, 2002, 176). Talk of extinction may well be exaggerated (Lomborg, 2001; Zimmerman, 2001, 243–5), but it does promote a sense of uncertainty. Likewise, as seas rise, the temperature of the atmosphere goes up, and the link between car emissions and climate becomes more clear, we can also expect a resurgence of animist thinking (Midgley, 2001, 7; Lovelock, 2000, 263). As humankind learns that it may not survive the adverse effects it is currently having on this planet, that is, the anthropological record suggests that a belief in an animated environment may re-emerge. Not in terms of phantom souls, but in terms of the natural environment's capacity to organize itself with regard to the whole.

The main evidence for thinking that Animist beliefs have already re-emerged is the Gaia hypothesis. Since it was first formulated, the Gaia hypothesis has become more scientifically respectable (Allaby, 1989; Joseph, 1990; Midgley, 2001; Lenton, 1998). Indeed, the concept covers a range of scientific hypotheses by now. The basic insight is Animist, however, despite a specific statement to the contrary by the physical chemist, James Lovelock, who first proposed the contemporary form of it (Lovelock, 1991a, 31).

Lovelock initially suggested the Gaia hypothesis (called Gaia on the advice of the novelist, William Golding) as a way of discussing the possibility that the Earth, as a whole, was alive, though he also said that the hypothesis that the Earth was in some sense alive was ". . . scientifically untestable." It could not be shown, he argued, either by logic or experiment, to be true (Lovelock, 1987 [1979], ix; Joseph, 1990, 162). Lovelock's long-term collaborator, the biologist Lynn Margulis, talks in similar terms of the Earth as a "huge set of interacting ecosystems." She also rejects any idea that the Earth is a single, living entity or organism. She does see the Earth's surface as having been a dynamic whole "for at least 3,000 million years," however, and humans as only one component of what is a huge, extremely old, and highly animated entity. Gaia for her is a "convenient name" for the way the planet's temperature, atmosphere, and acidity are regulated (Margulis, 1998, 150, 143).

At first glance, then, there would seem to be little of Animist significance here. Lovelock was initially interested in how the planet's systems of energy use worked. Impressed by the way the Earth's environment has remained either constant or close to a state "comfortable for life" over hundreds of millions of years, Lovelock saw in the mechanisms involved a level of synergy hitherto unsuspected. Perhaps the living (organic) and the non-living (inorganic) parts of the planet interact, he said. Perhaps living things do not just react to changes in the physical environment, but adapt in such a way as to change the physical environment so that it remains a suitable place to live. Perhaps, he conjectured, the Earth's "living matter, air, oceans, and land surface form a complex system which *can be seen* [emphasis added] as a single organism and which has the capacity to keep our planet a fit place for life" (Lovelock, 1987 [1979], x). Perhaps the temperature, and even the composition of the Earth's surface, are "actively regulated" by the sum of life on Earth. Perhaps the biota and the environment constitute a "single homeostatic system" that "opposes" (in some holistic fashion) changes detrimental to life (Margulis and Lovelock, 1989, 1, 6).

The slide into Animism begins when the planet's systems are seen to be purposive. This is something Rationalism sees manifest only in complex animal systems. The planet is a vegetable and mineral system, however. Rationalists do not see it as purposive, therefore.

Such a slide does have venerable antecedents. The Greek philosopher Pythagoras talked of the earth as an organism. In 1785, so did the geologist James Hutton (Lovelock, 1991a, 3), while in 1926, the minerologist, Vladimir Vernadsky, was already describing the biosphere as a living entity in scientific terms (Vernadsky, 1998 [1926], 52–3, 58).

Perhaps such thinking is merely metaphorical. The neo-Darwinists certainly think so (Gould, 1991, 339), particularly as the earth cannot breed, while Lovelock himself explicitly agrees with them, saying that the earth acts "as" a single organism, not that it is one. Then he starts to slide. He suggests, for example, that the earth acts in a life-like manner. He says that it is "difficult, without excessive circumlocution, to avoid talking of Gaia as if she were known to be sentient" (though he qualifies this at once by calling it engineer's talk, that is, the kind of talk used by engineers to say that a mechanical system is "dead" or "alive") (Lovelock, 1991a, 6). Any talk of "she," what is more, is just ". . . the appellation 'she,' " he says, "when given to a ship by those who sail in her, as a recognition that even pieces of wood and metal when specifically designed and assembled may achieve a composite identity with its own characteristic signature, as distinct from being the mere sum of its parts" (Lovelock, 1987 [1979], xii).

The earth is certainly a complex system with emergent properties, though what do we mean when we say this? A handful of watch parts are useless in themselves for chrono-calculation. Put them together in the appropriate way, however, and they whir, tick, and tell the time. That is an emergent property. It is a whole system function, not apparent from the mere sum of its parts. A frog, before and after it is put in a blender, is two very different things, even though the basic ingredients are exactly the same (Eisenberg, 1998, 45). The live frog manifests emergent properties that the blended frog does not. Likewise, Lovelock argues, the emergent properties of the Earth include those that are the result of the evolution of life on the planet's surface over eons of time. The whole-system capacity for self-regulation is the outcome of a development that took many millennia. It was achieved without "foresight . . . [or] planning," purpose or design (Lovelock, 1991a, 11), he says, but it acts nonetheless in a purposeful way to keep the planet habitable by keeping the climate, and the chemical composition of the atmosphere, within the narrow parameters congenial to life itself. Living things coevolved with the planet, he argues. They have the effect of changing the environment to suit themselves. They do not just passively adapt.

Now: we know that "simple agents following simple rules . . . [can] generate amazingly complex structures" (Johnson, 2001, 15), even though we cannot explain how these agents come upon their agency, and how these rules are set. We also know that living things can work together in such a way as to manifest outcomes we would not anticipate from knowing about what these things do in and of themselves. To wit, human cells make a human being, despite the way their local functioning suggests little of the sort (Lovelock, 1995, 18). Is this enough, however, to explain the way the Earth, looked at beside Mars and Venus, for example, has "faculties and powers" far enough beyond any mere sum of the parts of which it is composed. And is this enough to allow Lovelock to regard the Earth as possessing the attributes of a living system, that is, of a "single living entity, capable of manipulating the . . . atmosphere to suit its overall needs . . ." (Lovelock, 1987 [1979] xii, 9, 10)?

Lovelock says "living system." This certainly suggests that he thinks of the Earth as a single organism, or at least, as having a superorganism on its surface, one with its own distinctive physiology as well as its own distinctive chemistry and physics (Lovelock, 1995, 19, 1991b, 4–5). He calls Gaia, at one point, the "largest living creature on Earth" (Lovelock, 1987 [1979], 34). Elsewhere he even says that we should "recall our ancient sense of the Earth as an organism and revere it again." He even draws comfort from the idea that when he dies he will become part of the chemical components of a planet that, in some sense, is alive (Lovelock, 2000, 391–2). He also says that a Gaia-style awareness makes him think, "on happy days, in the right places, as if the whole planet were celebrating a sacred ceremony," going so far as to posit Gaia as a "religious as well as a scientific concept" (Lovelock, 1995, 193–4) (and quoting Bateson to the effect that the individual mind is part of a larger mind that is manifest in the planet's ecology, and is comparable to God) (Lovelock, 1995, 204). All of which is much more Animist than mere talk of complex systems organizing or regulating themselves to indeterminate ends (Jantsch, 1980, 8).

Much depends here, of course, on how we define life and the living. What does it mean, to be alive? Is it a thing? Is it a property of things? Is it an entity? Or is it a process that particular entities practice (which is why we find life usually defined in terms of what living involves, and what living things do)?

To the physicist, life is an antientropic event that contradicts, albeit only for a limited period, the Second Law of Thermodynamics. This is the one where time's arrow points in only one direction, that is, toward the heat death of the universe. In physical terms an animate being is able, for the time of its (un)natural life, to stem the entropic tide, turning energy into itself. Such a definition could just as well apply to a tornado, however. Something more than this definition would seem to be required, therefore.

To the biochemist, life is the process whereby energy becomes matter, in all of its material complexity. Like little chemical factories, living entities develop and reproduce. But then, little chemical factories do likewise. So something more than this definition would seem warranted, as well.

To the (neo-Darwinian) biologist, life is basically genes, and genetic mutation, and the natural selection of the most "fit." Central to the selection process is competition between organisms for the opportunity to reproduce, and though all life on earth is observed to do this, the earth as a whole does not. To some biologists, as noted earlier, this automatically precludes the Gaia hypothesis, for otherwise "there would have to be a set of rival Gaias, presumably on different planets." There would have to be reproduction, too, with those planets that fail to achieve what the Earth has achieved being those deemed extinct (Dawkins, 1982, 236).

To Lovelock himself, life happens at some point on the "hierarchy of intensity" from rock to Ralph. The "only difference between non-living and living systems" he argues "is in the scale of their intricacy," a distinction that becomes harder to make all the time as the "complexity and capacity" of such systems grows (Lovelock, 1987 [1979], 62). In his mind there is no clear line between what lives and what does not (Lovelock, 1995, 39). We know that there is life because it exists planet wide, lasts for cosmological eons, and can even create the conditions for its own continuance. We know that a line exists between life and non-life, too. We do not know where to draw that line, though, so as to define the one clearly apart from the other.

Twist and turn as he might, then, Lovelock does believe that the earth is alive. It may not be alive in the same way the ancient Greeks believed that Gaia, their earth goddess, was alive (Allaby, 1989, 5; Joseph, 1990, 223–30). But Lovelock does think that the earth is alive like a tree is alive, which is mostly dead wood, but has systems that allow it to take in energy across its perimeters, give back waste, grow, and reproduce (Lovelock, 1991a, 12). He calls Gaia "protolife" (Lovelock, 1987 [1979], 62) and likens it to a beehive or a coral reef or a whole forest. These are not sentient entities, however, they are intelligent entities in the sense that they can give the "correct answer to at least one question" (Lovelock, 1987 [1979], 146). They metabolize, evolve, keep their temperature and chemical balances constant, heal themselves, and even, despite what the neo-Darwinists say, reproduce. If human beings are able to render another planet habitable (by terra-forming Mars perhaps) then Gaia will have demonstrably sown its seeds elsewhere (Lovelock, 1991a, 31; Dawkins, 1982, 236).

In reviewing these assertions it becomes clear that the Gaia hypothesis is, indeed, a range of hypotheses now, not just one, and that these hypotheses make a number of rather different claims (Kirchner, 1991, 38). As the relatively weak idea that life on earth has a substantial influence on the composition and temperature of the atmosphere, or that life affects the environment, or that the environment constrains life by Darwinian means, the Gaia hypothesis is scientifically unexceptional. As the rather stronger idea that this coevolutionary interplay is characterized by homeostatic control systems, that is, by "stabilizing negative feedback loops" (Kirchner, 1991, 38), the Gaia hypothesis is more debatable. It remains plausible, however, as Lovelock's computer model of this process (Daisyworld) tries to show. Systemic stability is achieved in this model, while self-regulation emerges at a whole planetary level, from no more than natural selection operating on living parts (Lenton, 1998, 430–40). There are alternatives to Daisyworld, like Lupineworld, that result in systemic destabilization. The computer program test is not conclusive, then (Harte, 1991, 79). As the stronger idea again that the earth's control systems work purposefully for the biosphere's benefit, or that self-regulation is somehow inherent, the Gaia hypothesis is much more contentious. It is plausible even in this form, however, especially when it is argued that "purpose" might emerge as the property of a whole system itself. Most contentious of all is the idea that the biosphere manipulates the environment, not only to its own good, but also to its optimal good. Here the concept of emergent outcome strains the limits of scientific plausibility, some would say beyond all reasonable bounds.

The sticking point for modernist/Rationalists seems to be Lovelock's personal experience of the biosphere as a resourceful whole. They see this as imputing too much volition to things that do not have it.

When a physical chemist like Lovelock articulates his intuition that the whole earth is life-like, however, he is arguably doing no more than a biologist like McClintock does, when she says that she "listens" to her research material, "feeling for the organism" as a way to understand the complex forms of order that make it work, and then wins the Nobel Prize (Keller, 1985, 162, 165, 171). He is arguably doing no more than Salk, the bio-philosopher, does, when he imagines himself as a virus or as the human immune system, or sees himself dialoguing with nature by asking "it" questions in the form of experiments (Salk, 1983, 7). And he is arguably doing no more than an analyst like Duve does, when he talks of "vital dust" (Duve, 1995).

As Rationalists, modernists reject the emotions Lovelock expresses with regard to the English countryside, and with regard to his idea of reverting to star-stuff once he dies. They also dismiss McClintock's talk of being part of the biological system "right down there," where everything gets "big," and she can forget herself among her chromosomal friends to such an extent that they seem to become part of her (Keller, 1985, 165). And they are similarly dismissive of Salk, asking what he would do if he were a cancer cell (Salk, 1983, 7), or of Duve talking about cosmic matter as "awesome" (Duve, 1995). None of these people are talking about physics or chemistry or biology or physiology in a Rationalistic way. They are talking about other ways of knowing the world, non-Rationalist ways, and even anti-Rationalist ways. To Rationalists, however, these ways of knowing the world are not only radically different, they are also radically less likely to tell us what is true.

We know from the way the brain works that a feel for the world is necessary to know what is real about the world (Damasio, 2000, ch. 2, 1994). Someone whose brain is damaged, for example, who sees their mother but is unable to feel the requisite emotions, will think that their mother is a stranger impersonating their mother (Ramachandran and Blakeslee, 1999, ch. 8). Rational recognition alone is not enough, therefore. The requisite emotion is necessary to know what is real, since it is not only emotion that can result in illusion, rational recognition can too.

In a similar vein, there is support for using both Rationalist/objectifying and non-Rationalist/subjectifying ways to know how the environment works, and good reason to think that one result of doing so might be a better appreciation of what Gaia means. Impersonally appreciating the way an organism and its environment make a single field may not be enough, that is. It may require personal appreciation of Gaia's singularity, and a willingness to forego the carefully nurtured distinction between "matter, life and mind" (Lannoy, 1975, 272–4).

Margulis argues that "[a]t this late date" we can probably "shed our Cartesian mechanistic legacy at no risk to our scientific credibility" (Margulis and Sagan, 1997, 183). In line with the argument earlier, she seems to imply that if we complement our reason with other ways to know, we get not only a more comprehensive account of reality, but a more accurate and reliable one as well (Spretnak, 1986, 28–9).

Once more, we are probing the constraints set by Rationalism itself, though in this case, we may also be probing what these constraints might mean for the future of humankind. "Have we the intelligence" Margulis asks "to resist our tendency to grow without limit?" Can we recognize that: "We cannot put an end to nature; we can only pose a threat to ourselves" (Margulis, 1998, 161)?

Here human suffering is being put in the context of the planet as a whole. Lovelock debated this very issue with Mother Teresa at the Global Forum for Survival in 1988. He argued that our primary duty is to respond to general problems like overpopulation and deforestation. She argued that our primary duty is to respond to each other, and to each particular instance of human suffering (Joseph, 1990, 242). Lovelock was arguing as an Animist, while Mother Teresa was arguing as a Christian. Her position is a familiar one to those who practice contemporary world affairs, since it is a sacral conclusion that animates a wide range of global political and economic practices. What of Lovelock's Animistic insights, however? What do these have to offer the contemporary exponent of world affairs?

Basically, contemporary Animism highlights a key aspect of the discipline that has heretofore been marginalized. For human beings to survive, even in the short term, their effect on the planet as a whole has to be one that the earth can sustain. The natural environment must be one that supports human life in particular, not just planetary life as a whole, or there will be no human life, and there will be no global politics. And though acknowledging the importance of environmental concerns may not depend on the experience of Animism, Animist experiences do make such an acknowledgment much more compelling.

The extent to which global eco-crisis is a reality remains debatable, but Lovelock's feeling for the world as an organism suggests, to him, that "bad farming" (Lovelock, 1995, 168), deforestation, and industrial mono-cropping techniques, are causing global warming. He also sees the human consequences of allowing these techniques to spread to be serious—even terminal—for some or all of the human species. Insights like these heighten our awareness of the practices and processes that transcend the territorialized basis of global welfare. They also prompt a more internationalist, if not globalist, response to them.

A feeling for the world as one organism also prompts us to confront the capitalist nature of world production, and particularly the growth-based character of the liberal, free-market version of it. It provides a reason for re-examining the case for "steady-state" economics as an eco-viable planetary alternative (Daly, 1985). Perhaps, as Midgley says, "the profitable exchange of goods within the ship is a less urgent matter than how to keep the whole ship above water" (Midgley, 2001, 29). Since the free-market price of the ecological processes that sustain life itself are arguably not ones we can sensibly calculate (Lovelock, 1995, 225), this may not be a matter for the market alone.

A feeling for the world as one organism also highlights the individualist nature of personal identity on a global scale, as well as of nationalist and collectivist alternatives to it. It gives us a compelling reason to consider what planetary citizenship entails. Global citizenship as a concept is highly abstract. Our impact on the earth's ecology, however, forces us to think about what this means, who we are, and what we are doing. It confronts us with less species-centric alternatives to global ecology, and the need to develop a more sympathetic approach to the condition of the earth as a whole, one where we and it become "indivisible" (Midgley, 2001, 8).

A feeling for the world as one organism also highlights the bourgeois basis to global warming and the like, in as much as these environmental problems are not so much the responsibility of the world's workers, as of the world's owning and managing classes, who plan and run the productions systems that accumulate capital with little regard for ecological consequence. It gives us a compelling reason to look once more at whether a world of advanced communist societies, highly democratic, technologically sophisticated, and small in scale, would not be the one we should ultimately prefer.

A feeling for the world as one organism also highlights the male-made nature of the planet's ecological problems. This is a point put forcefully, but not exclusively, by Pagan feminists. It provides us with another compelling reason to confront the gendering practices that underlie all world affairs.

A feeling for the world as one organism is a feeling many indigenous peoples understand as well. Which is why the Rationalist move from humanism to Animism, even a scientized form of Animism, is one that often seems consistent with their own beliefs, and one they endorse. Einstein once said that "science without religion is lame, religion without science is blind" (Einstein, 1940, 605). Many indigenous peoples would disagree. They would argue that science without religion is blind, and that science proceeds only in the context of religious belief. As it happens, Einstein did not even agree with himself. He did not see science as lame without religion. Rather, he saw it as transcending personal hopes and desires. He saw it as leading to reverence for that in which reason inheres, and as spiritualizing our understanding of life (Einstein, 1940, 607).

A science with such a sacral impetus sounds like a Rationalist version of Animism, however. Tylor would be pleased.

Conclusion

A World Affairs for All the World

I knew nothing, and I persisted in the faith that the time of cruel miracles was not past.

— *Stanislaw Lem,* Solaris

Modernists articulate world affairs in a range of analytic languages, the most common of which are the realist, liberalist, individualist, materialist, and masculinist ones. Being modernist, all such languages are Rationalist, and being Rationalist, they bear the marks of their origins within European Christendom.

As the doctrines such languages espouse impinge worldwide, questions arise not only about what they say, but also about what they do not say. The same applies to the modernist project itself. It is becoming notably more apparent, that is, that the Rationalist epistemology the modernist project articulates sets limits to and distorts what can be known in this particular way. It is also becoming apparent that to transgress these limits, and to compensate for such distortions, the whole project needs to be located in non-modernist contexts, and in non-Christian ones as well.

This book began by systematically mapping the modernist project as it pertains to world affairs. It then attempted to deal with the shortcomings of this project, initially by subjectifying it.

It then went on to explore the terms set by communalist alternatives. Examining the world politics of world heritage, for example, provided an opportunity to show how the modernist concept of the human past, as a dead place of tangible products, is radically at odds with communalist conceptions of the human past, as a living process involving intangible practices. When modernist world affairs are brought to bear on heritage concerns, they result in reified conceptions of what humanity ought to bequeath. Establishing the priority of such conceptions is not cost-free, however. It comes at the expense of how human heritage might otherwise be conceptualized, for example, in non-reified terms, and while the assumptions that modernists and non-modernists make are incommensurable, allowing for both does make for a more cosmopolitan analysis of world affairs, and more diverse policy proposals.

This book subsequently explored the terms set by sacralist alternatives. Modernist states, markets, and civil societies, as well as modernist forms of class rule, value construction, gendering practice, and planetary sustainability, were discussed from Taoist, Buddhist, Muslim, Confucian, Hindu, Pagan, and Animist perspectives respectively. The argument was made that greater recognition of a range of sacral alternatives cannot fail to augment both the contemporary study of world affairs and the policy options available to practitioners, regardless of the incommensurability of the assumptions these alternatives entail.

Rationalists tend to reject both communalist and sacralist alternatives. They do not accept the challenge that either one represents, in part because of the stake they have in the discipline's epistemological status quo, and in part because of a sincere conviction that there has been epistemological progress, that Rationalism represents a high point in human achievement, and that the task ahead is to hold to these heights and to lift everyone else to them. They see any support for non-Rationalist knowing as compromising the theoretical integrity they have fought long and hard for, and as muddying the mind's waters in ways Rationalism alone can clarify.

Taking seriously insights from thought-worlds other than the Rationalist one does not necessarily mean abandoning the modernist search for analytic clarity, however. Putting modernist thinking in context makes it possible to pay greater deference to global human difference, and to highlight the contribution non- and antimodernist analyses can make. And while the incommensurability of the assumptions concerned does not help, moving through the cycle of knowing that these alternatives present allows ways of thinking to emerge different from those that limit and distort the modernist approach. A new and more inclusive form of world affairs emerges too.

The insights articulated by communalists are especially telling in this regard. Communalists directly contest the objectifying mind-gaze upon which modernity is based. This was exemplified by an account of the world debate about what constitutes world heritage, and more especially, by an account of the attempt made to include intangible practices as well as tangible products there.

The insights articulated by sacralists are telling too. Sacralists contest much more than the Rationalist mind-gaze. How much more was exemplified by a discussion of Taoist notions of non-action, Buddhist notions of right livelihood, Islamic notions of sacral mindfulness, Confucian notions of moral leadership, Hindu notions of the ground of all being, Pagan notions of achievable peace, and Animist notions of a living world.

Fukuyama once argued that modernist, and particularly liberalist, world affairs are the best of all possible world affairs. He saw the end of the Cold War as an end to all history, in the sense that this was the point at which Euro-American ("Western") liberalism could be said to have won (Fukuyama, 1992). He believed that this was the moment at which, after a protracted struggle, Euro-American liberals had achieved their final triumph, and were free to make the world over in democratic, liberal capitalist, internationalist terms. Because of this triumph there was no more left to do than to mop up. "[R]etrograde" areas, that still resist, might still have to be the focus of "rearguard" actions, Fukuyama said, while societies centered on diverse forms of "traditional existence" might still have to be subjected to modernist siege. But the strength of any backlash would merely be a measure of the significance of the overall victory. In his eyes, resistance would only be further evidence of the extent of Rationalist, liberalist success (Fukuyama, 2001, 21).

Huntington was similarly convinced of modernity's superiority, though he was not as convinced as Fukuyama that the global preponderance of modernist ways of living would last. Indeed, he saw this preponderance as already threatened by other thought worlds, some of which he defined in sacralist terms. Contra Fukuyama, Huntington posited a clash of "civilizations." In his view the "West" was far from destined to prevail. He saw it as continuing to compete against six or seven other major cultural entities (Huntington, 1993), which coexist with the "West." Far from having prevailed, the West had to keep struggling, he said. It had to circle its politico-strategic wagons if it wanted to prevent its preferred ways of knowing and being from being destroyed. And though in later accounts Huntington did begin to express views that allowed for a degree of inter-civilizational interaction (Huntington, 1996), the power political character of his vision of intercivilizational competition remained undimmed.

Contra both Fukuyama and Huntington, we have Dallmayr, who is much more equivocal about modernity's achievements, and much more concerned to highlight the ongoing significance of the ongoing dialogue between different global thought worlds (Dallmayr, 2002). Neither triumphant nor trepidated, Dallmayr thinks that the leading proponents of contemporary world affairs should appreciate the political potential that global difference provides, and act accordingly.

This book is in the Dallmayr tradition. It argues for a world affairs discipline worthy of the name, and a discipline that considers, as a matter of course, what all those who live in the world believe to be important there. This does not mean endorsing uncritically all of the world's ways of thinking and behaving, or every aspect of every way. After all, the modernist approach does oblige us at some point to objectify, and to exercise the critical judgment Rationalism requires. A world affairs worthy of the name does mean listening to communalist and sacralist attempts to account for world affairs, however, and does mean being prepared to entertain some at least of the attempts to craft world affairs with regard to what gets heard in these particular ways. It repudiates the imposition, whether by force, persuasion, or the setting of agendas, of any single set of ideas about the subject, including Rationalist/Christian ones. And it values human difference, without eschewing unity-in-diversity (which is the common ground we construct in the light of what we find universally to be true).

From this perspective, "world affairs" represents what it has always arguably represented, namely, global learning. Sometimes violent, though most of the time not, this process, whereby the world's peoples teach each other what they continue to learn about themselves, is a perennial and a pervasive one. It is also a process currently dominated by modernist Euro-Americans, who are wont to assume that their particular accounts of world affairs apply always and everywhere to everybody else. This assumption is ethnocentric, often inappropriate, and sometimes extremely dangerous. Most of the peoples on this planet contest many of these accounts, and usually for good reason. Euro-Americans fail in the main to hear these voices, or fail to consider them seriously enough to learn what they have to say about the worst the "West" can currently do. That is to eschew global learning to highly parochial effect, however, since it is one thing to grow up in a Rationalist culture, and to look at other cultures in the objectifying mental light that makes our mental windows into mirrors (Ames and Rosemont, 1998, x). It is quite another to modify this light so that the mind is able to pass through the glass into the worlds beyond.

As modernists "we" are familiar with Euro-American accounts of world affairs, with the particular concept of modernity that underpins these accounts, and with the "civilising mission" that modernity represents (Gong, 1984; Paris, 2002). "We" are also more familiar than "we" were once with the views of those whom modernists put on their putative margins, like feminists, the poor, indigenous peoples, postcolonials, and environmentalists.

"We" are still relatively unfamiliar, however, with accounts of modernist world affairs that articulate non-modernist perspectives. And "we" are least familiar of all with attempts to articulate antimodernist accounts of the "vastest things" that contemporary world affairs represent (Peake, 1975, 40).

Modernists tend to respond by saying that world politics is simply not about such things. They say it is about issues of war and peace, world production and consumption, global identity and self-realization. It is not about living or dying *per se*, or questions like how to burn with love. Nor is it about communalist ideas of cultural-purpose, or sacralist ideas about spiritual meaning.

World politics is far-reaching, however, and the longer the subject is studied, the better that begins to be understood. Which is why the old International Relations discipline is now defunct. This is not to say that the old discipline is no longer relevant, and no longer studied. It is to say that the discipline can no longer be preoccupied with issues of a politico-strategic nature only. There is a new International Relations now, which not only encompasses all the old military and diplomatic concerns, but encompasses politico-economic and politico-social, materialist and mentalist, feminist and environmentalist, and communalist and sacralist ones as well.

What might mastery of such a far-reaching subject mean? Peake thinks it is "pitiful" how modernists seem obliged to keep returning to those few things they can predict and control (Peake, 1975, 40). As a poet he tries to provide a more subjectifying account. More radically, Milbank sees Rationalist discourse articulating an "'ontology of violence,'" that places a "priority" on "force." This makes "counter-force" the only alternative (Milbank, 1990, 2), which is why Milbank himself advocates a return to

Rationalism's Christian roots. Christianity represents neither "original violence" nor infinite "chaos," he says, promoting instead "harmonic peace," and a profound respect for the *"sociality* of . . . . difference" (Milbank, 1990, 5). What of the analytic and policy significance of non-modernist and non-Christian thought worlds, then? A profound respect for "difference" cannot mean the preponderance of Christianity only, despite its promise of "harmonic peace." Nor can it mean the preponderance of Rationalism only, despite the explanatory and predictive power of the "metaphysics of presence" that Rationalism so powerfully promotes (Zizek, 2000, 101).

It can only mean respect for non-Rationalist, non-Christian ways of knowing as well as Rationalist/Christian ones. It can only mean a study of all the world (and not one globalizing part of it), in all of the ways in which that world is known (and giving those ways their due).

This is a world affairs for all the world. This is a world affairs worthy of the name. This is world politics.

References

Abe, Masao (1985) *Zen and Western Thought* (University of Hawaii, Honolulu).
Adler, Margot (1986) *Drawing Down the Moon: Witches, Druids, Goddess Worshippers, and other Pagans in America Today*, rev. ed. (Penguin/Arkana, Harmondsworth).
Adorno, Theodor (1973) *Negative Dialectics*, trans. E. Ashton (Seabury Press, New York).
Affifi, A. (1958) "The Rational and Mystical Interpretations of Islam" in Kenneth Morgan (ed.) *Islam—The Straight Path* (The Ronald Press, New York).
Agar, Nicholas (2001) *Life's Intrinsic Value: Science, Ethics, and Nature* (Columbia University Press, New York).
Agency for Cultural Affairs (2001) *Protection of Intangible Cultural Heritage in Japan*, Government of Japan.
Ahmed, Akbar (1992) *Postmodernism and Islam: Predicament and Promise* (Routledge, London).
Aikawa, Noriko (1999a) "The 1989 UNESCO Recommendation: Aims and Impact" in the *Symposium on the Protection of Traditional Knowledge and Expressions of Indigenous Culture in the Pacific Islands* (Secretariat of the Pacific Community and UNESCO, Noumea, February 15–16), Technical Paper No. 215.
—— (1999b) "The UNESCO Recommendation on the Safeguarding of Traditional Culture and Folklore (1989)—Actions Undertaken by UNESCO for its Implementation," *A Global Assessment of the 1989 Recommendation on the Safeguarding of Traditional Culture and Folklore: Local Empowerment and International Cooperation*, Washington, June 27–30 (UNESCO/Smithsonian Institution Centre for Folklife and Cultural Heritage).
Allaby, Michael (1989) *Guide to Gaia* (Optima, London).
Allen, Charlotte (1999) "Confucius and the Scholars," The Atlantic Monthly, http://www.theatlantic.com/issues/99apr/9904confucius.htm.
Ames, Roger (1994) *The Art of Rulership: A Study of Chinese Political Thought* (State University of New York Press, Albany).
—— and Rosemont, Henry (1998) *The Analects of Confucius: A Philosophical Translation* (Ballantine Books, New York).
Amoako-Atta, Boakye (1995) "Sacred Groves in Ghana" in Bernd von Droste et al. (eds.) *Cultural Landscapes of Universal Value* (Gustav Fischer Verlag, Stuttgart).
Anderson, Benedict (1991) *Imagined Communities: Reflections on the Origin and Spread of Nationalism*, rev. ed. (Verso, London).
Andreski, Stanislav (ed.) (1974 [1842]) *The Essential Comte: Selected from Cours de Philosophie Positive* (Croom Helm, London).
Angel, Leonard (1994) *Enlightenment East and West* (State University of New York, Albany).
Anikeer, Nikolai (1969) *Modern Ideological Struggle for the Ancient Philosophical Heritage of India* (Manish Granthalaya, Calcutta).
Ann, Martha and Imel, Dorothy (1993) *Goddesses in World Mythology* (ABC-Clio, Santa Barbara).

Arberry, A.J. (1950) *Sufism: An Account of the Mystics of Islam* (George Allen and Unwin, London).

—— (1957) *Revelation and Reason in Islam* (George Allen and Unwin, London).

—— (1968) *Mystical Poems of Rumi: First Selection, Poems 1–200* (The University of Chicago Press, Chicago).

—— (1979) *Mystical Poems of Rumi: Second Selection, Poems 201–400* (Westview Press, Boulder).

Arnold, Daniel (1998) "Mapping the Middle Way: Thoughts on a Buddhist Contribution to a Feminist Discussion," *Journal of Feminist Studies in Religion*, v. 14 no. 1 (Spring) pp. 63–84.

Aron, Raymond (1966) *Peace and War: A Theory of International Relations* (Doubleday, New York).

Asad, Muhammad (1984) *The Message of the Qur'an* (Dar Al-Andalus, Gibraltar).

Ayubi, Nazih (1991) *Political Islam: Religion and Politics in the Arab World* (Routledge, London).

Badcock, Christopher (2000) *Evolutionary Psychology: A Critical Introduction* (Polity, Cambridge).

Baker, Nicola and Sebastian, Leonard (1996) "The Problems with Parachuting: Strategic Studies and Security in the Asia/Pacific Region" in Desmond Ball, (ed.) *The Transformation of Security in the Asia/Pacific Region* (Frank Cass, London).

Baring, Anne and Cashford, Jules (1991) *The Myth of the Goddess: Evolution of an Image* (Viking Arkana, London).

Barnett, William (1992) review of Marija Gimbutas, *The Language of the Goddess* in *American Journal of Archaeology*, v. 96, pp. 170–1.

Barnhill, David and Gottlieb, Roger (eds.) (2001) *Deep Ecology and World Religions: New Essays on Sacred Grounds* (State University of New York Press, Albany).

Batchelor, Stephen (1990) "Buddhist Economics Reconsidered" in Allan Badiner (ed.) *Dharma Gaia: A Harvest of Essays in Buddhism and Ecology* (Parallax Press, Berkeley).

Batten, Juliet (1995) *Celebrating the Southern Seasons: Rituals for Aotearoa* (Tandem Press, North Shore City).

Beasley, W.G. and Pulleybank, E.G. (1961) *Historians of China and Japan* (Oxford University Press, London).

Benard, Elisabeth and Moon, Beverly (eds.) (2000) *Goddesses who Rule* (Oxford University Press, New York).

Bending, Tim (2002) "Power Versus Love: The Production and Overcoming of Hierarchic Repression," *Alternatives*, v. 27 no. 1 (Jan.–March) pp. 117–42.

Bennett, Tony (1995) *The Birth of the Museum: History, Theory, Politics* (Routledge, London).

Biardeau, Madelaine (1989) *Hinduism, the Anthropology of a Civilization* (Oxford University Press, Delhi).

Blake, Janet (1999) "Safeguarding Traditional Culture and Folklore: Existing International Law and future Developments," *A Global Assessment of the 1989 Recommendation on the Safeguarding of Traditional Culture and Folklore: Local Empowerment and International Cooperation*, Washington, June 27–30 (UNESCO/Smithsonian Institution Centre for Folklife and Cultural Heritage).

—— (2000) "On Defining the Cultural Heritage," *International and Comparative Law Quarterly*, v. 49 part 1 (January), pp. 61–85.

——— (2001) *Preliminary Study into the Advisability of Developing a New Standard-setting Instrument for the Safeguarding of Intangible Cultural Heritage ("Traditional Culture and Folklore").*

Bodian, Stephan (1995) "Simple in Means, Rich in Ends: An Interview with Arne Naess" in George Sessions (ed.) *Deep Ecology for the Twenty-first Century* (Shambhala, Boston).

Bohm, David and Hiley, B.J. (1993) *The Undivided Universe: An Ontological Interpretation of Quantum Theory* (Routledge, London).

Bolle, Kees (1987) "Animism and Animatism" in Mircea Eliade (ed.) *The Encyclopedia of Religion*, v. 1 (Macmillan Publishing Company, New York).

Boucher, David (1998) *Political Theories of International Relations* (Oxford University Press, Oxford).

Boulter, Michael (2002) *Extinction: Evolution and the End of Man* (Fourth Estate, London).

Boyer, Pascal (1994) *The Naturalness of Religious Ideas: A Cognitive Theory of Religion* (University of California Press, Berkeley).

——— (2001) *Religion Explained: The Evolutionary Origins of Religious Thought* (Basic Books, New York).

Brooks, E. Bruce and Brooks, A. Takeo (1997) *The Original Analects: Sayings of Confucius and his Successors, 0479-0249* (Columbia University Press, New York).

Brown, Chris (1997) *Understanding International Relations* (Macmillan, Basingstoke).

Bryson, Bill (2003) *A Short History of Nearly Everything* (Doubleday, London).

Bubna-Litic, David (1998) "Buddhist Ethics and Business Strategy Making" in Damien Keown et al. (eds.) *Buddhism and Human Rights* (Curzon, Richmond).

——— (2000) "Buddhism Returns to the Market Place" in Damien Keown (ed.) *Contemporary Buddhist Ethics* (Curzon, Richmond).

Budapest, Zsuzsanna (1989) *The Holy Book of Women's Mysteries* (Wingbow Press, Oakland).

Buddha (1959 [100 B.C.E.]) "Setting in Motion the Wheel of Truth (The First Sermon of the Buddha)" in Walpola Rahula, *What the Buddha Taught* (Grove Press, New York).

Buddhadasa, Bhikkhu (1989) *Me and Mine* (State University of New York Press, Albany).

Bugotu, Frances (1976) "Decolonizing and Recolonizing: The Case of the Solomon Islands" in Ron Moody (ed.) *The Indigenous Voice: Visions and Realities*, 2nd ed. (International Books, Utrecht).

Bull, Hedley (1966) "International Theory: The Case for a Classical Approach," *World Politics*, v. 18, pp. 361–77.

——— (1977) *The Anarchical Society: A Study of Order in World Politics* (Macmillan, London).

——— and Watson, Adam (eds.) (1984) *The Expansion of International Society* (Clarendon, Oxford).

Bull, Malcolm (1999) *Seeing Things Hidden: Apocalypse, Vision and Totality* (Verso, London).

Bunkazai hogo-bu, Bunka-cho, Monbusho [Department of Cultural Assets Protection, Agency for Cultural Affairs, Ministry of Education, Science, Sports and Culture] (Heisei 12 nendo [2000]), *Wagakuni no Bunkazai-hogoshisaku no gaiyo* [An Overview of Japan's Policies on the Protection of Cultural Properties] (Tokyo).

Burchill, Scott et al. (eds.) (2001) *Theories of International Relations*, 2nd ed. (Palgrave, Basingstoke).

Burkitt, Brian (1984) *Radical Political Economy: An Introduction to Alternative Economics* (Harvester Press, Brighton).

Burton, John (1968) *Systems, States, Diplomacy and Rules* (Cambridge University Press, Cambridge).

Bynner, Witter (1972 [1944]) *The Way of Life: According to Lao Tzu* (Berkeley Publishing Group, New York).

Cairo Declaration on Human Rights in Islam (1990).

Campbell, David (1992) *Writing Security: United States Foreign Policy and the Policies of Identity* (Manchester University Press, Manchester).

Carr, E.H. (1991 [1939]) *The Twenty Years' Crisis 1919–1939: An Introduction to the Study of International Relations* (Macmillan, London).

Carroll, Berenice (1972) "Peace Research: The Cult of Power," *Journal of Peace Research*, v. 16 no. 4, pp. 585–616.

Carse, James (1986) *Finite and Infinite Games* (Penguin, Harmondsworth).

Cavalli-Sforza, L. Luca (1997) "Genetic Evidence Supporting Marija Gimbutas' Work on the Origins of Indo-European People" in Joan Marler (ed.) *From the Realm of the Ancestors: An Anthology in Honor of Marija Gimbutas* (Knowledge, Ideas and Trends, Inc., Manchester CT).

Cavalli-Sforza, Luigi, Menozzi, Paolo, and Piazza, Alberto (1993) "Demic Expansions and Human Evolution," *Science*, v. 259 (January 29) pp. 639–46.

Chamberlin, T. (1890) "The Method of Multiple Working Hypotheses," *Science*, v. 15 no. 366, pp. 92–6.

Chan, Stephen et al. (eds.) (2001) *The Zen of International Relations: IR Theory from East to West* (Palgrave, Houndmills).

Chan, Wing-tsit et al. (1969) *The Great Asian Religions: An Anthology* (The Macmillan Company, Toronto).

Chaplin, Charlie (1978 [1936]) *Modern Times* (videorecording) (Magnetic Video, Michigan).

Christ, Carol (1996a) "Introduction: The Legacy of Marija Gimbutas," *Journal of Feminist Studies in Religion*, v. 12 no. 2 (Fall) pp. 31–5.

—— (1996b) " 'A Different World': The Challenge of the World of Marija Gimbutas to the Dominant World-view of Western Cultures," *Journal of Feminist Studies in Religion*, v. 12 no. 2 (Fall) pp. 53–64.

Cleere, Henry (1995) "The Evaluation of Cultural Landscapes: The Role of ICOMOS" in Bernd von Droste et al. (eds.) *Cultural Landscapes of Universal Value* (Gustav Fischer Verlag, Stuttgart).

Coakley, Sarah (2002) *Powers and Submissions: Spirituality, Philosophy and Gender* (Blackwell, Oxford).

Cohn, Carol (1987) "Sex and Death in the Rational World of Defense Intellectuals," *Signs*, v. 12 no. 4, pp. 687–718.

Convention Concerning the Protection of the World Cultural and Natural Heritage, November 16, 1972.

Conze, Edward (1962) *Buddhist Thought in India: Three Phases of Buddhist Philosophy* (George Allen and Unwin Ltd., London).

Cooper, John et al. (eds.) (2000) *Islam and Modernity: Muslim Intellectuals Respond* (I.B. Taurus, London).

Cosmides, Lena et al. (1995) "Introduction: Evolutionary Psychology and Conceptual Integration" in Jerome Barkow et al. (eds.) *The Adapted Mind: Evolutionary Psychology and the Generation of Culture* (Oxford University Press, New York).

Cottingham, John (1984) *Rationalism* (Paladin, London).

Cox, Robert (1987) *Production, Power and World Order: Social Forces in the Making of History* (Columbia University Press, New York).

Creel, Herrlee (1949) *Confucius and the Chinese Way* (Harper and Row, New York).

—— (1970) *What is Taoism? And Other Studies in Chinese Cultural History* (The University of Chicago Press, Chicago).

Dallmayr, Fred (2002) *Dialogue Civilizations: Some Exemplary Voices* (Palgrave Macmillan, New York).

Daly, Herman (1985) "Economics and Sustainability: In Defense of a Steady-state Economy" in Michael Tobias (ed.) *Deep Ecology* (Avant Books, San Diego).

Daly, Mary (1979) "Why Speak about God?" in Carol Christ and Judith Plaskow (eds.) *Womanspirit Rising: A Feminist Reader in Religion* (Harper and Row, San Francisco).

—— (1986) *Beyond God the Father* (The Women's Press, London).

Damasio, Antonio (1994) *Descartes' Error: Emotion, Reason and the Human Brain* (G.P. Putnam's Sons, New York).

—— (2000) *The Feeling of What Happens: Body, Emotion and the Making of Consciousness* (Vintage, London).

Darby, Phillip (1997) *At the Edge of International Relations: Postcolonialism, Gender and Dependency* (Pinter, London).

Dark, K.R. (ed.) (2000) *Religion and International Relations* (Palgrave, Houndmills).

Davidson, Donald (1984 [1974]) "On the Very Idea of a Conceptual Scheme" in his *Inquiries into Truth and Interpretation* (Clarendon Press, Oxford).

Dawkins, Richard (1982) *The Extended Phenotype: The Gene as the Unit of Selection* (W.H. Freeman and Company, Oxford).

Dawson, Miles (1915) *The Ethics of Confucius: The Sayings of the Master and his Disciples Upon the Conduct of "the Superior Man"* (G.P Putnam's Sons, New York).

de Bary, Wm. Theodore (1981) *Neo-Confucian Orthodoxy and the Learning of the Mind-and-Heart* (Columbia University Press, New York).

de Bary, Wm. Theodore et al. (1988) *Sources of Indian Tradition* (Motilal Banarsidass, Delhi).

Deleuze, Gilles and Guattari, Felix (1987) *A Thousand Plateaux: Capitalism and Schizophrenia*, trans. Brian Massumi (Athlone Press, London).

Devetak, Richard (1995) "The Project of Modernity and International Relations Theory," *Millennium*, v. 24 no. 1, pp. 27–51.

Diamond, Jared (1998) *Guns, Germs and Steel: A Short History of Everybody for the Last 13,000 Years* (Vintage, London).

Dirlik, Arif (1994a) "The Postcolonial Aura: Third World Criticism in the Age of Global Capitalism," *Critical Inquiry*, v. 20 (Winter) pp. 328–56.

—— (1994b) *After the Revolution: Waking to Global Capitalism* (Wesleyan University Press, Hanover).

—— (1995) "Confucius in the Borderlands: Global Capitalism and the Reinvention of Confucianism," *boundary 2*, v. 22 no. 3 (Fall).

Dupont, Alan (1995) "Concepts of Security" in Jim Rolfe, (ed.) *Unresolved Futures: Comprehensive Security in the Asia-Pacific* (Centre for Strategic Studies, Wellington).

Dussel, Enrique (1998) "Beyond Eurocentrism: The World-system and the Limits of Modernity" in Frederic Jameson and Masao Miyoshi (eds.) *The Cultures of Globalization* (Duke University Press, Durham).

Duve, Christian de (1995) *Vital Dust: The Origin and Evolution of Life on Earth* (Basic Books, New York).

Eagleton, Terry (1999) "Self-realization, Ethics and Socialism," *New Left Review*, no. 237 (September/October) pp. 150–61.

Eck, Diana (1981) *Darsan: Seeing the Divine Image in India* (Anima Books, Chamberburg).

Edkins, Jenny (1999) *Poststructuralism and International Relations: Bringing the Political Back in* (Lynne Rienner Publishers, Boulder).

Einstein, Albert (1940) "Science and Religion," *Nature*, v. 146 no. 3706 (November 9) pp. 605–7.

Eiseley, Loren (1988) "The Cosmic Orphan" in the *Propaedia* to *The New Encyclopaedia Britannica* (Chicago).

Eisenberg, Evan (1998) *The Ecology of Eden* (Alfred A. Knopf, New York).

Eisenstadt, S.N. (2000) "Multiple Modernities," *Daedalus*, v. 129 no. 1 (Winter) pp. 1–29.

Ernst, Carl (1997) *Sufism* (Shambhala Publications, Boston).

Esposito, John (1998) *Islam: The Straight Path*, 3rd ed. (Oxford University Press, New York).

Esteva, Gustavo and Prakash, Madhu (1998) *Grassroots Post-modernism: Remaking the Soil of Cultures* (Zed Books, London).

Farraq, Ahmad (1990) "Human Rights and Liberties in Islam" in Jan Berting et al. (eds.) *Human Rights in a Pluralist World: Individuals and Collectivities* (Meckler, Westport).

Fingarette, Herbert (1972) *Confucius—the Secular as Sacred* (Harper and Row, New York).

Finkelstein, David (2002) "The View from Beijing: U.S.–China Security Relations from Kosovo to September 11, 2001" in Andrew Scobel and Larry Wortzel, (eds.) *China's Growing Military Power: Perspectives on Security, Ballistic Missiles, and Conventional Capabilities* (Strategic Studies Institute, Carlisle).

Flood, Gavin (1996) *An Introduction to Hinduism* (Cambridge University Press, Cambridge).

Foucault, Michel (1994 [1966]) *The Order of Things: An Archaeology of the Human Sciences* (Routledge, London).

Fox, Jonathan (2001) "Religion as an Overlooked Element of International Relations", *International Studies Review*, v. 3 no. 3 (Fall) pp. 53–73.

Freeman, Michael (1995) "Are There Collective Human Rights?," *Political Studies*, v. 43, Special Issue, "Politics and Human Rights" (ed.) David Beetham, pp. 25–40.

Frykenberg, Robert (1991) "The Emergence of Modern 'Hinduism' as a Concept and as an Institution: A Reappraisal with Special Reference to South India" in Gunther Sontheimer and Hermann Kulke (eds.) *Hinduism Reconsidered* (Manohar, New Delhi).

Frymer-Kensky, Tikva (1992) *In the Wake of the Goddesses: Women, Culture, and the Biblical Transformation of Pagan Myth* (The Free Press, New York).

Fukuyama, Francis (1992) *The End of History and the Last Man* (Penguin, Harmondsworth).

——— (2001) "The West has Won" *The Guardian* (October 11) p. 21.

George, Jim (1994) *Discourses of Global Politics: A Critical (Re)introduction to International Relations* (Lynne Rienner Publishers, Boulder).

Geras, Norman (1983) *Marx and Human Nature: Refutation of a Legend* (Verso, London).

Gibson, Joan (1992) "Could Christ have been Born a Woman? A Medieval Debate," *Journal of Feminist Studies in Religion*, v. 8 no. 1 (Spring) pp. 65–82.

Giles, Herbert (1961 [1889]) trans., *Chuang Tzu: Taoist Philosopher and Chinese Mystic* (George Allen and Unwin, London).

Gill, Stephen (ed.) (1993) *Gramsci, Historical Materialism, and International Relations* (Cambridge University Press, Cambridge).

Gimbutas, Marija (1974) *The Gods and Goddesses of Old Europe: 7000 to 3500 BC, Myths, Legends and Cult Images* (Thames and Hudson, London).

—— (1982) "Women and Culture in Goddess-Oriented Old Europe" in Charlene Spretnak (ed.) *The Politics of Women's Spirituality: Essays on the Rise of Spiritual Power Within the Feminist Movement* (Anchor Books, New York).

—— (1989) *The Language of the Goddess* (Harper and Row, San Francisco).

—— (1991) *The Civilization of the Goddess: The World of Old Europe* (Harper, San Francisco).

—— (1999) *The Living Goddesses* (University of California Press, Berkeley).

Gilpin, Robert (1987) *The Political Economy of International Relations* (Princeton University Press, Princeton).

Godwin, William (1971 [1793]) *Enquiry Concerning Political Justice* (Clarendon Press, Oxford).

Gong, Gerrit (1984) *The Standard of "Civilization" in International Society* (Clarendon Press, Oxford).

Goodman, Steven (1994) "Transforming the Causes of Suffering" in Claude Whitmyer (ed.) *Mindfulness and Meaningful Work: Exploration in Right Livelihood* (Parallax Press, Berkeley).

Goody, Jacques (1993) "Safeguarding the Intangible Cultural Heritage," UNESCO International Consultation on New Perspectives for UNESCO's Programme: The Intangible Cultural Heritage, Paris, June 16–17.

Gould, Stephen (1991) *Bully for Brontosaurus; Reflections in Natural History* (W.W. Norton and Company, New York).

Graham, A.C. (1989) *Disputers of the Tao: Philosophical Argument in Ancient China* (Open Court, La Salle).

Gramsci, Antonio (1973) *Letters from Prison*, trans. Lynne Lawner (Harper and Row, New York).

Green, Ronald (1990) "Buddhist Economic Ethics: A Theoretical Approach" in Russell Sizemore and Donald Swearer (eds.) *Ethics, Wealth and Salvation: A Study in Buddhist Social Ethics* (University of South Carolina Press, Columbia).

Gross, Rita (1996) *Feminism and Religion: An Introduction* (Beacon Press, Boston).

Gruzinski, Serge (1993) "Protection of the Intangible Cultural Heritage: Survey and New Prospects," UNESCO International Consultation on New Perspectives for UNESCO's Programme: The Intangible Cultural Heritage, Paris, June 16–17.

Guthrie, Stewart (1993) *Faces in the Clouds* (Oxford University Press, New York).

Gupta, Akhil and Ferguson, James, (eds.) (1997) *Culture, Power, Place: Explorations in Critical Anthropology* (Duke University Press, Durham).

Gurnah, Ahmed (1997) "Elvis in Zanzibar" in Alan Scott (ed.) *The Limits of Globalization: Cases and Arguments* (Routledge, London).

Habermas, Jurgen (1978) *Knowledge and Human Interests*, trans. Jeremy Shapiro (Heinneman Educational, London).

Halbfass, Wilhelm (1988) *India and Europe: An Essay in Understanding* (State University of New York Press, Albany).

Hall, David and Ames, Roger (1987) *Thinking Through Confucius* (State University of New York Press, Albany).

Halliday, Fred (1995) "Relativism and Universalism in Human Rights: The Case of the Islamic Middle East," *Political Studies*, v. 43, Special Issue, "Politics and Human Rights" (ed.) David Beetham, pp. 152–67.

Hanh, Thich Nhat (1994) "The Art of Living" in Claude Whitmyer (ed.) *Mindfulness and Meaningful Work: Exploration in Right Livelihood* (Parallax Press, Berkeley).

Harding, Harry (1996) "A Chinese Colossus?" in Desmond Ball (ed.) *The Transformation of Security in the Asia/Pacific Region* (Frank Cass, London).

Harris, Ian (ed.) (1999) *Buddhism and Politics in Twentieth-century Asia* (Pinter, London).

Harte, John (1991) "Ecosystem Stability and Diversity" in Stephen Schneider and Penelope Boston (eds.) *Scientists on Gaia* (The MIT Press, Cambridge, Mass.).

Hayek, Friedrich (1991) *The Collected Works of F.A. Hayek* (ed.) William Bartley (University of Chicago Press, Chicago).

Heidegger, Martin (1977) *The Question Concerning Technology and Other Essays* (Harper Torchbooks, New York).

Heinemeijer, Willem (1990) "Islam and the Ideals of the Enlightenment" in Jan Berting et al. (eds.) *Human Rights in a Pluralist World: Individuals and Collectivities* (Meckler, Westport).

Heliotrope, Helen (1999) *God and Goddess in Conflict: The Argument for Modern Paganism* (Helen Heliotrope, Waikuku).

Hook, Glenn et al. (2001) *Japan's International Relations: Politics, Economics and Security* (Routledge, London).

Hooper-Greenhill, Eilean (ed.) (1995) *Museum, Media, Message* (Routledge, London).

Horkheimer, Max (1972) *Critical Theory: Selected Essays*, trans. Matthew O'Connell et al. (Herder and Herder, New York).

Horne, Donald (1984) *The Great Museum: The Re-presentation of History* (Pluto Press, London).

Hsiung, James Chieh (1970) *Ideology and Practice: The Evolution of Chinese Communism* (Praeger Publishers, New York).

Huang, Xiaoming (2001) "The Zen Master's Story and an Anatomy of International Relations Theory" in Stephen Chan et al. (eds.) *The Zen of International Relations: IR Theory from East to West* (Palgrave, Houndmills).

Hudson, Denneth (1975) *A Social History of Museums: What the Visitors Thought* (Macmillan, London).

Hunter, Anne (1992) "Numbering the Hairs of our Heads: Male Social Control and the All-seeing Male God," *Journal of Feminist Studies in Religion*, v. 8 no. 2 (Fall) pp. 7–26.

Huntington, Samuel (1993) "The Clash of Civilizations," *Foreign Affairs*, v. 72 no. 3, pp. 22–49.

—— (1996) *The Clash of Civilizations and the Remaking of World Order* (Simon and Schuster, New York).

Husserl, Edmund (1970) *The Crisis in European Sciences and Transcendental Phenomenology* (Northwestern University Press, Evanston).

I Ching (1968) *or Book of Changes*, 3rd ed., trans. R. Wilhelm (Routledge and Kegan Paul Ltd., London).

Jameson, Fredric (2000) "Globalization and Strategy," *New Left Review*, no. 4 (July/August) pp. 49–68.

Jantsch, Erich (1980) *The Self-Organizing Universe: Scientific and Human Implications of the Emerging Paradigm of Evolution* (Pergamon Press, Oxford).

Jaspers, Karl (1953) *The Origin and Goal of History* (Routledge and Kegan Paul, London).

Jensen, Lionel (1997) *Manufacturing Confucianism: Chinese Traditions and Universal Civilization* (Duke University Press, Durham).

Johnson, Steven (2001) *Emergence: The Connected Lives of Ants, Brains, Cities, and Software* (Scribner, New York).

Johnston, Alastair (1995) *Cultural Realism: Strategic Culture and Grand Strategy in Chinese History* (Princeton University Press, Princeton).

Jones, Charles (2001) "Christianity in the English School: Deleted by Not Expunged," a paper prepared for the International Studies Association annual conference, Chicago, February 21–4.

Joseph, Lawrence (1990) *Gaia: The Growth of an Idea* (Arkana, London).

Kant, Immanuel (1963 [1795]) "Perpetual Peace" in L. Beck (ed.) *Kant on History* (The Bobbs Merrill Co., Indianapolis).

Kaplan, Morton (1966a) "The New Great Debate: Traditionalism vs. Science in International Relations," *World Politics*, v. 19, pp. 1–20.

Kaplan, Robert (1966b) "Cultural Thought Patterns in Inter-cultural Education," *Language Learning*, v. 16 no. 1–2, pp. 1–20.

Katzenstein, Peter et al. (1998) "International Organization and the Study of World Politics," *International Organization*, v. 52, pp. 645–85.

Kawatake, Toshio (2001) "The Handing Down of the Succession of Classical Performing Arts," a paper presented to the UNESCO International Training Workshop on the Protection of Intangible Heritage—"Living Human Treasures" System, Tokyo, February 19–23.

Keller, Evelyn (1985) *Reflections on Gender and Science* (Yale University Press, New Haven).

Keller, Mara (1996) "Gimbutas's Theory of Early European Origins and the Contemporary Transformation of Western Civilization," *Journal of Feminist Studies in Religion*, v. 12 no. 2 (Fall) pp. 73–90.

Keohane, Robert and Nye, Joseph (1977) *Power and Interdependence: World Politics in Transition* (Little, Brown and Company, Boston).

Keynes, John Maynard (1926) *The End of Laissez-faire* (Hogarth Press, London).

Kindaichi, Haruhiko et al. (eds.) (1984) *Shinmeikai-kokugojiten* [Japanese Language Dictionary] (Sanseido, Tokyo).

King, Ursula (1987) "Goddesses, Witches, Androgyny and Beyond? Feminism and the Transformation of Religious Consciousness" in Ursula King (ed.) *Women in the World's Religions, Past and Present* (Paragon House, New York).

Kirchner, James (1991) "The Gaia Hypotheses: Are they Testable? Are they Useful?" in Stephen Schneider and Penelope Boston (eds.) *Scientists on Gaia* (The MIT Press, Cambridge, Mass.).

Klostermaier, Klaus (1998) *A Short Introduction to Hinduism* (Oneworld, Oxford).

Knott, Kim (1998) *Hinduism: A Very Short Introduction* (Oxford University Press, Oxford).

Kolakowski, Leszek (1972) *Positivist Philosophy, from Hume to the Vienna Circle* (Penguin, Harmondsworth).

—— (1990a) "The General Theory of Not-gardening: A Major Contribution to Social Anthropology, Ontology, Moral Philosophy, Psychology, Sociology, Political Theory, and Many Other Fields of Scientific Investigation," in his *Modernity on Endless Trial* (University of Chicago Press, Chicago).

—— (1990b) *Modernity on Endless Trial* (University of Chicago Press, Chicago).

Lacey, Robert and Danziger, Danny (1999) *The Year 1000: What Life was Like at the Turn of the First Millennium; an Englishman's World* (Little, Brown and Company, London).

Lannoy, Richard (1975) *The Speaking Tree: A Study of Indian Culture and Society* (Oxford University Press, Oxford).

Lao Tzu (1997 [480–222B.C.]) *Tao Te Ching*, trans. Arthur Waley (Wordsworth Editions, Ware).

Lau, D.C. (1979) *The Analects* (Penguin, Harmondsworth).

Lawrence, Bruce (1998) *Shattering the Myth: Islam Beyond Violence* (Princeton University Press, Princeton).

Layton, Robert and Titchen, Sarah (1995) "Uluru: An Outstanding Australian Aboriginal Cultural Landscape" in Bernd von Droste et al. (eds.) *Cultural Landscapes of Universal Value* (Gustav Fischer Verlag, Stuttgart).

Leclercq, Pascal and Havel, Christiane (2001) "Defining and Locating the Rare Know-how in the Field of the Crafts of Art to Nominate the Maitres D'Art (a title created by the Ministere de la culture et communication)," *UNESCO International Training Workshop on the Protection of Intangible Cultural Heritage*, Tokyo, February 19–23.

Leeming, David and Page, Jake (1994) *Goddess, Myths of the Female Divine* (Oxford University Press, New York).

Legge, James (1970 [1861]) *The Chinese Classics*, v. 1 (Hong Kong University Press, Hong Kong).

Lelwica, Michelle (1998) "From Superstition to Enlightenment to the Race for Pure Consciousness: Anti-religious Currents in Popular and Academic Feminist Discourse," *Journal of Feminist Studies in Religion*, v. 14 no. 2 (Fall) pp. 108–23.

Lem, Stanislaw (2003 [1961]) *Solaris* (Faber and Faber, London).

Lenton, Timothy (1998) "Gaia and Natural Selection," *Nature*, v. 394 no. 6692 (July 30) pp. 439–47.

Levinas, Emmanuel (n.d. [1961]) *Totality and Infinity*, trans. Alphonso Lingis (Duquesne University Press, Pittsburgh).

Levinson, David (1996) *Religion: A Cross-cultural Encyclopedia* (ABC-Clio, Santa Barbara).

Levi-Strauss, Laurent (2000) "Impact of Recent Developments in the Notion of Cultural Heritage on the World Heritage Convention" in *World Culture Report: Cultural Diversity, Conflict and Pluralism* (UNESCO, Paris).

Leys, Simon (1997) *The Analects of Confucius* (W.W. Norton and Company, New York).

Lin, Limin (2002) "Assessment in Economic and Strategic Perspectives," *Contemporary International Relations*, v. 12 no. 12 (December) pp. 36–40.

List, Friedrich (1966 [1885]) *The National System of Political Economy* (Augustus M. Kelley, New York).

Little, Richard (2000) "The English School's Contribution to the Study of International Relations," *European Journal of International Relations*, v. 6 no. 3, pp. 395–422.

Liu, Kang (1998) "Is There an Alternative to (Capitalist) Globalization? The Debate about Modernity in China" in Frederic Jameson and Masao Miyoshi (eds.) *The Cultures of Globalization* (Duke University Press, Durham).

Loewe, Michael (1990) *The Pride That was China* (Sidgwick and Jackson, London).

Lomborg, Bjorn (2001) *The Skeptical Environmentalist: Measuring the Real State of the World* (Cambridge University Press, New York).

Louie, Kam (1980) *Critiques of Confucius in Contemporary China* (The Chinese University Press, Hong Kong).

Lovelock, James (1987 [1979]) *Gaia: A New Look at Life on Earth* (Oxford University Press, Oxford).

—— (1991a) *Gaia: The Practical Science of Planetary Medicine* (Allen and Unwin, Sydney).

—— (1991b) "Geophysiology—the Science of Gaia" in Stephen Schneider and Penelope Boston (eds.) *Scientists on Gaia* (The MIT Press, Cambridge, Mass.).

—— (1995) *The Ages of Gaia: A Biography of Our Living Earth*, 2nd ed. (Oxford University Press, Oxford).

—— (2000) *Homage to Gaia: The Life of an Independent Scientist* (Oxford University Press, Oxford).

Lovibond, Sabina (1989) "Feminism and Postmodernism," *New Left Review*, no. 178 (November/December) pp. 5–28.

Mabbott, J.D. (1958) *The State and the Citizen* (Arrow Books, London).

Macdonald, Sharon and Fyfe, Gordon (1996) *Theorizing Museums: Representing Identity and Diversity in a Changing World* (Blackwell, Oxford).

Marett, Robert (1914) *The Threshold of Religion*, 2nd ed. (Methuen and Co., London).

Margulis, Lynn (1998) *The Symbiotic Planet: A New Look at Evolution* (Phoenix, London).

—— and Lovelock, John (1989) "Gaia and Geognosy" in Mitchell Rambler et al. (eds.) *Global Ecology: Towards a Science of the Biosphere* (Academic Press, Boston).

—— and Sagan, Dorion (1997) *Slanted Truths: Essays on Gaia, Symbiosis, and Evolution* (Copernicus, New York).

Marx, Karl and Engels, Friedrich (1971 [1848]) *Manifesto of the Communist Party* (Foreign Languages Press, Peking).

Mataatua Declaration, The (1993), adopted at the First International Conference on the Cultural and Intellectual Property Rights of Indigenous Peoples, Whakatane (June).

Mayeda, Sengaku (1979) *A Thousand Teachings: The* Upadesasahasri *of Sankara* (University of Tokyo Press, Tokyo).

Mayer, Ann (1991) *Islam and Human Rights: Tradition and Politics* (Westview Press, Boulder).

McFague, Sallie (1989) "God as Mother" in Judith Plaskow and Carol Christ (eds.) *Weaving the Visions: New Patterns in Feminist Spirituality* (Harper, San Francisco).

McGrath, Alister (2003) *The Re-echantment of Nature: Science, Religion and the Human Sense of Wonder* (Hodder and Stoughton, London).

Mehta, J.L. (1985) *India and the West: The Problems of Understanding* (Scholars Press, Chico).

Meisner, Maurice (1986) *Mao's China and After: A History of the People's Republic* (The Free Press, New York).

Mellaart, James (1965) *Earliest Civilizations of the Near East* (McGraw-Hill Book Company, New York).

—— (1967) *Catal Huyuk: A Neolithic Town in Anatolia* (Thames and Hudson, London).

—— (1975) *The Neolithic of the Near East* (Thames and Hudson, London).

—— (1978) *The Archaeology of Ancient Turkey* (Rowman and Littlefield, Totowa).

Metzger, Thomas (1977) *Escape from Predicament: Neo-Confucianism and China's Evolving Political Culture* (Columbia University Press, New York).

Midgley, Mary (2001) *Gaia: The Next Big Idea* (Demos, London).

Mignolo, Walter (1998) "Globalization, Civilization Processes, and the Relocation of Languages and Cultures" in Frederic Jameson and Masao Miyoshi (eds.) *The Cultures of Globalization* (Duke University Press, Durham).

Milbank, John (1990) *Theology and Social Theory: Beyond Secular Reason* (Blackwell, Oxford).

Millennium (2000) v. 29 no. 3, special issue, "Religion and International Relations."

Miller, Barbara (1986) *The Bhagavad-Gita: Krishna's Counsel in Time of War* (Columbia University Press, New York).

Mittal, Kewal (1974) *Materialism in Indian Thought* (Munshiram Manoharlal Publishers, New Delhi).

Mohanty, J.N. (1993) *Essays on Indian Philosophy: Traditional and Modern* (Oxford University Press, Delhi).

—— (2000) *Classical Indian Philosophy* (Rowman and Littlefield, Lanham).

Moore, Charles (ed.) (1968) *The Status of the Individual in East and West* (University of Hawaii Press, Honolulu).

Morgenthau, Hans (1972 [1948]), *Politics Among Nations: The Struggle for Power and Peace*, 5th ed. (Alfred A. Knopf, New York).

Morris, Brian (1994) *Anthropology of the Self: The Individual in Cultural Perspective* (Pluto Press, London).

Moussalli, Ahmad (2001) *The Islamic Quest for Democracy, Pluralism, and Human Rights* (University of Florida Press, Gainesville).

Muhaiyaddeen, M.R. Bawa (1987) *Islam and World Peace: Explanations of a Sufi* (The Fellowship Press, Philadelphia).

—— (1997) *To Die Before Death: The Sufi Way of Life* (The Fellowship Press, Philadelphia).

Munro, Donald (1996) *The Imperial Style of Inquiry in Twentieth-Century China: The Emergence of New Approaches* (The University of Michigan, Ann Arbor).

Muzaffar, Chandra (1998) "Cultures Under Attack: Key Issues" in Mohamed Hassan (ed.) *A Pacific Peace: Issues and Responses* (ISIS Malaysia, Kuala Lumpur).

Naess, Arne (1989) *Ecology, Community and Lifestyle: Outline of an Ecosophy* (Cambridge University Press, Cambridge).

—— (1995) "The Deep Ecological Movement: Some Philosophical Aspects" in George Sessions (ed.) *Deep Ecology for the Twenty-first Century* (Shambhala, Boston).

Needham, Joseph (1956) "History of Scientific Thought," *Science and Civilisation in China*, v. 2 (Cambridge University Press, Cambridge).

Niebuhr, Reinhold (1936) *Moral Man and Immoral Society: A Study in Ethics and Politics* (Charles Scribner's Son's, New York).

Nikhilananda, Swami (1964) *The Upanishads* (Harper and Row, New York).

Nivison, David (1972) "Communist Ethics and Chinese Tradition" in John Harrison (ed.) *China* (The University of Arizona Press, Tucson).

Nozick, Robert (1974) *Anarchy, State, and Utopia* (Blackwell, Oxford).

O'Flaherty, Wendy (ed.) and trans. (1981) *The Rig Veda: An Anthology* (Penguin Books, Harmondsworth).

Onuf, Nicholas (1989) *Worlds of Our Making: Rules and Rule in Social Theory and International Relations* (University of South Carolina Press, Columbia).

Operational Guidelines for the Implementation of the World Heritage Convention, March 1999.

Organ, Troy (1975) *Western Approaches to Eastern Philosophy* (Ohio University Press, Athens).

Oxford English Dictionary (OED), on-line.

Paris, Roland (2002) "International Peacebuilding and the 'Mission Civilisatrice,' " *Review of International Studies*, v. 28 no. 4 (October) pp. 637–56.

Parrinder, Geoffrey (1977) *The Wisdom of the Early Buddhists* (Sheldon Press, London).

Passmore, John (1970) *The Perfectibility of Man* (Duckworth, London).

Payutto, Ven P.A. (1994) *Buddhist Economics: A Middle Way for the Market Place* (Buddhadhamma Foundation, Bangkok).

Peake, Mervyn (1975) *Selected Poems* (Faber and Faber, London).

Pearce, Susan (1992) *Museums, Objects and Collections: A Cultural Study* (Leicester University Press, Leicester).

Pereira, Jose (ed.) (1976) *Hindu Theology: A Reader* (Image Books, New York).

Pettman, Jan Jindy (1996) *Worlding Women: A Feminist International Politics* (Allen and Unwin, St. Leonards).

Pettman, Ralph (1993) *Going for a Walk in the World*, http://www.vuw.ac.nz/~ralph/aikido.html.

—— (1998) "Sex, Power, and the Grail of Positive Collaboration" in Marysia Zalewski and Jane Parpart (eds.) *The "Man" Question in International Relations* (Westview Press, Boulder).

—— (2000) *Commonsense Constructivism, or the Making of World Affairs* (M.E. Sharpe, New York).

Petty, Bruce (n.d.) *The Money Game* (Australian Broadcasting Corporation, Sydney).

Phillips, Stephen (1995) *Classical Indian Metaphysics* (Open Court, Chicago).

Piaget, Jean (1929) *The Child's Conception of the World* (Kegan Paul, Trench, Trubner and Co. Ltd., London).

Pinker, Steven (2002) *The Blank Slate: The Modern Denial of Human Nature* (Allen Lane, London).

Plotkin, Henry (1998) *Evolution in Mind: An Introduction to Evolutionary Psychology* (Penguin, London).

Pound, Ezra (1933) *Confucian Analects* (Peter Owen Limited, London).

Pressouyre, Leon (1996) *The World Heritage Convention, Twenty Years Later* (UNESCO, Paris).

Prott, Lyndel (1999) "Some Consideration on the Protection of the Intangible Heritage: Claims and Remedies," a paper presented at the conference on *A Global Assessment of the 1989 Recommendation on the Safeguarding of Traditional Culture and Folklore: Local Empowerment and International Cooperation,*

Washington, June 27–30 (UNESCO/Smithsonian Institution Centre for Folklife and Cultural Heritage).

Prott, Lyndel (2001) "An International Legal Instrument for the Protection of the Intangible Cultural Heritage" in Claus Classen et al. (eds.) *"In einem vereinten Europe dem Frienden der Welt zu dienen"* (Duncker and Humbolt, Berlin).

Pye, Michael (1979) *The Buddha* (Duckworth, London).

Radhakrishnan, Sarvepalli and Moore, Charles (eds.) (1957) *A Source Book in Indian Philosophy* (Princeton University Press, Princeton).

Rahula, Walpola (1959) *What the Buddha Taught* (Grove Press, New York).

—— (1994) "Buddhism in the 'Real World' " in Claude Whitmyer (ed.) *Mindfulness and Meaningful Work: Exploration in Right Livelihood* (Parallax Press, Berkeley).

Ramachandran, Vilayanur and Blakeslee, Sandra (1999) *Phantoms in the Brain: Human Nature and the Architecture of the Mind* (Fourth Estate, London).

Rawlinson, Andrew (1997) *The Book of Enlightened Masters: Western Teachers in Eastern Traditions* (Open Court, Chicago).

Ree, Jonathan (2000) "Apocalypse Unbound," *New Left Review* no. 4 (July/August) pp. 163–7.

Roessler, Mechtild (1995) "UNESCO and Cultural Landscape Protection" in Bernd von Droste et al. (eds.) *Cultural Landscapes of Universal Value* (Gustav Fischer Verlag, Stuttgart).

Rothbard, Murray (1973) *For a New Liberty* (The Macmillan Company, New York).

Rozman, Gilbert (ed.) (1991) *The East Asian Region: Confucian Heritage and its Modern Adaptation* (Princeton University Press, Princeton).

Ruether, Rosemary (1983) *Sexism and God-talk; Toward a Feminist Theology* (Beacon Press, Boston).

—— (1989) "The Feminist Critique in Religious Studies" in Charles Fu and Gerhard Spiegler (eds.) *Religious Issues and Interreligious Dialogues: An Analysis and Sourcebook of Developments Since 1945* (Greenwood Press, New York).

Rule, Paul (1986) *K'ung-tzu or Confucius? The Jesuit Interpretation of Confucianism* (Allen and Unwin, Sydney).

Ryckmans, Pierre (1986) *The Chinese Attitude Towards the Past*, The Forty-seventh George Ernest Morrison Lecture in Ethnology (The Australian National University, Canberra).

Salk, Jonas (1983) *Anatomy of Reality: Merging of Intuition and Reason* (Columbia University Press, New York).

Sanday, Peggy (1981) *Female Power and Male Dominance: On the Origins of Sexual Inequality* (Cambridge University Press, Cambridge).

Satha-Anand, Chaiwat and Wongwaisayawan, Suwanna (1979) "Buddhist Economics Revisited," *Asian Culture Quarterly*, v. 7 no. 4, pp. 37–45.

Schram, Stuart (1989) *The Thought of Mao Tse-Tung* (Cambridge University Press, Cambridge).

Schumacher, Ernst (1973) "Buddhist Economics," in Herman Daly (ed.) *Towards a Steady-State Economy* (W.H. Freeman, San Francisco).

Seeger, Anthony (1999) "Summary Report on the Regional Seminars," a paper presented at the conference on *A Global Assessment of the 1989 Recommendation on the Safeguarding of Traditional Culture and Folklore: Local Empowerment and International Cooperation*, Washington, June 27–30 (UNESCO/Smithsonian Institution Centre for Folklife and Cultural Heritage).

Senior Policy Seminar (2001) *Key Issues in Asia Pacific Security* (East-West Center, Hawaii).

Sessions, George (ed.) (1995) *Deep Ecology for the Twenty-first Century* (Shambhala, Boston).

Seth, Sanjay (2000) "A 'Postcolonial World'?" in Greg Fry and Jacinta O'Hagan (eds.) *Contending Images of World Politics* (Macmillan, Houndmills).

Shankaracharya, Shri [Sankara] (1974) *Vivekachudamani* ["Crest Jewel of Discrimination"] (Advaita Ashrama, Calcutta).

Sharman, Arvind and Young, Katherine (eds.) (1999) *Feminism and World Religions* (State University of New York Press, Albany).

Sharp, Martin (1947) "Aggression: A Study of Values and Law," *Ethics*, v. 57 no. 4 Part II (July).

Sheldrake, Rupert (1981) *A New Science of Life: The Hypothesis of Formative Causation* (J.P. Tarcher, Inc., Los Angeles).

——— (1990) *The Rebirth of Nature: The Greening of Science and God* (Century, London).

Sherkin, Samantha (1999) "A Historical Study on the Preparation of the UNESCO 1989 Recommendation on the Safeguarding of Traditional Culture and Folklore," a paper presented at the conference on *A Global Assessment of the 1989 Recommendation on the Safeguarding of Traditional Culture and Folklore: Local Empowerment and International Cooperation*, Washington, June 27–30 (UNESCO/Smithsonian Institution Centre for Folklife and Cultural Heritage).

Short, Philip (1999) *Mao: A Life* (Hodder and Stoughton, London).

Shweder, Richard and Levine, Robert (eds.) (1984) *Culture Theory: Essays on Mind, Self, and Emotion* (Cambridge University Press, New York).

Simon, Bradford (1999) "A Legal Assessment of the 1989 Recommendation on the Safeguarding of Traditional Culture and Folklore," a paper presented at the conference on *A Global Assessment of the 1989 Recommendation on the Safeguarding of Traditional Culture and Folklore: Local Empowerment and International Cooperation*, Washington, June 27–30 (UNESCO/Smithsonian Institution Centre for Folklife and Cultural Heritage).

Simos, Miriam *alias* Starhawk (1979) "Ethics and Justice in Goddess Religion" in Charlene Spretnak (ed.) *The Politics of Women's Spirituality: Essays on the Rise of Spiritual Power Within the Feminist Movement* (Anchor Books, New York).

——— (1988) *Dreaming the Dark: Magic, Sex and Politics*, 2nd ed. (Beacon Press, Boston).

——— (1989) *The Spiral Dance: A Rebirth of the Ancient Religion of the Great Goddess*, 2nd ed. (Harper and Row, San Francisco).

Sinari, Ramakant (1970) *The Structure of Indian Thought* (Charles C. Thomas, Springfield).

Smart, Ninian (1989) *The World's Religions: Old Traditions and Modern Transformations* (Cambridge University Press, Cambridge).

Smith, Adam (1892 [1776]) *An Inquiry into the Nature and Causes of the Wealth of Nations* (George Routledge and Sons, London).

Smith, Linda Tuhiwai (1999) *Decolonizing Methodologies: Research and Indigenous Peoples* (Zed Books, London).

Smith, Steve et al. (eds.) (1996) *International Theory: Positivism and Beyond* (Cambridge University Press, New York).

——— (2002) "The United States and the Discipline of International Relations: 'Hegemonic Country, Hegemonic Discipline,' " *International Studies Review*, v. 4 no. 2 (Summer) pp. 76–85.

Spencer, Herbert (1904) *First Principles*, 4th ed. (Williams and Norgate, London).

Spretnak, Charlene (1982) "The Politics of Womens's Spirituality" in Charlene Spretnak (ed.) *The Politics of Women's Spirituality: Essays on the Rise of Spiritual Power within the Feminist Movement* (Anchor Books, New York).

—— (1986) *The Spiritual Dimension of Green Politics* (Bear and Company, Santa Fe).

—— (1996) "Beyond the Backlash: An Appreciation of the Work of Marija Gimbutas," *Journal of Feminist Studies in Religion*, v. 12 no. 2 (Fall) pp. 91–8.

Stevenson, Leslie and Haberman, David (1998) *Ten Theories of Human Nature*, 3rd ed. (Oxford University Press, New York).

Stietencron, Heinrich von (1991) "Hinduism: On the Proper Use of a Deceptive Term" in Gunther Sontheimer and Hermann Kulke (eds.) *Hinduism Reconsidered* (Manohar, New Delhi).

Stone, Merlin (1976) *When God was a Woman* (Harvest/HBJ, San Diego).

Sugarman, Susan (1987) *Piaget's Construction of the Child's Reality* (Cambridge University Press, Cambridge).

Suva Declaration, The (1995), adopted by the South Pacific United Nations Development Programme (UNDP) Consultation on Indigenous Peoples' Knowledge and Intellectual Property Rights, Suva, April.

Taber, John (1983) *Transformative Philosophy: A Study of Sankara, Fichte, and Heidegger* (University of Hawii Press, Honolulu).

Tagore, Rabindranath (1967 [1930]) "The Four Stages of Life" in William Gerber (ed.) *The Mind of India* (Southern Illinois University Press, Carbondale).

Takashina, Shuji (1996) "The Heritage of Memory," *Japan Echo*, v. 23 no. 4 (Winter), see http://www.japanecho.co.jp, on request....

Tallis, Raymond (2002) "The Truth About Lies: Foucault, Nietzsche and the Cretan Paradox," *Times Literary Supplement*, no. 5151 (December 21) pp. 3–4.

Tamney, Joseph and Chiang, Linda (2002) *Modernization, Globalization, and Confucianism in Chinese Societies* (Praeger, Westport).

Taylor, Charles (1989) *Sources of the Self: The Making of Modern Identity* (Cambridge University Press, Cambridge).

Terada, Yoshitaka (2000) "Asian Music in a Globalizing World," *Japan Echo*, v. 27 no. 4 (August) pp. 55–9.

Teson, Fernando (1997) *Humanitarian Intervention: An Inquiry into Law and Morality*, 2nd ed. (Transnational Publishers, New York).

Tibi, Bassam (1998) *The Challenge of Fundamentalism: Political Islam and the New World Disorder* (University of California Press, Berkeley).

Titchen, Sarah (1995) *On the Construction of Outstanding Universal Value: UNESCO's World Heritage Convention* (Convention concerning the Protection of the World Cultural and Natural Heritage, 1972) *and the Identification and Assessment of Cultural Places for Inclusion in the World Heritage List*, a thesis submitted for the degree of Doctor of Philosophy, the Australian National University.

—— and Roessler, Mechtild (1995) "Tentative Lists as a Tool for Landscape Classification and Protection" in Bernd von Droste et al. (eds.) *Cultural Landscapes of Universal Value* (Gustav Fischer Verlag, Stuttgart).

Tobias, Michael (ed.) (1985) *Deep Ecology* (Avant Books, San Diego).

Tringham, Ruth (1993) Review of Marija Gimbutas, *The Civilization of the Goddess: The World of Old Europe* (Harper Collins, San Francisco) in *American Anthropologist*, v. 95 no. 1 (March) pp. 196–7.

Trungpa, Chogyam (1973) *Cutting Through Spiritual Materialism* (Shambhala, Boston).

Tse-Tung, Mao (1965 [1938]) "The Role of the Chinese Communist Party in the National War," *Selected Works of Mao Tse-Tung*, v. II (Foreign Languages Press, Peking).

Tu, Wei-ming (ed.) (1996) *Confucian Traditions in East Asian Modernity: Moral Education and Economic Culture in Japan and the Four Mini-dragons* (Harvard University Press, Cambridge).

Tylor, Edward (1903 [1871]) *Primitive Culture: Researches into the Development of Mythology, Philosophy, Religion, Language, Art, and Custom*, 4th ed., vols. 1 and 2 (John Murray, London).

Ueki, Yukinobu (2001) "Preservation and Perpetuation of Folk Performing Arts," a paper presented to the UNESCO International Training Workshop on the Protection of Intangible Heritage—"Living Human Treasures" System, Tokyo, February 19–23.

United Nations Educational, Scientific and Cultural Organisation [UNESCO] (1984) "Final Report," *Meeting of Experts to Draw up a Future Programme Concerning the Non-Physical Heritage*, November 28–30, CLT-84/CONF.603/COL.2.

——— (1987) "Final Report," *Meeting of the Working Group for the Preparation of a Plan of Action to Safeguard the Non-Physical Heritage*, October 5–8, CC-87/CONF.609/COL.1.

——— (1999a) *Operational Guidelines for the Implementation of the World Heritage Convention*, March (WHC.99/2).

——— (1999b) "Action Plan for the Safeguarding and Revitalisation of Intangible Cultural Heritage," *A Global Assessment of the 1989 Recommendation on the Safeguarding of Traditional Culture and Folklore: Local Empowerment and International Cooperation*, Washington, June 27–30 (UNESCO/Smithsonian Institution Centre for Folklife and Cultural Heritage).

——— (1999c) "Final Report," *A Global Assessment of the 1989 Recommendation on the Safeguarding of Traditional Culture and Folklore: Local Empowerment and International Cooperation*, Washington, June 27–30 (UNESCO/Smithsonian Institution Centre for Folklife and Cultural Heritage).

——— (2000a) Bureau of the World Heritage Committee, Twenty-fourth Extraordinary session, Cairns, Australia, *Information Document: Evaluations of Shey-Phoksundo National Park (Nepal) by IUCN [World Conservation Union] and ICOMOS [International Council on Monuments and Sites]*.

——— (2000b) *World Culture Report* (UNESCO, Paris).

——— (2001) Bureau of the World Heritage Committee, Twenty-fifth session, Paris, Convention Concerning the Protection of the World Cultural and Natural Heritage, *Report of the Rapporteur*, June 25–30 (WHC-2001/CONF.205/10).

——— (2001) Bureau of the World Heritage Committee, Twenty-fifth session, Paris, Convention Concerning the Protection of the World Cultural and Natural Heritage, *Discussion Paper on the Application of Cultural Criterion (vi)*, June 27 (WHC-2001/CONF.205/INF.8).

——— (2001) "UNESCO's Contribution to the International Decade of the World's Indigenous People (1995–2004)," *Executive Board*, August 9 (162 EX/17).

——— (2001) "Report on the Proposed World Heritage Indigenous Peoples Council of Experts (WHIPCOE)," *Convention Concerning the Protection of the World Cultural and Natural Heritage*, Bureau of the World Heritage Committee, June 25–30 (WHC-2001/CONF.205/WEB.3).

United Nations Educational, Scientific and Cultural Organisation [UNESCO] (2001) "Report on the Preliminary Study on the Advisability of Regulating Internationally, Through a New Standard-setting Instrument, the Protection of Traditional Culture and Folklore," *Executive Board*, May 16 (161 EX/15).

—— (2001) "Universal Declaration on Cultural Diversity," *General Conference*, November 2 (31C/Resolution 30).

—— (2002) Third Round Table of Ministers of Culture, "Intangible Cultural Heritage—a Mirror of Cultural Diversity," *Discussion Guidelines*, Istanbul, September 16–17.

—— (n.d.) *Proclamation of Masterpieces of the Oral and Intangible Heritage of Humanity, Implementation Guide*.

Universal Islamic Declaration of Human Rights (1981).

Uyeshiba, Kisshomaru (1963) *Aikido* (Hozansha Publishing, Tokyo).

Vernadsky, Vladimir (1998 [1926]) *The Biosphere* (Copernicus, New York).

Vincent, John (1986) *Human Rights and International Relations* (Cambridge University Press, Cambridge).

Vivekananda, Swami (1964) *Teachings of Swami Vivekananda* (Advaita Ashrama, Calcutta).

von Droste, Bernd et al. (eds.) (1995) *Cultural Landscapes of Universal Value: Components of a Global Strategy* (Gustav Fischer Verlag, Stuttgart).

—— (1995) "Cultural Landscapes in a Global World Heritage Strategy" in Bernd von Droste et al. (eds.) *Cultural Landscapes of Universal Value* (Gustav Fischer Verlag, Stuttgart).

Waever, Ole (1996) "The Rise and Fall of the Inter-paradigm Debate" in Steve Smith et al. (eds.) *International Theory: Positivism and Beyond* (Cambridge University Press, Cambridge).

Waley, Arthur (1934) *The Way and Its Power: A Study of the Tao Te Ching and Its Place in Chinese Thought* (George Allen and Unwin, London).

—— (1989 [1938]) *The Analects of Confucius* (Vintage Books, New York).

Wallerstein, Immanuel (1974–80) *The Modern World-System* (Academic Press, New York).

Walsh, Kevin (1992) *The Representation of the Past: Museums and Heritage in the Postmodern World* (Routledge, London and New York).

Waltz, Kenneth (1979) *Theory of International Politics* (Addison-Wesley, Reading MA).

Wang, Jisi (2002) "Assessment of China's International Environment," *Contemporary International Relations*, v. 12 no. 12 (December) pp. 1–7.

Watanabe, Michihiro (1998) "Cultural Policies in Japan," *World Culture Report: Culture, Creativity and Markets* (UNESCO, Paris).

Weber, Cynthia (2001) *International Relations Theory: A Critical Introduction* (Routledge, London).

Weber, Max (1930) *The Protestant Ethic and the Spirit of Capitalism*, trans. Talcott Parsons (Allen and Unwin, London).

—— (1951) *The Religion of China: Confucianism and Taoism* (The Free Press, Glencoe).

—— (1958) *The Religion of India: The Sociology of Hinduism and Buddhism* (The Free Press, Glencoe).

—— (1968) *Economy and Society: An Outline of Interpretive Sociology*, Guenther Roth and Claus Willich (eds.) (Bedminster Press, New York).

White, Lynn (1967) "The Historical Roots of Our Ecologic Crisis," *Science*, v. 155 no. 3767 (March 10) pp. 1203–7.

Wight, Martin (1967) "Western Values in International Relations" in Herbert Butterfield and Martin Wight (eds.) *Diplomatic Investigations* (Allen and Unwin, London).

Wilson, Edward (1984) *Biophilia: The Human Bond With Other Species* (Harvard University Press, Cambridge, Mass.).

Wittgenstein, Ludwig (1961 [1921]) *Tractatus Logico-Philosophicus* (Routledge and Kegan Paul, London).

Wurm, Stephen (2001) *Atlas of the World's Languages in Danger of Disappearing*, 2nd ed. (UNESCO Publishing, Paris).

Yao, Xinzhong (2000) *An Introduction to Confucianism* (Cambridge University Press, Cambridge).

Young, Serinity (ed.) (1993) *An Anthology of Sacred Texts by and about Women* (Crossroad Publishing Co., New York).

Zalewski, Marysia and Parpart, Jane (eds.) (1998) *The "Man" Question in International Relations* (Westview Press, Boulder).

Zimmerman, Michael (2001) "Ken Wilber's Critique of Ecological Spirituality" in David Barnhill and Roger Gottlieb (eds.) *Deep Ecology and World Religions: New Essays on Sacred Ground* (State University of New York Press, Albany).

Zizek, Slavoj (2000) "Class Struggle or Postmodernist? Yes, Please!" in Judith Butler et al., *Contingency, Hegemony, Universality: Contemporary Dialogues on the Left* (Verso, London).

Index

Abe, Masao, 81
Absolute, 131
adhyasa [superimposition], 130
Adler, Margot, 136
adoration, 7
Adorno, Theodor, 29
Advaita Vedanta, 125, 128, 131, 132, *see also*
    Hinduism
Affifi, A., 111
Agar, Nicholas, 145
Agency for Cultural Change (Japan), 72
Ahmed, Akbar, 110
Aikawa, Noriko, 59, 66, 67
aikido, 88
    and Japanese foreign policy, 89
alchemy, 1
alienation, 29, 103, 136, 140, *see also*
    individuation, of individuals
    compensation for, 110
Allaby, Michael, 150, 153
Allen, Charlotte, 118
Ames, Roger, 9, 83, 86, 116, 117, 118, 119,
    122, 160
analytic languages, *see* language,
    analytic
anarchism, 19
Anderson, Benedict, 24, 70
Andreski, Stanislav, 1–2
Angel, Leonard, 32
Anikeev, Nikolai, 128
animism, 156
    as danced out, 148
    as thought out, 148
    definition of, 146
    pagan, 145
    pre-, 148
    scientized form of, 156
animist
    spiritualism, 146
Animist environmentalism, 11, 145–156

Ann, Martha, 136
anti-modernity, *see* modernity, anti-
Arberry, A.J., 80, 110, 112, 113
archaeologists, 139
Aristotle, 4
Arnold, Daniel, 101
Aron, Raymond, 17
Asad, Muhammad, 104, 105
Asia Pacific Economic Cooperation
    (APEC), 91
Asian Development Bank, 91
associations, 26
astrology, 1
astronomy, 1
Atman [the inner Self], 127, 128, 129,
    130, 132
avidya [ignorance], 130
Ayubi, Nazib, 106

Badcock, Christopher, 30
"behavioralist revolution", 2
Baker, Nicola, 91
Baring, Anne, 137, 142, 143, 144
Barnett, William, 139
Barnhill, David, 149
Batchelor, Stephen, 97, 98
Bateson, Gregory, 152
Batten, Juliet, 137
Bawa Muhaiyaddeen, *see* Muhaiyaddeen,
    M.R. Bawa
Beasley, W.G., 121
being, 3
"behavioralists"
    American, 17
Benard, Elisabeth, 137
Bending, Tim, 112
Bennett, Tony, 70
Beyond, the, 7, 129, 132
    access to, 80
Bhagavad Gita, 126, 128

bhakti, 128
Biardeau, Madelaine, 125, 127
biology, 4
Blake, Janet, 61, 62, 63, 64
Blakeslee, Sandra, 154
Bodian, Stephan, 149
Bohm, David, 149
Bolle, Kees, 148
Boucher, David, 32
Boulter, Michael, 149
Boyer, Pascal, 148
Brahma Sutra, 128
Brahman [the absolute], 127, 128, 129,
    130, 131
Brooks, E. Bruce, 116, 117, 118
Brooks, A. Takeo, 116, 117, 118
Brown, Chris, 32
Bryson, Bill, 5
Bubna-Litic, David, 97, 99
Budapest, Zsuzsanna, 149
Buddha, the, 94, 98
    first sermon of, 95
    Four Noble Truths of, 95
    Middle Way of, 95
    Noble Eightfold Path of, 95
    promise of Enlightenment by, 95
Buddhadasa, Bhikku, 97, 98
Buddhism, 137
    definition of, 94
Buddhist economics, 11, 93–102
    and Right Action, 99
    and Right Livelihood, 99
    and Right Mindfulness, 96
    as a contradiction in terms, 94
Buddhists, 128
Bugotu, Frances, 18
Bull, Hedley, 17
Bull, Malcolm, 15
Burchill, Scott, 32
Burkitt, Brian, 26
Burton, John, 25
Bynner, Witter, 84

Cairo Declaration on Human Rights, The,
    109
Campbell, David, 9
Capgras syndrome, 9
Carr, E.H., 23
Carroll, Berenice, 81
Carse, James, 10

Carvata/Lokayata, 128
Cashford, Jules, 137, 142, 143, 144
cause, 3
cause and effect
    patterns of, 6
Cavalli-Sforza, Luigi, 141
Chalcolithic era, 137
Chamberlin, T., 32
Chan, Stephen, 33
Chan, Wing-tsit, 33, 86
Chaplin, Charlie, 41
chemistry, 1, 4, 152
Chiang, Linda, 115, 116, 118, 122
Chinese
    classical, 9
Christ, Carol, 139, 142
Christendom, 146
    European, 157
Christianity, 7, 33, 79, 126, 138, 140,
    145, 161
    and world affairs, 80
citizenship
    planetary, 156
civics
    Islamic, *see* Islamic civics
civilisations, 139
    clash of, 159
civil society
    global, 103
class struggle, 28
Cleere, Henry, 54
Coakley, Sarah, 139
Cohn, Carol, 83
Cold War, 158
collectivism, 21, 26, 103, 112, 113
commonsense
    emotional, 30
    phenomenological, 30
communalism, 8, 49
communalists, 158
communication, 28
communists, 4
communitarianism, 110
compassion
    true, 97, 102
Comte, Auguste, 1–4, 13
Confucian
    Analects, 117, 121
    bureaucracy, 123
    Marxism, 11, 115–124

Confucianism
   as advocating order, 115
   as effective government, 116
   as "ethically correct" behavior, 115
   as the *ren* way [honourable;
      authoritative; benevolent], 116
   as the nexus of education,
      morality and political
      power, 116
Confucius, 74, 115
conservatism, 17
constitutions, 103
constructivism, 21, 29–30, 93
   as anti-marxism, 30
   as anti-postmodernism, 30
   conservative and "hard-line", 30
   conservative and "soft-line", 30
   Hindu, *see* Hindu constructivism
   "Miami Group", 30
constructivists
   as Rationalists, 131
consumption, 100
context
   Animist, 7
   Buddhist, 7
   Christian, 7
   communalist, ix
   Confucian, 7
   Hindu, 7
   Islamic, 7
   Pagan, 7
   politico-cultural, 11
   politico-spiritual, 7, 113
   sacral, 113
   sacralist, ix
   social, 6
   Taoist, 7
contract, 25, 103
Conze, Edward, 94
Cooper, John, 111
copyright, 58
corporations
   international, 65
   transnational, 134
cosmic consciousness, 112
Cosmides, Lena, 30
Cottingham, John, 2
Cox, Robert, 29
Creel, Herrlee, 84, 86, 87, 118
Crete, 142

Critical Theory, 29
Cultural Revolution, 121
culture
   cunning of, 81
   global, 93
   strategic, *see* strategic culture
cultural landscapes, 54
cure-alls
   use of, 1

Daisyworld, 153
Dallmayr, Fred, 159
Daly, Herman, 156
Daly, Mary, 143, 144
Damasio, Antonio, 154
Danziger, Danny, 52, 143
Darby, Phillip, 17
Dark, K.R., 79
Dawkins, Richard, 153
death, 83, 133
de Bary, Wm. Theodore, 94, 95, 96,
    98, 122
deduction, 2
deforestation, 145
Deleuze, Gilles, 32
democracy, 25
   liberal, 123, 124
Deng Xiaoping, 91
Descartes, 2
detachment, 5
Devetak, Richard, 6
Diamond, Jared, 27
difference
   human, 159
Divine, the
   as male, 137
   as female, 138, 144
dharma [universal and eternal
    law], 125
dhikr [remembering the name of
    god], 113
dimensions
   metaphysical, 3
   scientific, 3
   theological, 3
Dirlik, Arif, 121, 122, 123
disabled, the, 4
Dupont, Alan, 90
Dussel, Enrique, 81
Duve, Christian de, 154

Eagleton, Terry, 28
Earth
    as an organism, 152
Eck, Diana, 128, 132
ecology
    planetary, 145, 152
economics
    Buddhist, *see* Buddhist economics
Edkins, Jenny, 8, 9
Einstein, Albert, 156
Eiseley, Loren, 145
Eisenberg, Evan, 151
Eisenstadt, S.N., 13, 51, 65
emergent properties, 151, *see also*
    organised complexity
emotion, 8
emotivism, 7
Engels, Friedrich, 28
English, 9
environment
    planetary, 145
environmentalism, 18–19, 160
    Animist, *see* Animist environmentalism
epistemology
    post-Euro-American, 132
    non-Rationalist, 5
    Rationalist, 157
Ernst, Carl, 111
Esposito, John, 111
essence, 3
Esteva, Gustavo, 17
ethnocentricism, 18
evil, 136
exchange, 100
experimentation
    empirical/deductive, 2

"facts", 2
faith, 131
falsification, 4
Farraq, Ahmad, 109
fascism, 103
feminism, 18
    Pagan, *see* Pagan feminism
    radical, 93
feminists, 135, 160
    Christian, 139
    Goddess, 138
    liberal, 140
    marxist, 139

modernist, *see* modernist feminists
    Pagan, 140, 141, 142, 143, 144, 148, 156
    postmodernist, 139
Ferguson, James, 8, 35
Fichte, 133
final causes
    belief in, 2
Fingarette, Herbert, 116
Finkelstein, David, 91
"first peoples", 17, *see also* indigenous
    peoples
Flood, Gavin, 126, 129, 132
folklore, 58, 61
Foucault, Michel, 16
Fox, Jonathan, 79
Frankfurt School, 29
Freeman, Michael, 109
Frykenberg, Robert, 125, 126
Frymer-Kensky, Tikva, 137, 138, 143
Fukuyama, Francis, 110, 158, 159
Fyfe, Gordon, 70

Gaia, 151, 155
    as a hypothesis, 150, 153, 154
    as a range of hypotheses, 153–154
Galileo, 2
Gauda Pada, 130
gays, 4
gender equity, 144
George, Jim, 2, 17
Geras, Norman, 28
Gibson, Joan, 136
Giles, Herbert, 85
Gill, Stephen, 29
Gimbutas, Marija, 137, 138, 139, 140,
    141, 142
Gilpin, Robert, 21
global
    civil society, 26
    (con)federation, 27
    governance, 26
    government, 26
    learning, 159
    warming, 145
Global Form for Survival, 155
globalism, 20, 26, 83, 89
globalization, ix
    marxist account of, 122
God, 9, 79, 84, 97, 111, 112, 128, 139, 152
    as *Allah*, 103, 104, 109

as a woman, 141
as a verb, 143
as not a noun, 143
Christian, 136, 140
eye of, 132
Father, 141
female, 140
gender of, 138
male, 140
name of, 113, *see also dhikr*
Goddess, the, 140, 141, 142
as absolute foundation, 137
as Bad, 137
as binding force, 137
as fertility, 137
as Good, 137
as Great Mystery, 137
as holder of the Blood Mysteries, 137
as Killer-Regeneratrix, 137
as living Earth, 137
as living unity, 137
as Mother Nature, 137
as Mother of the Dead, 137
as Mother of the Living, 137
as sanctioning the sovereignty of
    kings, 137
as the Tree of Life, 137
as warrior, 137
belief in, 139
feminists, *see* feminists, Goddess
Godwin, William, 25
Golding, William, 150
Gong, Gerrit, 160
Goodman, Steven, 100
Goody, Jacques, 61
Gottlieb, Roger, 149
Gould, Stephen, 151
Graham, A.C., 83, 84, 85
Gramsci, Antonio, 29
Green, Ronald, 102
Gross, Rita, 137
Gruzinski, Serge, 60–61
Guattari, Felix, 32
Gupta, Akhil, 8, 35
Gurnah, Ahmed, 81
Guthrie, Stewart, 147, 148
gypsies, 4

Haberman, David, 5
Habermas, Jurgen, 29

Halbfass, Wilhelm, 132
Hall, David, 122
Halliday, Fred, 105, 110
Hanh, Thich Nhat, 99
Harding, Harry, 90
Harris, Ian, 100
Harte, John, 154
Havel, Christiane, 77
Hayek, Friedrich, 25
hegemony, 27
    American, 90
    Christian, 105
    contemporary liberal, 122
    modernist, 33, 51
    non-modernist (communalist)
        challenge, 33
Hegel, 29
Heidegger, Martin, 3, 9, 133
Heinemeijer, Willem, 109
Heliotrope, Helen, 137
heresy
    neo-pagan, 79
heritage, 157
    as intangible practices, 57, 58
    as intangible products, 57–58
    as tangible practices, 57
    as tangible products, 57
    definition of, 51–52
heroes, 143
Hiley, B.J., 149
Hindu
    constructivism, 11, 125–134
    schools, 128
Hinduism, 137
    Advaita Vedanta, 131, *see also Advaita
        Vedanta*
Hook, Glenn, 89
Hooper-Greenhill, Eilean, 70
Horkheimer, Max, 29
Horne, Donald, 70
Hsiung, James, 120, 121
Huang, Xiaoming, 81
Hudson, Denneth, 70
human nature, 20–27, 133
    as essentially bad, 20, 22–26
    as essentially calculating, 20,
        24–26
    as essentially good, 20, 26–27
human nurturing practices, 27–30, 133
    as essentially materialist, 27–28

human nurturing practices—*continued*
   as essentially materialist and mentalist,
     28–29
   as essentially mentalist, 29–30
humanism, 156
humanity
   survival of, 5
Humanity
   Religion of, 1
human rights, 16, 25, 103, 108, 112, 140
   as heretical, 109
Hunter, Anne, 136
Huntington, Samuel, 159
Husserl, Edmund, 15
Hutton, James, 151
hybridity, 81

I *Ching*, 1
idealism
   as mentalism, 30
   as the globalist alternative to realism,
     30
   as the internationalist alternative to
     realism, 30
identity, 3
illusion
   Rationalist, 154
   non-Rationalist, 5
Imel, Dorothy, 136
imperialism
   European, 120
indigenous peoples, 156, 160
individualism, 21, 24–25, 103, 108, 110,
     113, 122
individuation, 15, 85
   absolute, 8
   double, 16
   of individuals, 6–7, 103, 110, 143, 147
   process, 7
   relative, 8
induction, 2
industrial
   pollution, 145
   revolution, 142
infantilism, 3
intellect
   hypertrophy of, 9
   primacy of, 7
intellectuals
   defense, 83
International Monetary Fund, 91

internationalism, 20, 25, 83, 89
   "English School", 17
   American, 17
intervention
   Taoist, 87
Isa Upanishad, 127
Islam, 126, 137
   conservationists of, 106–107
   radical conservationists of, 107
   reformists of, 106–107
Islamic civics, 11, 103–114

Jainas, 128
Jameson, Frederic, 8
Jantsch, Erich, 152
Jaspers, Karl, 15
Jensen, Lionel, 115, 119, 120
Jews, 4
Johnson, Steven, 151
Johnston, Alastair, 91
Jones, Charles, 79
Joseph, Lawrence, 150, 153, 155
Judaism, 126, 136
judo, 88
juyo mukei bunkazai hojisha [important
     intangible cultural asset-holder], 72

Kant, Immanuel, 2, 27
Kaplan, Morton, 17
Kaplan, Robert, 35
Katzenstein, Peter, 30
Kawatake, Toshio, 76
Keller, Evelyn, 154
Keller, Mara, 141, 142
Keohane, Robert, 17, 25
Keynes, John, 25
Kindaichi, Haruhiko, 71
King, Ursula, 144
Kirchner, James, 153
Klostermaier, Klaus, 125, 130
Knott, Kim, 127
knowing
   as gardening, 10
   as tower climbing, 10
   cycles of, 10
   externalised, 2
   metaphysical, 1
   "negativist", 10
   non-Positivist, 4
   non-Rationlist, 4
   phenomenological, 11

Positivist, 1, 10
Rationalist, 4, 10
romantic, 10
scientific, 3
Theological, 1
knowledge
reliable, 4
Kolakowski, Leszek, 1, 5
Kongzi [Master Kong], *see* Confucius
Kurgan
incursions, 143
invaders, 142
victories, 143

Lacey, Robert, 52, 143
language
analytic, 2, 5, 16, 19, 31–32, 103, 157
as analytic dialect, 2
as not neutral, 9
of communal privilege, 64
of human rights, 64
Lannoy, Richard, 155
Lao Tzu, 84, 86, 88
Lau, D.C., 118
Lawrence, Bruce, 80, 105, 106, 107
Layton, Robert, 58
Leclercq, Pascal, 77
Leeming, David, 137
Legalists, 116
Legge, James, 118
Le Guin, Ursula, 135
Lelwica, Michelle, 140
Lem, Stanislav, 157
Lenton, Timothy, 150
levels of analysis, 23
Levinas, Emmanuel, 8
Levine, Robert, 3
Levinson, David, 149
Levi-Strauss, Laurent, 53
Leys, Simon, 116, 118, 121
liberalism, 3, 21, 25, 93, 97, 140
triumphal, 158, *see also* Fukuyama,
Francis
life, 133
as an anti-entropic event, 152
as energy become matter, 152
as gene transmission and selection, 152
as intricacy, 153
Lin, Limin, 92
List, Friedrich, 24
Little, Richard, 17

Liu, Kang, 122
Living Human Treasures project, 65–66
Loewe, Michael, 84
logics
non-modernist, *see* non-modernist
logics
Lomborg, Bjorn, 149
Louie, Kkam, 120, 121
Lovelock, James, 149, 150, 151, 152, 153,
155, 156
Lovibond, Sabina, 139
Lun yu [selected sayings], *see* Confucian
Analects
Lupineworld, 153

Mabbott, J.D., 10
Macdonald, Sharon, 70
Mahabharata, 126
Mao Tse-Tung, 91, 119
Mandela, Nelson, 116
Marett, Robert, 148
Margulis, Lynn, 150, 155
market, the, 21, 24, 25, 97
non-liberal accounts of, 96
Marx, Karl, 28
Marxism, 21, 27–28, 93, 122
classical, 123
Confucian, *see* Confucian Marxism
neo-, *see* neo-marxism
Masterpieces of the Oral and Intangible
Heritage of Humanity project, 66–67
Mataatua Declaration, The, 61
materialism, 29
marxist, 28, 115
non-marxist, 27
scientific, 146
May Fourth Movement, 120
maya [illusion], 128
Mayeda, Sengaku, 128, 129, 130
Mayer, Ann, 110
McClintock, Barbara, 154
McFague, Sallie, 136
McGrath, Alister, 79, 80
medicine, 1
meditation, 7
Buddhist, 98
Hindu, 131
Taoist, 85
Sufic, 111
Mehta, J.L., 15, 133
Meisner, Maurice, 121

Mellaart, James, 141, 143
mentalism, 29
   constructivist, 115
mercantilism, 20, 23–24, 93
   autarkic, 24
Metaphysica, the, 4
metaphysical
   alphabet of, 138
   reflection, *see* reflection, metaphysical
metaphysics, 4
   definition of, 3
   of presence, 161, *see also* Rationalism
   Taoist, 86
method
   hypothetico-deductive, 4
Metzger, Thomas, 119, 120
"Miami Group", *see* constructivism
Midgley, Mary, 149, 150, 156
Milbank, John, 19, 31, 79, 160, 161
Millennium, 79
mind-gaze
   objectifying, 5, 98, 129
   Rationalist, 8, 13, 52, 145
mind-move, *see* mind-gaze
Mittal, Kewal, 128
mode of production
   agricultural, 142
   pre-industrial, 142
modernism, 107
modernist
   analyses, x
   analytical languages, 19
   citizen, 103
   construction of these world affairs, 13
   culture, ix
   feminists, 139
   self, 6
   society, 6
   way of knowing, 132
   world affairs, ix
modernist project, x, 13–33, 79, 157
   as ethnocentric, 18
   as gendered, 17–18
   as indifferent to the environment,
      18–19
   as marginalizing anarchists, 19
   as marginalizing the poor, 19
   Japan's acceptance of, 71
modernist self
   map, 6–7

modernity, 7, 13, 133, 140, 142, 158, 160
   anti-, 7, 160
   as a politico-cultural project, 33
   as a politico-spiritual project, 33
   as ethnocentric, 160
   extreme, 7
   extreme anti-, 7
   margins of, 17–19, 140
   moderate, 7
   moderate anti-, 7
   non-, 6, 49, 160
   post-, 7, 17, 133
   pre-, 6, 17
Mohanty, J.N., 3, 126
Mohists, 116
Moon, Beverly, 137
Moore, Charles, 119, 127
Morgenthau, Hans, 17, 22
Morris, Brian, 80, 84, 96, 101
Mother Teresa, 155
Mousalli, Ahmad, 109
Muhaiyaddeen, M.R.Bawa, 111–112, 113
multiple modernities, 13, 69
Munro, Donald, 122
museums, 70
Muzaffar, Chandra, 33
mystic, 113

Naess, Arne, 149
national interests, 23
nationalism, 21, 24, 103, 106, 107, 110, 112,
      113, 122
nation-making, 103
natural action
   definition of, 87–88
nature, 97
Needham, Joseph, 85, 86
neti, neti [thisness and thatness], 130
neo-Hegelianism, *see* constructivism
Neolithic era, 137
neo-Pagans, 138, 139
neo-marxism, 21, 28–29, 93, 115,
      122, 123
neo-realism, 17, 23
Niebuhr, Reinhold, 24
Nikhilananda, Swami, 126
ningen kokuho [living national treasures]
      program, 65, 72
nirvana [Enlightenment], 95
Nivison, David, 119, 121, 122

non-modernist logics
  convergent, 35
  mosaic, 35
  multiple, 35
  parallel, 35
  spiral, 35
non-modernist perspectives, 160
non-modernity, *see* modernity, non-
non-Rationalists, 5
nonscience, 4
Nyaya, 128
Nozick, Robert, 25
Nye, Joseph, 17, 25

objectification, 136
objectifying, 5, 85
Objectivism, 15, 16
O'Flaherty, Wendy, 127
ontology, 7
  of violence, 160
Onuf, Nicholas, 30
Opium Wars, 120
Organ, Troy, 125
organised complexity, 146

pacifism, 85
Pagan
  animism, *see* animism
  feminism, 11, 135–144, *see also* feminism,
    Pagan
Pagan, 136, 137
  neo-, *see* neo-Pagans
  post-, see postpagan
Paganism
  Old European, 139
Page, Jake, 137
Pali Canon, *see Tripitaka*
paradigm policing, 25
Paris, Roland, 160
Parpart, Jane, 18
Parrinder, Geoffrey, 95
participant observation, 35
participant understanding, 35
Passmore, John, 113
patriarchy, 136, 140
Payutto, Ven. P.A., 97, 98, 102
Peake, Mervyn, 160
peace
  as a lull between wars, 23
Pearce, Susan, 70

Pereira, Jose, 130
Pettman, Jan Jindy, 18
Pettman, Ralph, 30, 89
Petty, Bruce, 37
phallic fiat, 128
Phillips, Stephen, 130
Physica, the, 4
physics, 4, 152
Piaget, Jean, 146, 147
Pinker, Steven, 31
Pleistocene, the, 145
Plotkin, Henry, 31
politics
  definition of, 20
poor, the, 17, 160
positivism
  small "p", 2
Positivism
  capital "P", 2, 15
  extreme, 5
postcolonialism, 18, 160
postmodernity, *see* modernity, post-
postpagan, 139
poststructuralism, 9
Pound, Ezra, 117, 119
Prakash, Madhu, 17
prayer, 7
pre-modernity, *see* modernity, pre-
Pressouyre, Leon, 54, 56
production, 100
  capitalist, 156
project
  modernist, *see* modernist, project
  Rationalist, 5
property
  commodified views of, 52
protectionism, *see* mercantilism
Prott, Lyndel, 64–65
Pulleybank, E.G., 121
Puranas, 126
Purva Mimamsa, 128
Pye, Michael, 93, 94
Pythagoras, 151
quantum indeterminacy, 5
Qur'an [Koran], 103, 104, 110
  and reason, 107

Radhakrishnan, Sarvepalli, 127
Rahula, Walpola, 96, 99, 100, 102

Ramachandran, Vilayanur, 154
Ramanuja, 130
Ramayana, 126
rationalism
    sacral, 107
    small "r", 2
Rationalism, 16, 17, 31, 35, 79, 98, 107, 131,
        133, 142, 158, 159, 151
    American, 5, 16
    anti-, 133, 134, 154
    as a way to know, 35, 154
    as the metaphysics of presence, *see*
        metaphysics
    British, 5, 16
    capital "R", 2, 8
    Christian context of,
        79–80, 161
    constraints set by, ix, 155
    Continental, 5
    definition of, 15
    European, 16
    extreme, 5
    "invisible shadow" of, 9
    limits set by, ix, 155
    moderate, 5
    modernist, 93, 140
Rationalist, 85
    modernist, 132
    principles, 103
    rejection of emotion, 154
    self, 6
    Western, 129
rationalist, 2, 13
Rawlinson, Andrew, 101
realism, 3, 20, 22–23, 83, 89
    classical, 17
    neo- , *see* neo-realism
reality, 3
    virtual versions of, 8
realpolitik, 23, 92
reason, 110, 147
    as an end in itself, 16, 49
    culture of, 13
    embedded, 7
    embodied, 7
    prioritisation of, ix
Ree, Jonathan, 5
reflection
    abstract/deductive, 2
    metaphysical, 3

"regimes"
    as arrangements, 26
religion, 4, 156
research
    non-Rationalist, 5
    proximal, 35
resource depletion, 145
revelation, 110, 147
rhizomes, 32
Rig Veda, 127
rhizomatic analysis, 32
Roessler, Mechtild, 54, 56
Rosemont, Henry, 9, 116, 117, 119, 160
Rothbard, Murray, 25
Rozman, Gilbert, 116
Ruether, Rosemary, 138, 139, 143
Rule, Paul, 115, 119
rule of law, 25
Rumi, Jalal al-Din, 110, 112
Ryckmans, Pierre, 74, 75

Sagan, Dorion, 155
saints, 7
Salk, Jonas, 154
salvation, 128
Samkhya, 128
Sanday, Peggy, 138, 142, 143
Sankara, *see* Shankaracharya
Sartha-Anand, Chaiwat, 96
Satanists, 136
Savepalli Radhakrishnan, 132
satisfaction, 100
scepticism, 5
Schopenhauer, 133
Schram, Stuart, 119, 120, 121
Schumacher, Ernst, 97
science, 4, 131, 133, 146, 156
    horizon of, 5
    the naughty thumb of, 143
    the only alternative to (Spring), 143
scientific analysis
    meta-language for, 2
scientific method, 4
scientific materialism, *see* materialism
scientism
    hypothetico-deductive, 2
Sebastian, Leonard, 91
security
    collective, 90
    common, 90

comprehensive, 90
cooperative, 90
human, 90
national, 90
Seeger, Anthony, 61, 62
seers, 146
self-determination, 24, 109
self
    as an illusion, 96
    decentred, 8
    doubt about, 136
    individuated, 8
    multiple, 8
    modernist, *see* modernist self
    objectifying, 8
    relational, 8
    sense of, 112
Self, 128
    inner, 130
    larger, 149
    sacral, 130
    sense of, 112
sentiment
    primacy of, 7
Sessions, George, 149
Seth, Sanjay, 17
sex, 83
shamans, 146
Shankaracharya, Shri, 128, 129, 130
Sharman, Arvind, 139
Sharp, Martin, 22
Sheldrake, Rupert, 149
Sherkin, Samantha, 59
Short, Philip, 121
Shweder, Richard, 3
Simon, Bradford, 60, 61
Simos, Miriam, 137, 138
Sinari, Ramakant, 132
sites
    cultural, 53
    mixed, 53
    natural, 53
Smart, Ninian, 104, 116
Smith, Adam, 25, 96
Smith, Linda Tuhiwai, 3, 17, 18
Smith, Steve, 17, 32
social movements, 26, 103, 109,
    111, 134
socialism, 21, 26, 93, 96, 97
    Chinese-style, 122

marxist, 21, 27
non-revolutionary (democratic), 26
soul, 146
space, 3
species extinction, 145
Spencer, Herbert, 148
spirit, the, 146
spiritualism
    animist, *see* animist spiritualism
Spretnak, Charlene, 141, 143,
    144, 155
Sri Aurobindo, 132
Ssu-ma Kuang, 121
star-stuff, 154
state sovereignty, 55
"steady-state" economics, 156
Stietencron, Heinrich von, 125, 126
Stone, Merlin, 139
strategic culture
    Chinese, 91
    Confucian-Mencian, 91
    Taoist, 91–92
structures
    as patterns of whole system
        practice, 23
substance, 3
Sugarman, Susan, 146
sutra [thread/strand], 128
Suva Declaration, The, 61
stages
    metaphysical, 3
    scientific, 3
    theological, 3
Starhawk, *see* Simos, Miriam,
Stevenson, Leslie, 5
strategics
    Taoist, *see* Taoist strategics
Sufism, 111–114
systems
    living, 153
    non-living, 153

Taber, John, 133
Tagore, Rabindranath, 132
tai chi chuan, 88
Takashina, Shuji, 74, 75
Tallis, Raymond, 17
Tamney, Joseph, 115, 116, 118, 122
Taoist strategics, 11, 83–92
Tao Te Ching, 84, 87, 135

Taylor, Charles, 16, 25
te [virtue; power], 87
technology, 28, 133
Terada, Yoshitaka, 71
Teson, Fernando, 25
Tibi, Bassam, 109
time, 3
Titchen, Sarah, 53, 54, 58
Tobias, Michael, 149
tourism, 63, 76
tradition
    Chinese sense of, 75
"traditionalists"
    British, 17
transport, 28
Treaty of Westphalia, 55
Tringham, Ruth, 138, 139
Tripitaka, 94, 95
Trungpa, Chogyam, 80, 111
Truth
    absolute, 10
    contingent, 109
    empirically tested, 109
    enlightened, 128
    eternal, 10
    Muslim, 104
    revealed, 109
    ultimate, 127
    universal, 10
Tse-Tung, Mao, *see* Mao Tse-Tung
Tu, Wei-ming, 116, 117, 120
turiya [pure consciousness], 130
Tylor, Edward, 146, 147

Ueki, Yukinobu, 76
umma [community], 105
    global Islamic, 103
understanding
    Rationalist, 131
United Nations Education, Scientific and
    Cultural Organization [UNESCO],
    33, 53–56, 74, 75
United States, 2
*Universal Islamic Declaration of Human
    Rights*, 109
universalism
    Catholic, 1
Upanishads, 127, 128, 130
Uttara Mimamsa, 128

Uyeshiba, Kisshomaru, 89
Uyeshiba, Morihei, 88

Vaisesika, 128
Vedanta, 128
Vedas, 126, 128, 129, 130, 131
Vernadsky, Vladimir, 151
Vincent, John, 110
Visnu, 130
Vivekananda, Swami, 132
Voltaire, 133
von Droste, Bernd, 54, 56
Vyakarana, 128

Waever, Ole, 25
Waley, Arthur, 84, 85, 87, 117, 118
Wallerstein, Immanuel, 28
Walsh, Kevin, 70
Waltz, Kenneth, 17, 23, 25
Wang, Jisi, 92
war
    democracies and, 4
    Taoist conception of, 85–86
Watanabe, Michihiro, 78
Watson, Adam, 17
Weber, Cynthia, 32
Weber, Max, 84, 97, 98, 122
Western canon, 2
White, Lynn, 79, 145
Wight, Martin, 20, 21
Wilson, Edward, 145
wisdom
    received, 52
    sacral, 52
Wittgenstein, Ludwig, 80
Wongwaisayawan, Suwanna, 96
World Bank, 91
World Intellectual Property
    Organization (WIPO), 59, 65
world heritage
    as dead things, 66
    as living practices, 66
    communalist conceptions of, 56–58, 158
    in Japan, 69–78
    world politics of, 33, 51–68, 157
World Heritage Committee, 53, 70
World Heritage List, 53, 56, 57, 70, 75
World Trade Organization, 91
World War II, 2, 71

worship, 7
Wurm, Stephen, 65
wu-wei [no unnatural action], 86–87, 88, 90

Yao, Xinzhong, 116, 117, 120, 122
Yoga, 128, 130

Young, Katherine, 139
Young, Serinity, 138

Zalewski, Marysia, 18
Zimmerman, Michael, 149
Zizek, Slavoj, 161

Printed in the United States
118342LV00002B/61-75/P